Betrayal of the Homeland

Columbia Studies in Middle East Politics

Columbia Studies in Middle East Politics
MARC LYNCH, SERIES EDITOR

Columbia Studies in Middle East Politics presents academically rigorous, well-written, relevant, and accessible books on the rapidly transforming politics of the Middle East for an interested academic and policy audience.

Varieties of Power: Women's Political Representation in Arab Parliaments, Marwa Shalaby

Twilight of the Saints: The History and Politics of Salafism in Contemporary Egypt, Stéphane Lacroix, translated by Jeremy Sorkin

Surviving the Islamic State: Contention, Cooperation, and Neutrality in Wartime Iraq, Austin Knuppe

Mayors in the Middle: Indirect Rule and Local Government in Occupied Palestine, Diana B. Greenwald

Smugglers and States: Negotiating the Maghreb at Its Margins, Max Gallien

The Suspended Disaster: Governing by Crisis in Bouteflika's Algeria, Thomas Serres

Syria Divided: Patterns of Violence in a Complex Civil War, Ora Szekely

Shouting in a Cage: Political Life After Authoritarian Cooptation in North Africa, Sofia Fenner

Security Politics in the Gulf Monarchies: Continuity Amid Change, David B. Roberts

Classless Politics: Islamist Movements, the Left, and Authoritarian Legacies in Egypt, Hesham Sallam

Lumbering State, Restless Society: Egypt in the Modern Era, Nathan J. Brown, Shimaa Hatab, and Amr Adly

Friend or Foe: Militia Intelligence and Ethnic Violence in the Lebanese Civil War, Nils Hägerdal

For a complete list of books in the series, please see the Columbia University Press website.

Betrayal of the Homeland

Disloyal Subjects
in Wartime Syria

SAMER ABBOUD

Columbia
University
Press
New York

Columbia University Press
Publishers Since 1893
New York   Chichester, West Sussex
cup.columbia.edu

Copyright © 2026 Columbia University Press
All rights reserved

Library of Congress Cataloging-in-Publication Data
Names: Abboud, Samer Nassif author
Title: Betrayal of the homeland : disloyal subjects in wartime Syria / Samer Abboud.
Description: New York, NY : Columbia University Press, 2026. | Series: Columbia studies in Middle East politics | Includes bibliographical references and index.
Identifiers: LCCN 2025031979 (print) | LCCN 2025031980 (ebook) | ISBN 9780231215329 hardcover | ISBN 9780231215336 trade paperback | ISBN 9780231564595 epub | ISBN 9780231565868 PDF
Subjects: LCSH: Conflict management—Political aspects—Syria | Postwar reconstruction—Political aspects—Syria | Allegiance—Syria | Treason—Syria | Syria—History—Civil War, 2011- —Political aspects
Classification: LCC DS98.6 .A225 2026 (print) | LCC DS98.6 (ebook)
LC record available at https://lccn.loc.gov/2025031979
LC ebook record available at https://lccn.loc.gov/2025031980

Cover design: Elliott S. Cairns
Cover image: Vagabjorn / Shutterstock.com

GPSR Authorized Representative: Easy Access System Europe, Mustamäe tee 50, 10621 Tallinn, Estonia, gpsr.requests@easproject.com

To Sonia, Kalila, Nadim, and Maysa

Contents

Acknowledgments ix
List of Abbreviations xiii

Introduction   1

1 The Astana Process and the Regional Context of Conflict Management   37

2 The Spectral Terrorist as State Enemy   62

3 The Reconciliation Process: Transforming Enemies Into Friends   86

4 Settling Friends, Unsettling Enemies: The Settlement Process and Civilian Subjectivity   112

5 Absence as Disloyalty   137

6 The Regime Falls: Managing Syria's Transition   162

Conclusion: Authoritarian Conflict Management and Its Legacies   182

Notes   195
Bibliography   217
Index   235

Acknowledgments

My entire professional life has been dedicated to researching, writing, and thinking about contemporary Syria. For more than two decades I have been learning from Syrians who have graciously given me their time, opened their homes, and treated me with care. Some people, like Jihad Yazigi and Zaher al-Sgheer, have quite literally been on this journey with me from day one. I feel totally incapable of expressing the depth of my debt and gratitude to them, and to all the Syrians who have welcomed me into their lives over the last two decades.

I have been fortunate to have received several invitations to present different parts of the material that makes up this book. I am thankful to colleagues at Georgetown, Stanford, Northwestern, Carleton, McGill, and the London School of Economics, where portions of this book were presented virtually and in person over the last few years. Special thanks to Daniel Neep, Marwa Daoudy, Hesham Sallam, Shayna Silverstein, James Milner, Laura Madokoro, Megan Bradley, and Rim Turkmani for facilitating these talks. I would also like to thank participants at a workshop I co-organized with Alexa Firat on the future of Syrian studies who provided me with excellent feedback on a paper that forms part of the introduction: Rimun Murad, Rula Jabbour, Christa Salamandra, Fadi Skeiker, Ghada al-Atrash, and Sumaya Malas. My writing buddies—Kunle Owolabi, Brie Radis, and Jen Riggan—always gave me conversations to look forward to as I trudged my way through this book. Their kindness and comradery fueled me to the finish line. Caelyn Cobb at Columbia University Press made sure this entire process was both smooth and humane. Marc Lynch's excitement for this project and critical eye toward various drafts helped me sharpen the analysis and figure out how to make sense of the book's arguments. He has been an enthusiastic supporter and helped shape a lot of my thinking about how to incorporate the fall of the regime into the book's overarching story.

I tried not to bore those around me with constant book talk, but I am nevertheless indebted to the many people who knowingly and unknowingly supported me on this journey: my karate crew, new and old hockey teammates, and all the others I am lucky enough to call my friends. Brie Radis and Shelley Hedlund allowed me to use their house for several days for a writing retreat during a particularly acute period of writer's block; I still can't imagine having finished this book without that time to think and write. Bassam Haddad and Omar Dahi are two of the smartest, kindest, people on earth, and they have taught me so much about Syria and how to uplift those around them. I am deeply indebted to them, even if I often forget to text them back. Benjamin Muller is a caring person who I deeply admire as an academic, father, and friend. His presence in my life is a blessing.

I am so grateful for the wonderful staff at the various libraries where much of this writing happened: Haverford and St. Joe's University Libraries and the Lovett Public Library in Philadelphia, and the Carlingwood Public Library and MacOdrum Library at Carleton University in Ottawa. Special thanks to the Happy Goat Coffee Co. on Laurel Street in Ottawa for always playing an eclectic mix of Arabic music during my many long writing sessions there.

My department is an incredible space where I have always felt nourished and supported. My Villanova colleagues Hibba Abugideiri, Boris Briker, Andra Cain, Gordon Coonfeld, Kevin Fox, Anusha Hariharan, Raúl Diego Rivera Hernández, Christine Kalleeny, Elizabeth Kolsky, Yumi Lee, Katie Lenehan, Dana Lloyd, Mary Mullen, Cera Murtagh, Thomas Noel, Jonathan O'Neil, Kunle Owolabi, Mark Schrad, Kayo Shintaku, Kathryn Getek Soltis, Catherine Warrick, and HaiLin Zhou are genuinely wonderful people to work with. I am especially grateful to Nate Badenoch for the giggles and language lessons, Maghan Keita for coffee chats and mentorship, and to Chiji Akoma for being an extraordinary department chair. His unwavering support has allowed me to grow into the kind of teacher-scholar I always hoped to be.

My deepest gratitude is reserved for my family, who are all I will ever need in this world. My in-laws, Fred and Rabia Rosen, have provided so much support over the years and continue to fill our lives with love and puns. My parents, Rabab and Nassif, remain my backbone and the two people I lean on most. They created a world for me to flourish and be loved in. Being around them is a constant reminder of the immense power of love, family, and community. My incredible children, Kalila, Nadim, and Maysa, give me so much to look forward to in this world. It was always so hard to take time away from being with them to write this book. Watching Kalila grow into a dancer, singer, actor, performer, and robotics nerd has been one of the greatest joys of my life. Her smile, passion, and giggly laugh fill my heart. Nadim embodies the Arabic meaning of his name in profound ways: He is the ultimate friend and companion in this world. He is such a talented, curious person whose excitement about anything from a new card game he invented, trick soccer moves he just perfected, or a math problem he solved at school, is infectious. Maysa's sass, joy, mischievousness, and intense love for those around them serves as a daily reminder of how powerful it can be to walk through the world with careless wonder. I really enjoy trying to keep up with Maysa even if I am always two steps behind. I am incredibly lucky to share this precious life with my spouse, Sonia Rosen. Sonia helped guide me through this book in a million different ways. Her presence is a gift to me, our children, and the world.

Abbreviations

ACM	authoritarian conflict management
CRC	Civil Registry Centers
CTC	Counter-Terrorism Court
CWC	Chemical Weapons Convention
DDR	disarmament, demobilization, and reintegration
ESCWA	Economic and Social Commission for West Asia
FSA	Free Syrian Army
GWOT	global war on terror
HLP	housing, land, and property rights
HNC	High Negotiation Committee
HTS	Hayat Tahrir al-Sham
ISSG	International Syrian Support Group
ISIS	Islamic State of Iraq and al-Sham
JAN	Jabhat an-Nusra
LAS	League of Arab States
NDF	National Defense Forces
OPCW	Organisation for the Prohibition of Chemical Weapons
SANA	Syrian Arab News Agency
SCC	Syrian Constitutional Committee
SCND	Syrian Congress of National Dialogue
SDF	Syrian Democratic Forces

SNA	Syrian National Army
SNC	Syrian Negotiation Committee
SSG	Syrian Salvation Government
SSSC	Supreme State Security Court
UNHCR	United Nations High Commissioner for Refugees
UNSC	UN Security Council
UNSCRs	UN Security Council resolutions
YPG	Yekîneyên Parastina Gel (People's Defense Units)

Betrayal of the Homeland

Introduction

Nearly everywhere the political order is reconstituting itself as a form of organization for death. Little by little, a terror that is molecular in essence and allegedly defensive is seeking legitimation by blurring the relations between violence, murder, and the law, faith, commandment, and obedience, the norm and the exception, and even freedom, tracking, and security.

—ACHILLE MBEMBE

In a February 2019 speech celebrating ongoing military victories against armed groups, President Bashar al-Assad called Syria's enemies traitors, people without souls who sold their homeland, who profited from their country's destruction and sold themselves as "slaves" to do America's bidding, but who ultimately failed. Those who enacted that plan were terrorists working in the interests of foreign entities intent on destroying Syria: "today, and in the future, we must realize that the war was between us Syrians and the terrorists. We triumph together, not against each other, and any victory is exclusively over terrorism."[1] President al-Assad's defiant tone reiterated the state's official narrative of a conflict between a steadfast, nationalist Syria, on the one hand, and a coalition of external and internal enemies, on the other hand. The political hatred fueling al-Assad's conflation of state enemies with terrorism was the most important bifurcating line in the loyalist narration of conflict. To stand against the state was to stand with terrorism; conversely, to stand with the state was to demonstrate loyalty, steadfastness, and a love of the homeland.

President al-Assad's speech was one of several that celebrated a "victory" in Syria's war against terrorism. Such a celebration would not have been possible without the decisive Russian military intervention in September 2015 that altered the trajectory of the conflict. Barely a year after the intervention began the entire landscape of the conflict had changed. Activists had begun to acknowledge the painful reality that the revolution had failed, and that new, long-term strategies for change were needed. Regime loyalists began declaring victory and speaking openly about punishing "those who betrayed the homeland," a catchall reference to state enemies. Syrians living in neighboring countries slowly began to return home. To do so, they had to risk presenting themselves to security officials and submit to a settlement process whereby the state would only sanction their repatriation if they were deemed a loyal returnee.[2] Armed fighters and civilians under the government's control were forced to "reconcile" with the state after military defeat and either accept displacement to Idlib or remobilization within the official counterinsurgency apparatus. State-backed civil committees worked alongside the local security apparatus in areas formerly held by armed groups to begin surveying recaptured areas and identifying disloyal residents, who were then targeted for punishment through asset expropriation. Settling civilians, reconciling with fighters, and producing new legal regimes to punish those deemed disloyal were pillars of the state's conflict management strategies that materialized a political order that rested on the bureaucratization of conflict and its absorption into the machinations of the state. *Betrayal of the Homeland* seeks to understand how the state's conflict management strategies were absorbed into the state apparatus and how this absorption institutionalized the enmity and punishment borne out of the Syrian regime's own professed "war on terrorism."

The Syrian uprising that began in 2011 broke the wall of authoritarian fear that millions of Syrians had lived with for decades. But the uprising also created the conditions for a violent conflict that engulfed the country, fragmented large swaths of territory, displaced half of the population, and led to widespread physical destruction. This tragedy had not prevented the regime from declaring victory in the conflict. The narrative of victory was taken up by Syria's allies and enemies, and the question of how to deal with the regime dominated international policy discussions about Syria until the collapse of the al-Assad regime in December 2024. In Syria, unlike in many other conflicts around the world, Western states, the United Nations, and other international liberal institutions had been wholly peripheralized in the country's transition to a post-conflict order after the Russian intervention. There was no serious, deliberative process by which Syrians could negotiate political order in the wake of the fighting. The regime was able to construct victory and a transition to a post-conflict order according to its own vision without external pressure or demands from Syrian oppositionists. For all intents and purposes, the war was fought as a zero-sum game in which one side was going to win, and another was going to lose. The state's narration of conflict as a zero-sum game between the state and terrorists was absorbed into the subsequent order as several political processes, laws, institutions, courts, and practices that seek to extend enmity against state enemies through punishments that cast disloyal Syrians out of the body politic. The proclamations of "victory" concealed deeper underlying changes to the political order that sought to strengthen the state by eliminating enemies, but which ultimately weakened the state's ability to govern.

This is a book about how the Syrian regime managed conflict and how it sought to construct a political order that absorbed the war's logic into the machinations of the state. As we now know from the regime's collapse in December 2024, that political order was unsustainable. Nevertheless, the period of conflict that this book is interested in provides important insights into how authoritarian states fight wars, how they extend the battlefield to the state bureaucracy, and how conflict management strategies materialize a narrative of conflict that reshapes bureaucracies, laws, and courts around the punishment of disloyal populations. In the following chapters, I ask two principal questions: First, how did the Syrian regime manage conflict? And second, what kind of political order emerged from the state's conflict management strategies? Drawing on and contributing to literature interested in authoritarian conflict management,[3] illiberal peacebuilding,[4] and state repression in the Middle East,[5] I argue that the Syrian regime's conflict management strategies sought to bifurcate Syrian society into the loyal and the disloyal and to orient the state apparatus around the management, control, and punishment of recalcitrant populations broadly understood as those who had betrayed the homeland. The bifurcation of loyal and disloyal citizens emerged from the state's narration of the conflict as a terrorist attack against Syria. This narration materialized in several discursive legal categories that indexed disloyalty, such as the terrorist, deserter, or absentee. These subjectivities were given political meaning as targets for state punishment. How the state narrated conflict created these legal and political categories that were subjectivized as punishable. The state absorbed these categorizations of disloyal citizens through the creation of new laws, institutions, courts, and practices, by which it sought to manage the conflict. Such strategies contributed to an illiberal peace that comprises "the reification of a sovereign center and the construction of an internal friend/enemy divide as the constitutive basis of a system of conflict management."[6]

Post-conflict order and the bifurcation of society into friends and enemies, loyal and disloyal, materialized through three conflict management practices that were absorbed into the state. The first mechanism is the *reconciliation process* that provided a legal and political structure for the alchemic transformation of former fighters from enemies into friends. The reconciliation process created new conflict subjectivities (reconciled fighters) and new geographies (reconciled areas) that had to be managed through the integration of former fighters into the regime's counterinsurgency apparatus and laws that governed reconciled areas. These areas became spaces for the state's production of knowledge about loyal and disloyal populations and the enactment of punishment against the former through asset appropriation. The reorganization of Syria's housing, land, and property rights regimes undergirded new legal regimes directed toward the punishment of disloyal citizens through the erasure of their legal identities, appropriation of their properties, and forbidding their return to Syria. These new legal regimes codified disloyalty by producing categorizations that were targeted for punishment. These categorizations subjectivized Syrians relative to their presumed roles in the conflict. The third mechanism is a *settlement process* created to give disloyal subjects an opportunity to reverse the state's suspicion and resolve their status vis-à-vis the state through what was effectively a loyalty test. As I argue in this book, these mechanisms were at the core of the conflict management strategies by which the Syrian regime bifurcated society into loyal and disloyal, reoriented post-conflict state building around illiberal practices, and created the conditions for an illiberal political order. These practices created "loyal" but uncommitted populations whose allegiance to an illiberal political order increasingly defined by a hollowed-out state, extreme poverty, and the pervasive threat of violence, was fleeting at best.

While liberal ideas about peace are premised on the elimination of civil violence and power sharing between former belligerents, an illiberal peace opens the possibility for understanding violence as constitutive of an order that suppresses dialogue, deliberation, and a diffusion of power to different groups. In this sense, an illiberal "peace" more accurately refers to the type of political order that emerges after civil violence in which an illiberal state authority seeks to consolidate power through the elimination of enemies and other threats. There are two major distinctions between authoritarian conflict management (ACM) and illiberal peace as analytical frameworks for understanding conflict, with some seeing ACM as a practice of illiberal peace and others seeing it as producing illiberal peace teleologically.[7] I understand the relationship between ACM and illiberal peace to be co-constituted. Salwa Ismail argues that a "civil war regime" has existed in Syria since the 1970s whereby the state has always been at war with its population and is oriented around permanent civil war.[8] This civil war regime is oriented around rendering populations legible and acting upon state-defined subversives violently. Understanding state violence after 2011 within the broader trajectory of the civil war regime encourages us to see how conflict management strategies and forms of illiberal peace cannot be distinguished as temporal periods but are instead (re)produced through a regime of violence directed against citizens. State practices of punishment after 2011 have antecedents in the pre-conflict period. There is more continuity than not in Syrian state practices toward enemy populations. I argue that conflict management strategies analyzed in this book are in fact extensions of Syria's pre-2011 civil war regime, which similarly sought to divide and act violently upon disloyal subjects. In this sense, conflict and peace are inseparable as the state is engaged in permanent violence and punishment. War, as Ismail reminds us, is not an event but a set of social relations.[9]

In the Syrian context, these social relations were determined not by a strict separation of the regime and the population but by the attempted carving out of disloyal subjects from the body politic and the political embrace of loyalist populations. This book is interested in how disloyal subjects were discursively created and acted upon by the state. In making arguments about conflict management and disloyal subjectivity, my intention is not to suggest a strict distinction between regime and population. There were many segments of the Syrian population who could be considered loyalists in the traditional sense of supporting the regime and its conflict management efforts, even if they did acknowledge the brutality of such practices. Wedeen's "uncommitted centrists" in Syria who did not necessarily support the regime but nonetheless refused or failed to mobilize in support of the opposition represents another segment of the population whose political orientations were, effectively, buttressing regime power, if not explicitly so. The point here is that the regime had many opponents and many loyalists, but that most Syrians sat somewhere in between the two poles. This book is interested in how the regime constructed disloyalty in relation to its supposedly "loyal" subjects (committed or otherwise).

The regime could not maintain a loyalist base without also reconstituting the basis of neo-patrimonial rule that directed the spoils of war to networks of loyalist elites. These elites were cultivated from the lower strata of the business community, first as intermediaries and then as major players in the Syrian war economies. Other elites were recruited through the civil and settlement committee structures that gave local notables institutional expression as a collective loyalist body capable of enacting state power and generating knowledge about disloyal populations. These new centers of regime power were intimately connected to the security apparatus. Other loyalist networks emerged through various local militias that were eventually institutionalized as the National Defense Forces. In all these cases, the regime was able to cultivate political loyalty (or at the very least ambivalence) by redirecting the spoils of war to these networks. Appropriating the property and assets of the disloyal, and redirecting them to loyalist networks, was central to this process.

The chapters in this book explore how the state constructs citizen subjectivity through political hatred. This political hatred was certainly shared by segments of the Syrian population for whom the threat of regime collapse represented an existential, objective threat. This hatred demarcates politically relevant cleavages that materialize into a set of laws, institutions, and practices that extend the enmity of war beyond the battlefield and into the state bureaucracy. Enmity against the state's enemies has become the generative condition of Syrian statehood after 2011. The conditions for illiberal statehood, societal bifurcation and punishment, and the practices that sustain both, are explored throughout this book.

The Syrian Catastrophe

The scale of the Syrian catastrophe is impossible to adequately quantify or make sense of. Half of the prewar population is estimated to have been killed or displaced, with many of the latter forced into several displacements as they moved from one location to another. Overlapping humanitarian crises, economic contraction, fear of conscription, simmering violence, COVID-19, the 2023 earthquake, and gradual ecological change have all placed immense pressures on Syrians since the outbreak of conflict in 2011. In this context, it is extremely difficult to quantify the number of deaths or the different forms of mobilities people engage in to avoid one form of insecurity or another. Existing estimates point to the scale of the humanitarian crisis. The Internal Displacement Monitoring Center estimated in mid-2023 that there had been 19.5 million internal displacements (defined as "each new forced movement of person within the borders of their country") since 2011 and 6.9 million internally displaced as of the end of 2022.[10] The total figure of Syrian refugees registered with either the Government of Turkey (under temporary protection) or the United Nations High Commissioner for Refugees (UNHCR) is estimated at 5.2 million,[11] and that does not include either unregistered or resettled Syrian refugees, or the estimated 1 million Syrians who are in Europe as refugees and asylum-seekers. Estimates of war casualties vary widely, with the UNHCR estimating just over 300,000 casualties by mid-2023,[12] while the Syrian Observatory for Human Rights estimated that by 2021 more than 600,000 Syrians had perished during the war.[13] The Syrian government did not officially record the number of war casualties, although it did classify deaths in some cases involving military or security personnel. While millions of Syrians are displaced, thousands were confined in the regime's notorious prison system.[14]

Syria's territorial fragmentation during the conflict induced multiple movements across regime and opposition space. Many Syrians who remained in the country and had to flee to families' homes found themselves on the move several times as violence ebbed and flowed and new authorities (or old ones) assumed control of specific areas. Many people gravitated to the relative safety of Damascus and the coastal areas, which were much quieter compared to urban centers such as Aleppo, Homs, and Hama, despite dwindling resources and no government-sponsored support system for the internally displaced. Families were torn apart as opportunities for movement presented themselves differentially throughout the conflict. Some remained in Syria, others were able to settle in neighboring countries, and a select few were able to settle in Western countries.

The majority of displaced Syrians live in the neighboring countries of Lebanon, Jordan, and Turkey under differential rights regimes and increasingly hostile political environments in which forced repatriation has become normalized. The Lebanese government does not define Syrian refugees *as* refugees, instead referring to them as "displaced," a legal category that does not confer any rights of protection. Syrians in Lebanon thus cannot formally be acknowledged as refugees by the UNHCR. Instead, their flight is characterized as "refugee movement,"[15] without any rights or legal protections being assigned to the individuals that undertake this movement. Initially, Turkey had an "open border" policy for Syrians that made the country much more hospitable than Lebanon. As a site of both settlement and transit for Syrians, Turkey's evolving legal and security regime differentially impacted Syrian refugees' sense of security and safety. Caught in the spaces between "precarity, differential inclusion, and negotiated citizenship," Syrians are subject to a legal framework that grants them certain citizenship rights while simultaneously rendering their status impermanent.[16] Syrian refugee life in Turkey remains defined by discourses of "guesthood" that shape policy,[17] and which have enabled calls for forced repatriation. In Jordan, most Syrian refugees are registered with the UNHCR. Most Syrians (around 80 percent) live outside of the two main camps, Za'atari and Azraq. Jordan refuses to forcibly repatriate Syrians, but economic and living conditions in the country, as well as a stalled resettlement process, have led to many Syrians wishing to return home.

Many Syrians have used regional countries, especially Turkey, as transition points on their way to Europe. The often harrowing and deadly trip across the Mediterranean from Turkey or North Africa via exploitative smuggling networks has subjected Syrians to untold insecurities and fears, as well as familial separations. The deadly trip is compounded by violent, restrictive policies on the European side that actively prevent boats from landing on European shores. The European Union's coast guard, Frontex, actively patrols and surveils the Mediterranean looking for boats to intercept and turn back. The Missing Migrants Project estimated that between 2016 and 2023 more than 1.7 million migrants attempted to cross the Mediterranean, of whom more than 20,000 died or disappeared, close to 500,000 were intercepted and returned, with the remaining 1.2 million having arrived on European shores.[18] Life in Syria's neighboring countries has been difficult amid constrictive rights regimes, and those able to reach Europe often find themselves in complicated and similarly restrictive rights regimes that do not easily confer residency.

Understanding Syria's Conflict

This book inquires into the state's management of conflict and thus departs from most accounts of post-2011 Syria that attempt to explain the conflict's trajectory with reference to the relational interactions between domestic, regional, and international actors. Alongside Sosnowski and Szekeley's work cited below, this is one of the only lengthy studies to focus almost exclusively on the post–Russian intervention period. This is also the first major study to explore how the Syrian war was fought away from the battlefield, through the machinations of state power and bureaucracy and their orientation around the punishment of disloyal subjects. In the aftermath of the Russian intervention, little, if any, scholarly attention has been paid to these more granular workings of state power. This book thus seeks to expand our understanding of the Syrian conflict by shifting our attention to how the state apparatus was oriented around conflict management. Doing so makes significant contributions to understanding how regime power was refracted through the state bureaucracy to punish official enemies and helps us answer the question of how the regime was able to maintain some semblance of coherence throughout the course of the conflict despite its hollowing out, the territorial fragmentation of Syria, and economic collapse. The emergent discursive, legal, and political tools deployed to manage conflict required a radical reorientation of the bureaucracy to bifurcate and act upon a host of state enemies. Reducing Syria's conflict to its battlefield or carceral realities ignores a mostly invisible, yet fundamentally important, form of warfare that was absorbed into the state bureaucracy. In trying to understand the war as something that was also fought away from the battlefield, this book provides a unique perspective on the nature of Syrian warfare—one that has largely been overlooked in most research on the conflict.

In my previous books on Syria, I sought to understand first how a political and military stalemate took root,[19] and second how the Russian military intervention in 2015 broke the stalemate and made an authoritarian peace possible.[20] The broader, panoramic view of the conflict to which I aspired in these texts mirrored that found in many of the books published in the initial years of the conflict, which sought to understand it as a product of competing political projects and alliances that produced profound violence and human tragedy. Much of this work focused on the nature and structure of the uprising itself and concentrated on the initial years when a movement to overthrow the regime first took shape.[21] This work asks and answers questions about the outbreak of the uprising and the social and political structure of the opposition. Other books focused on battlefield shifts and the nature of international responses and intervention in the conflict.[22] These contribute to our understanding of a dynamic and shifting battlefield and how this impacted the formation of state-state and state–armed group alliances by exploring questions of geopolitics and political alignments, but they tell us little, if anything, about how state power was deployed to buttress the regime's battlefield strategies (and realities). Battlefield analysis dominated research in the first years of the conflict as questions about regime survival, battlefield alliances, the rise and fall of brigades and fronts gave insight into the bigger questions about the conflict's trajectory.

In contrast, several books have since shaped our understanding of the Syrian conflict by highlighting Syrian narratives and experiences of the war away from the battlefield. This literature ranges from a focus on the role of (social) media in narrating the conflict,[23] for example, to highlighting the experiences and voices of refugees and the displaced.[24] Journalistic and personal accounts have similarly documented how the war was experienced from multiple sides of growing Syrian divides.[25] Several ethnographic studies have explored refugee ontologies and the experiences of Syrians as shaped by fluid state policies and an ineffectual global refugee rights regime.[26] Charlotte al-Khalili's ethnographic study of revolutionary Syrians in Turkey explores how time and distance affected Syrian's subjectivity in relation to the revolution and provides important insight into how the uprising's residues exist within the lives of Syrians. Şule Can's study of Syrian-Turkish encounters in Antakya similarly shows how refugee precarity and host state policies shape the everyday experiences of displaced Syrians.[27] Ethnographic insights into the lives of displaced Syrians help us understand the cascading effects of war, exile, and constricted rights regimes that govern the lives of displaced Syrians.

Research into the individual experiences of war contrasts with an extensive body of scholarship devoted to the international dimensions of the Syrian conflict. Much of this literature has focused on the role that regional states have played in perpetuating the conflict through the pursuit of competing political projects. This work, however, pays virtually no attention to the inner machinations of state power and the punishment of disloyal subjects—forces that have had such a profound effect on people's displacement and ability to return. Fragmented and overlapping interests in Syria comprised one of the main contributions to the stalemate that existed until late 2015. Christopher Phillips has argued that a new regional order emerged after 2011 in which the United States, Russia, Iran, Saudi Arabia, Turkey, and Qatar competed for influence in Syria,[28] thereby contributing to the stalemate. The dynamics of this regional order have been explored in several collections and case studies that juxtapose the interventions of regional actors into Syria's conflict, giving more nuance to our understanding of how external factors shaped the conflict's trajectory.[29] A major area of inquiry has been the failure of international diplomacy to resolve the conflict. Bâli and Rana identified two common arguments explaining the failure of the United Nations to negotiate a political solution to the conflict: the insistence on a "grand bargain" between all major parties and the legitimization of the Syrian regime as a credible negotiating partner.[30] Similarly, both Bellamy and Nassar have devoted book-length studies to the failure of peace processes in Syria from the perspective of the United Nations and international diplomacy.[31] This literature reflected the specific geopolitical dynamics of the conflict prior to Russian intervention.

After 2015, an extensive body of both policy and academic literature sought to explain the Russian intervention and its geopolitical aftermath,[32] but none of this work accounted for how this period created the political conditions for the punishment of disloyal subjects off the battlefield.

Literature on opposition and rebel politics during the war focused on either the organizational structure of opposition violence or the bureaucratization of rebel governance. The rise (and rapid fall) of the Islamic State of Iraq and al-Sham was the focus of extensive policy and scholarly work interested in both the group's battlefield strategies and its governance.[33] Various iterations of rebel governance strategies have been the focus of different studies interested in their structure and durability. Baczko and colleagues show how different social orders emerged in relation to the war around specific armed groups.[34] These orders tethered residents to armed groups through unique political economies and governance structures. Still other work focused on the organizational structure of the uprising and its manifestation in (temporary) governance structures that sought to institutionalize the revolution.[35] Yasser Munif's work, for example, shows how a revolutionary politics materialized outside of regime control and was ultimately undermined by counterrevolutionary forces.[36] Others have asked how Western support influenced rebel governance structures.[37] The principal concern of this research was to understand how social networks, foreign alliances, political economies, and battlefield shifts produced competing governance projects. Despite this interest in governance in wartime, little attention was paid to how state power was oriented around meeting battlefield needs.

Literature on Syria's evolving battlefield often understood state violence in relation to these post-2011 patterns at the expense of more nuanced, historically sensitive analysis of historical continuities. Marwa Daoudy's book, for example, offers unique insight into the failures of state environmental policies that predated and shaped the trajectory of the conflict.[38] Important correctives historicizing state violence have also emerged to counter narratives claiming that the post-2011 violence is somehow exceptional. Shaery-Yazdi and Üngör, for their part, see the post-2011 violence as an extension of "long-standing histories and practices that predate the current civil war."[39] Mass violence in Syria should be understood both in terms of how it unfolds during the armed struggle between military actors and how it is directed against civilians who are not part of the battlefield.[40]

The use of torture and mass incarceration, for example, were central tools of authoritarian governance for decades, but these took on renewed relevance in the context of the state's counterinsurgency campaign.[41] Jaber Baker and Ugur Ümit Üngör's magisterial *Syrian Gulag: Inside Assad's Prison System* is a haunting, meticulous mapping of the country's prisons and the system's effects on Syrians.[42] There is no other text in English that provides such a comprehensive study of the Syrian prison system. Üngor's analysis of the organizational structure of regime violence has also been productive in helping us think about regime responses to the conflict. He argues that the regime's "well-equipped coercive apparatus" consists of four major pillars: the army, intelligence agencies, special forces, and militias.[43] These pillars are vertically and horizontally linked in ways that allow a core regime elite to manage their destructive potential without risking internal dissent. The design and operation of this structure of violence predated the conflict and is a primary explanation for regime continuity after 2011. My book contributes to this research by showing how state practices likewise aimed at punishing disloyal subjects were extended into the post-2011 period to target new subjects (such as the terrorist, the absentee, or the deserter) who emerged during the conflict. In other words, violence was not the sole strategy deployed to punish state enemies.

Research on Syrian violence prior to and during the conflict often takes violence as a problem to be explained and understood. While my argument does not rest on making significant claims about mass violence as such, I am nevertheless interested in similar questions about how the state governs through enmity that materializes in both physical violence and bureaucratic punishment. Ora Szekeley's book on patterns of violence in Syria's civil war is a useful departure point for my own analysis. Szekely argues that "both the overall patterns of violence in the Syrian war and the use of performative violence in particular have been shaped in part by a conflict over what the war is truly about."[44] The argument that conflicting understandings of the civil war shape how actors conduct warfare is interesting in its tethering of narrative to violence. That "narratives have powerful effects in the context of civil war in general and in Syria in particular" suggests that how war is framed, narrated, presented, and understood has serious implications for how it unfolds.[45] Szekely argues that there are five major narratives of the conflict that shape the actual and performative violence of the war: "the conflict between dictatorship and democracy; a sectarian conflict between Sunnis and Alawites (or Shi'ites); a related conflict between secularists and fundamentalists; an ethnonationalist conflict between Kurds and Arabs; and a narrative of the war as a series of interrelated proxy conflicts."[46] I am interested in how narratives materialize in war, but unlike Szekely I am concerned with this as a bureaucratic and institutional problem and not one solely relegated to the battlefield. The question of how the regime narrates the war and how this is reflected in laws, practices, and institutions *away* from the battlefield is what most interests me here.

The categorization of disloyal subjects was the direct outcome of how the state narrated the conflict and produced state enemies as targets for punishment. Drawing on a case study of the Aleppo countryside in 2013, Josepha Wessels asks a chilling but important question about state violence: Why kill defenseless women, children, and elderly people? The answer does not merely relate to sectarianism. Wessels argues that state ideas about rurality and subaltern othering, along with retribution, opportunism, and strategic military calculations, all converged in the brutal violence inflicted on the inhabitants of the small village of Rasm al-Nafl.[47] The fifty-seven people needlessly massacred there were ultimately "dispensable" to the regime and rationalized as worthy victims of state violence through overlapping justifications, some of which, such as rurality and subalternity, predated the conflict. The complex processes subjectivizing the victims at Rasm al-Nafl are relevant to understanding how state institutions absorb and materialize a logic of enmity. As I argue below, the disloyal subject is itself a dispensable category in which other forms of punishing state violence—property appropriation, refusing repatriation, displacement, loss of public benefits, and so on—inflict something like a social, if not physical, death on Syrians. Citizens who are legally categorized and indexed as disloyal become dispensable to the state. In this book, then, I am interested in the political conditions in which certain people are rendered dispensable. While scholarly interest in these processes predates the conflict and extends into the post-2011 period, my study is the first to situate this within the post–Russian intervention period and to understand the punishment of disloyal subjects as a political project correlated to the battlefield.

Research on mass violence in Syria gives nuance to our understanding of state violence and the important role that categorization and narration play in its unfolding. Disaggregating and localizing our understanding of state violence in Syria is important if we are to see how macro- and microdynamics fuel violence against specific targets.[48] Salwa Ismail's work extends our understanding by framing this violence as *governmental*, residing at the very core of how the state governs society. Ismail's argument that Syrian governance constitutes a "civil war regime" in which the state is constantly at war with its citizens captures the complex continuities of violent state practices against the population.[49] For decades, the state was oriented toward the naming, management, and punishment of a fluid set of enemies. An enduring feature of Syria's civil war regime is the state's bifurcation of society and the punishment of perceived enemies through a coercive apparatus underpinned by mass incarceration and the constant threat of massacre. These two apparatuses of government were deployed to maintain friend/enemy distinctions and to "convey the message that violence is the primary and organizing modality of action in dealing with domestic opposition."[50] Ismail's work is central to my arguments here as she takes the state construction and infliction of violence on enemies as the starting point for understanding Syrian governmentality. For her, these official apparatuses directed toward "extermination and annihilation" are nothing less than a mode of government, and not some aberration. In making this argument Ismail is trying to understand the role that violence plays in shaping subjects and subjectivities. Throughout this book, I contend that similar processes of categorization of state enemies, the inflicting of punishment, and the creation of subjects and subjectivities necessary for post-conflict governance have occurred through conflict absorption. I argue that the production of subjects necessary for durable order occurs through both violence and the bureaucratization of punishment directed against state enemies.

The arguments in this book show how violence is extended through the bureaucratization of enmity as an expansion of the state's capacity to punish people who are categorized as enemies. Research into mass violence recognizes the role that both discursive dehumanization and state institutions play in perpetrating violence.[51] Bureaucratic capacity, or what Uzonyi calls "quality,"[52] is necessary to commit mass violence and fight wars but also to ensure the durability of an authoritarian order in the context of simmering conflict. The state cannot simply fight, bomb, or destroy its way to security and stability; rather, an apparatus of both control and exclusion must be erected to manage state enemies while ensuring that friends, no matter how temporary they are, acquiesce to authoritarian order. State practices exclude through bureaucratic practices that render segments of the population as enemies to be acted upon. Thus, while I agree with Ismail that "the enactment of ... political violence is grounded in the polarization of the body politic and in the introduction and continual nurturing of a breaking through it—the 'us' and 'them' divide"[53]—I wish to understand how this bifurcation extends to state practices that are not always recognized under the rubric of physical violence. Throughout this book, I show how these practices sometimes involve the violent displacement of people, such as in the case of reconciliations, and at other times the mundanely bureaucratic practice of rendering someone absent and forbidding their return to Syria. These seemingly banal categorizations can have profound effects on politics, statehood, and citizen subjectivity.

One area of inquiry that brings together the various analytical threads described above relates to how the war was understood, narrated, and conducted by the various actors. Literature that seeks to understand regime behavior has often focused on the exercise of violence and the role that the regime's external allies (Hizballah, Russia, and Iran) have played in ensuring its stability. My book seeks to extend this area of inquiry by asking how the state absorbed the logic of enmity and punishment. Despite the importance of the bureaucratization of enmity to the state's conflict management strategies, most research has focused almost exclusively on the reorganization of housing, land, and property (HLP) rights to provide various forms of bureaucratic punishment. Unruh's argument that the HLP system has been weaponized as a tool of war to both exclude populations deemed disloyal and reward loyalist elites captures the bureaucratic conflict management strategies I am interested in.[54] By extending our understanding of regime behavior to how state institutions absorbed the conflict's logic, I seek to show how violence and exclusion materialize beyond the prison and the battlefield. The reorientation of state practices around enmity and punishment provides insight into the circumstances in which a politics of reconciliation is eschewed in favor of a politics of enmity.

The relationship between mass violence and the bureaucratization of conflict is symbiotic, complementary, and interdependent. My arguments seek to expand our understanding of state violence by inquiring into the institutional apparatus of exclusion that parallels it. Societal bifurcation and political hatred did not simply materialize in prisons and on the battlefield; they also come about through appropriations, settlement decisions, repatriation politics, counterterrorism courts, laws, and the general chaos and uncertainty that accompanies each new decision that the state makes in managing conflict. This raises the question of who the state targets as enemies in the context of conflict. Simplistic explanations see this as a sectarian conflict in which an Alawi minority–dominated regime targets a Sunni-majority population. If this were the case, then the line between "us" and "them" would be easy to delineate. Sectarian narratives, however, are based on "false assumptions" about Syrian political identity,[55] on the one hand, and the logic of state repression, on the other. Without delving into these reductive debates, I believe it suffices to say that sectarianism plays a role but is not the determining factor in producing state enemies.[56] The argument that the regime is the protector of Syria's minorities certainly has resonance among a population that fears regime change, yet violence and exclusion has also been directed against minority communities in the very name of protection.[57] The dividing line between state friends and enemies is not sectarian but one produced politically and affectively by the state's targeting of anyone deemed an enemy.

Understandings of Syria's civil war as a purely sectarian conflict obfuscate alternative cleavages that subjectivize populations along strictly political lines. Sectarianism was certainly an important factor in how the regime ruled and governed and thus, in turn, how people understood and narrated the conflict. However, to reduce the conflict to one between the regime as either an "Alawi regime" or a presumed defender of minority populations and an exclusively Sunni opposition obscures the many other cross-cutting cleavages that shaped political loyalties during this period, including class, geography, demographics, and political beliefs. The subject that the state sought to render as disloyal throughout the conflict was thus not a purely Sunni subject, just as loyalist subjects were not reduced to Alawi or minority identities. Citizen subjectivity in wartime Syria was narrated and materialized as a political subjectivity whose bifurcating distinction was loyal and disloyal identities. Even if we were to take loyalty and disloyalty as proxies for sectarian identities, we would have to explain why so many Sunni loyalists were enriched during the war or why so many Christian and Alawi citizens were subject to asset forfeiture, imprisonment, torture, and murder. The disloyal subject that the state was acting upon in wartime Syria was one whose identity and "enemy" status were determined by a series of acts, non-acts, feelings, and other betrayals that constituted disloyalty, regardless of sect.

Betrayal of the Homeland explores how the relationship between mass violence and the bureaucratization of enmity produced the conditions for an illiberal political order. It is thus situated within a broader interest in how the Syrian regime conducted warfare and how the conflict trajectory from 2011 created the conditions for a new form of statehood. This is the first book to think beyond the Syrian battlefield in such a comprehensive way and to argue that conflict management strategies help explain the regime's durability, until 2024, amid metastasizing conflict. To understand the relationship between conflict management strategies and their impacts on statehood I draw on the authoritarian conflict management literature. This body of work has its foundations in the study of Eurasian conflict management and the central role that Russia, China, and other countries played in securing regime stability and preventing liberal political transitions. The ACM literature highlights how conflict management strategies produce illiberal outcomes while developing approaches for understanding how states manage simmering violence and political opposition.

Authoritarian Conflict Management and State Enmity

One of the principal arguments of this book is that the Syrian regime's conflict management strategies created state practices away from the battlefield oriented around the exclusion and punishment of state enemies. I am thus interested in what discourses, laws, practices, and institutions, were erected to ensure the durability of enmity and punishment. Throughout this book, I contend that conflict management strategies created new subjectivities, legalities, and practices that tethered citizenship and belonging to the conflict. The durable order that the regime envisioned creating was one in which new forms of legality produce durable forms of violence and exclusion. The question of how these practices bifurcated and acted upon Syrians is an important one. I argue that broad categories of loyalty and disloyalty informed the state's strategies toward different populations.

Some people are considered loyal, others disloyal, but these categories were never fixed, universal, or knowable. The chapters below detail the processes of categorization that produce subjects indexed as disloyal and how these politically relevant cleavages laid the foundation for an illiberal political order.

The distinction between authoritarian conflict management and illiberal state building is a relevant one taken up by scholars of conflict in recent years. Lewis and colleagues define authoritarian conflict management as "the prevention, de-escalation or termination of organised armed rebellion or other mass social violence such as inter-communal riots through methods that eschew genuine negotiations among parties to the conflict, reject international mediation and constraints on the use of force, disregard calls to address underlying structural causes of conflict, and instead rely on instruments of state coercion and hierarchical structures of power."[58] Authoritarian conflict management seeks to ensure regime security through social and political stability. Stabilizing measures are always intended to suppress opposition demands and to disincentivize rebellion. These measures rely on the actual and possible exercise of state violence against enemies. State institutions are oriented around stabilization, and a networked elite overlapping economic, security, and political spheres ensure the continuity of a regime's social base. In Syria's case, however, stabilization was always precarious because of the country's territorial fragmentation and continued economic pressures and isolation.

Authoritarian conflict management is not simply a temporary set of practices meant to quell armed rebellion; it can in fact foundationalize post-conflict order: "Not only does this model combine multiple practices and initiatives in different domains of state and social activity, it also acts as a *sustained mode of governance* that encompasses different phases of a conflict, including cessation of armed violence, post-conflict settlement and reconstruction processes, and on-going conflict prevention mechanisms."[59] Throughout this book, I show how the state's conflict management practices created the conditions for an illiberal political order. Conflict management practices are not turned on or off like a switch but instead become a part of the governance structure of authoritarian states as constitutive of the "civil war regime." The durability of the state's practices is evidenced in the reconciliation and settlement processes, the erection of a legal architecture of appropriation, the marshaling of new legal forms of punishment, and the enactment of a "social death" on Syrians whose political and legal categorizations index disloyalty.

The emergence of literature on authoritarian conflict management recognizes the growing, if not quite cohesive, alternatives to the externally led liberal management of conflict transition. Sometimes conflicts do not evolve into neat power-sharing agreements. The expectation of liberal peace proponents that they should follow such a trajectory has been undermined by an international order that is increasingly hostile to liberal interventions. While a coherent alternative to global liberalism has not emerged, alternative norms and practices to manage conflict have, and these practices reflect what scholars broadly refer to as authoritarian or illiberal conflict management. Scholars working with these ideas have identified three domains in which we can identify the theory and practice of authoritarian conflict management: a *spatial* politics in which both military and civilian controls are enacted; *economic* practices that distribute resources toward political outcomes, such as elite recruitment; and a *discourse* consisting of state propaganda, information control, and knowledge production.[60]

As a set of discursive practices, authoritarian conflict management seeks to create a hegemonic narrative of conflict that suppresses alternative narrations. State officials seek to create a "commonsense narration" of the conflict that rejects inclusivity and plurality as opportunities for oppositionists to articulate grievances.[61] The hegemonic conflict narrative seeks to undermine oppositionists and to prevent their inclusion in politics. Authoritarian states attempt to achieve this through coercion or repressing alternative interpretations of events, controlling news, limiting knowledge production, and generating official discourse about the war that undermines opposition grievances.[62] One of the most prevalent strategies of authoritarian states is to deploy the discourse of "terrorism" to undermine opponents. As we will see throughout this book, the spectral terrorist became the subject around which state discourse revolved and disloyal/loyal categories were constructed. Syrian officials acted not only on terrorist enemies, but also on a whole set of other subject categories that were created to justify punishment of civilians. The bifurcation of society into loyal and disloyal subjects made it easier to act upon the latter through the law as "Friend/Enemy discourses also allow the identification of internal 'fifth columns,' which are portrayed as aiding and abetting the enemy."[63] ACM scholarship treats discourse as constituting a world that state officials materialize through violence and the institutionalization of political hatred.

The spatial organization of conflict and the erasure of opposition presence is a second identifiable authoritarian conflict management strategy. The aim of spatial control is to prevent alternative political projects that can challenge state power. As such, authoritarian states "view space as a resource that can be used by would-be rebels, not only to organise, to recruit and to extract resources, but also to impose their own normative order on a part of the population, potentially strengthening their discursive appeal to a wider community. Authoritarian regimes therefore seek to penetrate, close or dominate space through military patrols, encampment and occupation, by the forced resettlement of civilians."[64] Space is controlled through military practices, reconstruction policy, repatriation politics, and urban planning. As I argue below, the regime's ability to control space was made possible by the Russian military intervention and the subsequent Astana process that carved Syria's territory into several de-escalation zones patrolled by Russian and Turkish forces. Meanwhile, the shifting battlefield allowed the state to develop forced displacement practices under the guise of "reconciliation" agreements with civilians and fighters in formerly rebel-held areas. These agreements gave fighters and civilians two options: either accept displacement to Idlib Governorate or stay and "settle" their status with the state. Anyone engaged in opposition politics typically chose displacement out of fear of state retribution. While these practices cleansed areas of disloyal subjects, a legal infrastructure emerged to erase the vestiges of opposition rule through the reorganization of HLP rights and prevent the return of subjects deemed disloyal by the state.

Spatial control of territory was requisite for the state's political economy of conflict management. In the economic domain, states seek to control resources both to prevent oppositionists from acquiring them but also to distribute them to elite and clientelist networks. As Lewis and colleagues write, "such measures of economic control and co-optation often provide the most durable practices of conflict management" because they create an economic order that reflects the political management of conflict.[65] Post-2011 legal changes in Syria aimed at reversing any possibility of integrating opposition governance structures into the post-conflict order. New laws after 2016 were especially targeted toward an erasure of the political economy of non-regime rule through the annulment of property transfers. As I discuss in chapter 4, these annulments rendered wartime political economies invisible while also creating legal ambiguities around ownership that ultimately led to property and asset forfeiture by the state. The appropriation and auctioning off of absentee subjects' property has become an important mechanism to reward loyalists. The intertwining of discursive, economic, and spatial practices served to punish enemies and create a durable order through the exclusion of disloyal subjects. The point, so to speak, of authoritarian conflict management is to suppress alternatives to state power, whether in the realm of memory politics or land ownership.

The ACM literature is nascent and open to theoretical and empirical innovations. Throughout this book I engage with a lacuna in the ACM literature identified by Chalermsripinyorat, who shows how the Thai state's approach to separatist movements in the South involved forms of "legal bargaining" to co-opt or neutralize opponents.[66] The legal tools deployed by the state largely revolved around forms of surrender through amnesty programs and pardons. The question of how legal tools are deployed as forms of conflict management is largely peripheral to the ACM framework. In this book, I centralize legal tools as part of the Syrian state's conflict management and identify the myriad ways in which the law is not only used to co-opt or transform enemies into friends but also deployed as a technique of punishment. In the case of the reconciliation process, for example, the law serves to formally transform former fighters and integrate them into the counterinsurgency apparatus. While fighters and civilians are given opportunities to prove their loyalty to the state, others are punished for their supposed disloyalty. These forms of punishment are primarily enacted against the displaced through various legal measures. The counterterrorism courts that were created to try those suspected of terrorism are an example of an altogether new legal infrastructure established during the conflict so as to bifurcate society and punish enemies.

The area of inquiry most relevant to this book, but which is largely peripheral to the ACM literature, is the relationship between law and categorization. Enemy categories are given legal expression through various subjectivities—absentee, unsettled, martyr, missing, terrorist, deserter, and so on—that carry attendant rewards and punishments that materialize illiberal political order. These categorizations give specific meaning to disloyal and loyal subjects, producing reward and punishment regimes that affectively and politically tie Syrians to the state through relations of enmity.[67] The processes through which these subjects are rendered legible and how collective identities were institutionalized and acted upon through specific punishments is my principal interest here. Legible communities were constructed around specific acts rather than prescribed geographic, linguistic, sectarian, or class identities. Broad categorizations of communities around acts of disloyalty lacked any precision, such that a person was easily identified as disloyal. Syrian officials circumvented the problem of precision by rendering disloyalty through a series of acts, such as displacement, posting on social media, or simply a denunciation from a neighbor.

Enmity, Subjectivity, and the Punishment of "Legible" Populations

If war is a set of social relations, then enmity is part of its structuring economy. How does political hatred and enmity become institutionalized? What practices serve to punish enemy populations? How do state officials' narration of the conflict materialize as laws, practices, and institutions that punish Syrians? These questions are at the heart of this book. German jurist and political theorist Carl Schmitt is the starting point for any discussion of political hatred and enmity. An avowed and committed Nazi, Schmitt advanced a theory of politics that revolved around the "friend-enemy distinction." For Schmitt, "the specific political distinction to which political actions and motives can be reduced is that between friend and enemy."[68] There is no mistaking Schmitt's authoritarian, illiberal politics. His theory of politics was developed to advance the basis for an exclusionary political order. Schmitt's advancing of an illiberal politics has paradoxically helped scholars understand the machinations of authoritarian politics. Lewis identifies three ways that Schmitt helps us understand authoritarian conflict management: first, in his claims that pluralist political orders are inherently destabilizing and conflict-producing, and that sustainable political order therefore requires centralized power;

second, in his denial that conflict can be resolved through liberal dialogue and consensus; and, finally, by arguing that politics is rooted in spatial control and not universalist liberal norms.[69] Schmitt's critique of liberal politics is also a blueprint by which to understand illiberal states.

Achille Mbembe has engaged Schmitt's concept of enmity as it relates to postcolonial states, Israeli occupation, and the proliferating violence of borders, walls, and security practices in the early twenty-first century. His engagement with Schmitt takes the concept of enmity as an analytical framework through which to understand how states construct political order. Mbembe advances the idea of a "society of enmity" in which enemies are produced and acted upon to create regimes of separation. To live in a society of enmity is to live amid violent practices intended to separate and exclude, a society "whose functioning paradoxically depends on an intimate proximity with those who have been separated."[70] The enemy is not a distant abstraction, but rather a knowable, proximate subject who must be carved out of the body politic.

Mbembe draws on Schmitt to deepen how we understand enmity as structuring politics in the contemporary age:

> If our world today is an effectuation of Schmitt's, then the concept of enemy is to be understood for its concrete and existential meaning, and not at all as a metaphor or an empty lifeless abstraction. The enemy Schmitt describes is neither a simple competitor, nor an adversary, nor a private rival whom one might hate or feel antipathy for. He is rather the object of a *supreme antagonism*. In both body and flesh, the enemy is that individual whose physical death is warranted by their existential denial of our own being.[71]

Moreover, "the contemporary age can be seen to embody the fundamental character of the political as a hatred of the enemy, the need to neutralize him, and a generalized desire to avoid the sorts of dangers and contagion he is perceived to bring."[72] I ask how the Syrian state constructs hatred against enemies and materializes this enmity through various punishments that attempt to carve out disloyal subjects from Syrian political order. The materialization of a supreme antagonism against state enemies creates the conditions for a type of illiberal state oriented toward exclusion and violence.

Enmity and political hatred have structured how the Syrian state has been reoriented around political order in the wake of simmering conflict. The Syrian state has eschewed political deliberation and instead constructed a durable political order from the remnants of conflict by maintaining friend/enemy distinctions. The discursive construction of these distinctions relies on several indexical framings that are repeated over and over again in state discourse: enemies of the homeland, misguided citizens, terrorists, and so on. These categorizations index disloyalty and materialize in punishments that effectuate what Mbembe calls a form of "social death."[73] Antagonism does not in and of itself produce this social death; rather, the outcome is a comprehensive punishment regime linking discourse, laws, institutions, and practices to the political project of excluding Syrian state enemies.

How did the Syrian regime render the population legible during the conflict and how did these categorizations correspond to punishment and reward regimes? The discursive processes through which state officials render populations legible during wartime materialize in legal regimes that distribute rewards and punishments accordingly. Categories of loyal and disloyal produce political and legal subjectivities around which the state can act to both punish and reward. The family of a "martyr," for example, may be entitled to a state pension, whereas the family of a "missing person" may have their property appropriated by the state, while someone who was "absent from state territory because of terrorism" will be allowed to return without punishment. State categorization is tied to narratives of responsibility and victim/perpetrator binaries.

The Syrian population was rendered legible through the deployment or expansion of existing categories of disloyalty (such as missing person) and the creation of altogether new categories tied to the conflict, such as absentee, unsettled, or reconciled. Such political categorizations correspond with legal subjectivities that inform punishment and reward regimes. Categorizations are determined by acts and non-acts that are legalized and punishable as disloyal. A displaced person, for example, was often considered to be disloyal because they had left the country and had not returned. Their property may be appropriated by the state for this presumed act of disloyalty. Similar punishments were aimed at deserters or people accused of "terrorism." As a series of punishable acts (e.g., deserting) and non-acts (e.g., not returning) these categorizations cut across sectarian and ethnic affiliations. Disloyalty was not explicitly codified by sect or region, but rather through act or non-act.

The counter-subject to the disloyal Syrian was the loyalist subject who was presumably supportive of the state's conflict management practices. Wedeen, Ismail, and others have contributed to complicating our understanding of citizen loyalty and the affective dimensions of regime rule. Consequently, it is simply too reductionist to reduce "loyalty" to a core set of beliefs or commitments. There were indeed many Syrians who supported the regime's conflict management strategies out of the objective fear of opposition violence. Many Syrians rejected both the opposition groups and the regime. Many of those who were forcibly subject to seizure and other forms of violence by armed groups saw in the regime a source of protection. These complexities cannot be ignored or lost in the subsequent discussion of the state's production of the disloyal subject. Regime power and support from the population was always tenuous throughout the conflict. Moreover, the regime's ability to project power was always limited by the strength of the opposition and the limited resource base on which the regime could draw to reconstruct areas under its control. Thus, the story told here is not one of an all-encompassing regime capable of shape transforming Syrians into loyal or disloyal subjects, but rather a story of a regime deploying various conflict management strategies in order to retain political control. As the collapse of the regime in December 2024 demonstrates, this control was always unstable.

Conflict Absorption and Illiberal Political Order

My inquiry into the management of the Syrian conflict through the state's reorientation around the identification and punishment of enemy populations reflects an interest in what Khoury calls "war as a form of everyday bureaucratic governance."[74] Understanding conflict as a set of policy and bureaucratic problems that exist in relation to, but nevertheless apart from, the battlefield provides insight into how war's horrors are normalized, bureaucratized, and absorbed into the state apparatus. Moreover, we can gain insight into how populations are rendered legible in conflict terms and acted upon through the machinations of the state such that war emerges "as a way of governing that structures everyday lives."[75] The state's transformation around counterinsurgency required the wholesale reorganization of the state apparatus to develop new models, methods, and strategies of governance aimed at the management of the Syrian population. The processes through which the state identified, rendered legible, and acted upon different segments of the population through bureaucratic policy decisions are the central focus of this book.

The execution of the war on the battlefield and through regional alliances (principally with Hizballah, Iran, and Russia) occurred alongside the absorption of the war into the state as a mode of governing. This governance model established the criteria through which society could be bifurcated and acted upon through systems of punishment that extended from imprisonment through to asset seizure to forms of social death via the erasure of legal identity and the legal basis of Syrian citizenship. To enact these different forms of punishment against disloyal, treasonous, and recalcitrant subjects, the state absorbed battlefield practices honed through the reconciliation and settlement processes by which the loyal were bifurcated and divided from the disloyal and new techniques of punishment extended against the latter. The logic of enmity and political hatred that fueled conflict had slowly been absorbed into the state apparatus. Paradoxically, as the state's capacity to govern and reconstruct the country diminished, its capacity to enact punishment increased.

These new techniques of governing a population during war required innovations in the state's epistemological, carceral, and legal practices to determine who was and was not a disloyal enemy.

How did the Syrian regime conceptualize, codify, and act upon ideas of loyalty? Unlike the Iraqi regime, which measured loyalty by attitude,[76] the Syrian regime enacted laws that measured specific acts as constituting disloyalty. In Iraq, measuring attitudes relied on various surveillance methods and information relayed to the state security apparatus about an individual's or family's politics and social proclivities. Generating knowledge about someone's attitudes depended on ever-changing assumptions about what constituted proper or problematic attitudes and complicated surveillance methods that relied on denunciations, cadre reports, and other forms of informing that required some corroboration. In Syria, acts and non-acts constituted the basis of categorization alongside attitudes (as measured by denunciations, engagement in opposition politics, or social media posts, among other forms of evidence) to determine who was a disloyal subject.

I want to illustrate the phenomenon of conflict absorption through a truncated version of a story that unfolds over several chapters of the book.[77] In 2012, a new state ministry called the Ministry of National Reconciliation was created. The stated aim of the new ministry, as its name suggested, was to foster national reconciliation between Syrians and to serve as an institutional platform for deliberation. This liberal intent, of course, belied the violence and exclusionary practices wielded by the ministry toward real and spectral regime enemies via the reconciliation agreements. These reconciliation agreements were at first negotiated by local actors in civil committees, but when Russian military forces entered Syria in September 2015 they began to standardize, oversee, and monitor their negotiations. Russia established the Russian Reconciliation Center for Syria for the monitoring of national reconciliations, located at the Hmeimin Air Base, through which its personnel would guide the work of the civil committees.

The civil committees largely operated outside of state oversight. So wide was the gap between the ministry and the civil committees that a parliamentary body reporting directly to the Council of Ministers was created to oversee the work of these committees, including appointing new members (who were always local notables), although the Ministry of National Reconciliation was created to do precisely what the committees were doing. As Russian military advances brought more and more territory under state control after 2015, the importance of the civil committees relative to the Russian military presence and the state apparatus increased considerably. Specifically, the civil committees emerged to take on important state functions, including generating knowledge about the Syrian population that could then be marshaled to punish state enemies. They became the principal actor for the identification of friends and enemies and the deployment of state power against the disloyal. Meanwhile, the Ministry of National Reconciliation was dissolved in 2019.

Civil committees henceforth assumed the responsibility for generating knowledge about Syrians and their property. To this end, they sought information on various questions, the answers to which would determine whether and how Syrians could live in their own country: Who is displaced?

What properties have been abandoned or damaged? How did people die? Who engaged in "terrorism"? Who can return? and so on. The committees' role in categorizing acts corresponded to a post-2011 legal architecture that sought to punish Syrians for their "betrayal of the homeland." To enact punishment, Syrians were to be categorized and acted upon accordingly. Once categorized, the names of citizens were then sent to the Ministry of Finance, which issued circulars denouncing individuals for specific crimes and measures for property appropriation. Categorization and punishments extended to a series of crimes that broadly fell under the category of acts of disloyalty. Anyone caught in this web of categorization and punishment risked losing not only their assets but their social identity as a Syrian who could own property, work, or reside in the country. Punishment was also extended to kin in various ways, such as the unexplained deactivation of close to 600,000 smart cards used to distribute state subsidies.[78]

The relational power dynamics linking civil committees, the Russian military, and state institutions is one example of the process of conflict absorption through which the state is reoriented around the gradual bureaucratic process of punishing Syrians. The question that I am interested in, then, is how we understand categorization and punishment as a form of government in Syria that was reliant on the objective power (and fear) of violence, but which was nevertheless enacted through the slow bureaucratic process of appropriation and exclusion. I contend that conflict absorption in Syria should be understood in terms of war's normalization and institutionalization as a set of practices that seek to extend the enmity of war to the future.

Conflict Absorption and Political Order

One of the principal arguments I make in this book is that violence in Syria was transmuted to create more highly institutionalized, bureaucratic mechanisms of punishment. I refer to this process as *conflict absorption* and locate it within the emergence of state practices that identified, bifurcated, and punished citizens deemed disloyal. As such, I am interested less in questions about whether or not Syria was in a post-conflict stage after Russian intervention than about how violence persists, how enmity and punishment get absorbed into the state apparatus, and how a political order centered around exclusion and that extends political hatred into the future emerged out of these processes. Although 2011 was indeed a spectacular moment of revolutionary upheaval in which the "wall of fear" was toppled, state practices after the outbreak of protests had their roots in decades of authoritarian state building. The regime, in other words, had learned how to engage in conflict with its own population.

Anthropologists of conflict have taught us that wars have no easily defined beginnings or ends. Thinking of war as part of a continuum rather than a singular, temporally delimited process can help us uncover the antecedents of a state's practices toward its citizenry in moments of conflict, low- or high-intensity violence, or "peace." The start of the Syrian conflict is (rightly) dated to early 2011 when the first protests calling for political reforms began, with most identifying the imprisonment and torture of school children in Dar'aa as the start of the conflict. Yet, the Syrian state's conflict management strategies were not born out of the post-2011 period but instead have their antecedents in what Salwa Ismail calls a "civil war regime."[79]

I am interested in the conditions of possibility for the durability of conflict, not its cessation. This means tracing the forms of institutionalization, legality, discourse, and violence that perpetuated rather than ended conflict. Creating a durable order out of the ashes of conflict by creating new subjects, legalities, subjectivities, and practices tethers citizenship and belonging to the conflict. I take these processes as productive of illiberal state building emerging out of a particular kind of "peace" that had persisted through more than a decade of conflict. The persistence of the regime during this time amid mass violence, fragmentation, and economic collapse demands a deeper explanation that this book tries to provide. In particular, the "peace" that emerged after the Russian intervention was one that demanded the continued reproduction of political hatred and punishment against disloyal subjects to sustain itself. This substituted for a genuine political process or reconciliation. The conflict management strategies explored in this book should thus help us explain how "peace" persisted for years and how the regime was able to maintain power during the conflict until it ultimately collapsed in December 2024. The peace that the regime sought contrasts with liberal assumptions about what conflict resolution and peace entail in the aftermath of conflict and can best be described as authoritarian, illiberal, or repressive because of the continuity of enmity, punishment, and violence into the supposed post-conflict period.[80]

Liberal peace assumes that the suppression of future conflict occurs through power sharing, whereas an authoritarian peace can be understood as a form of peace oriented around regime stability and the suppression of opposition politics. Both forms of peace emerge from radically different approaches to peacebuilding. Smith and colleagues draw three important distinctions between liberal and illiberal peacebuilding: "In place of Western powers, illiberal peace-building is dominated by domestic actors. In place of economic neo-liberalism, illiberal peace-building runs on clientelism, cronyism and corruption. In place of liberal ideals of equality and liberty, illiberal peace-building emphasises illiberal norms of inequality and order."[81] Moreover, "what characterises the core of illiberal peace-building is the prioritisation of regime security and stability over accountability, human rights and social inclusion."[82] The objective of illiberal peacebuilding is to create a durable order that suppresses alternatives to incumbent regimes while managing conflict within the elite networks and social bases that constitute state power. The political impulse is to exclude alternatives.

How Do We Study the Regime? How Do We Study the State?

How do we study the Syrian regime when its inner workings are opaque and invisible while its effects are profoundly known, felt, and feared among Syrian society? This is an extremely difficult question to answer without access to a vast state archive such as that of the Ba'th Arab Socialist Party of Iraq, the Hizb al-Ba'th al-'Arabi al-Ishtiraki Records, 1968–2003, held at the Hoover Institution at Stanford University before being repatriated to Baghdad. This archive provided scholars with robust material around which to understand the machinations of Iraqi state power, the role of specific individuals and institutions within that constellation of power, and how the Iraqi state "saw" and acted upon the citizenry.[83] Without such access we are left to explore different ways of understanding how a political order emerged in Syria during the conflict.

Although in the case of Syria we as researchers do not have access to a comprehensive state archive, the regime remains methodologically and politically accessible because "the covers are off and the will to exclude, marginalize, and brutalize is not concealed but celebrated."[84] I am motivated by Chatterjee's own struggles working with "an archive that wears its politics on its sleeve" and where political norms are explicit and undenied. How do we research and understand governance systems when state officials, courts, ministries, and elites willfully expressed their desire to violently exclude perceived enemies? Drawing on the works of Annelise Riles and Ann Stoler, Chatterjee calls for an "along the grain" reading of documents and archives that "emphasizes densities, regularities, and distributions" that also pays attention to the materialities of what is being said and done. My arguments in this book are derived from my understanding of these kinds of dense patterns across the post-2011 period. I take seriously what state officials say, what institutions are created and how they operate, how laws function, and I do so alongside material derived from a long-term interview study of Syrians seeking to understand fear and insecurity under authoritarian rule.

What, then, does it mean to read along the grain of documents and archives of the Syrian state? I take several methodological and empirical approaches to this question. First, following the ACM literature, I take state discourse seriously as a way of imagining and ordering the world. Analysis of state officials' discourses allows us to notice patterns and relationships in the narration of conflict.[85] I refer to these discourses collectively as the commonsense narration of conflict. Much like Szekely, I wish to see how narrative materializes. Second, tracing the materialization of this discourse through institutions and laws reveals dense, regular patterns from which to understand conflict absorption. Searching for consistencies across these different material and institutional forms allows us to understand how the commonsense narration of conflict materializes as a governance system. Third, tracing the legal, rather than just bodily, effects of state violence as a form of exclusion are made possible by the state's insistence on rendering appropriation and exclusion legal and thus subject to public dissemination. The state gazette, for example, contains all the information on individuals and why they are targeted for punishment.

Tracing the institutionalization of a commonsense narrative about the conflict through government bodies, elite networks, laws, and courts allow us to address "what forms of legality, sociality, and politics transform spectacular violence into durable order."[86] I am interested not in how the battlefield shifts but in how a logic of enmity seeps into bureaucracy and institutions and orients the state apparatus around the punishment of enemies. These punishments most obviously take the form of murder, torture, and imprisonment and have (rightly) been the focus of much research about the conflict. The understanding of punishment I advance here refers more to the social death of the Syrian citizen.[87]

Structure of the Book

There are two distinct periods defining the Syrian conflict. The first period lasted from 2011 until late 2015 and was characterized by a political and military stalemate. In these years, violence proliferated, and Syrian territory fragmented among competing armed groups and their attendant governance projects. International efforts to resolve the conflict failed miserably at bringing about any meaningful cessation of violence or serious political negotiations to end the conflict. The second period was defined by the breaking of the military and political stalemate after Russian military intervention in September 2015. This intervention was a major inflection point in the conflict and created the conditions of possibility for regime stability and new forms of conflict management. The post-2015 period was also characterized by unresolved territorial issues in the northwestern and northeastern parts of the country. A third period began in December 2024 after the regime collapsed, creating entirely new paths for Syria's political trajectory.

This book is predominantly focused on the period after the Russian intervention when the stalemate was broken and renewed authoritarian conflict management practices were made possible. These practices helped sustain regime rule until its collapse in December 2024. The first chapter focuses on this period of transition from stalemate to the Astana process and shows how the changing battlefield was reflected in a regionally negotiated agreement between Iran, Turkey, and Russia to manage the Syrian conflict through trilateral consensus. The innovative battlefield strategies that emerged from tripartite negotiations allowed the regime to cleanse areas of disloyal subjects through reconciliation agreements and settlements while reestablishing control over territory formerly held by rebels. The emergence of Astana as the principal regional forum to manage the Syrian conflict peripheralized the United Nations and other international actors and prevented from playing a major role in shaping Syria's political future. It is in this context of Astana's hegemonic role that the regime's authoritarian conflict management strategies could unfold.

Chapter 2 focuses on the state's construction of a conflict narrative around the subject of the spectral terrorist. Situating the Syrian conflict within a global war on terrorism discourse, Syrian officials sought to present both violent and nonviolent opposition as terroristic. Such discourses suppressed any possibility for engaging with serious opposition grievances or in political negotiations. The spectral terrorist gave rise to a series of discourses around terroristic acts of betrayal that constituted harms against the homeland. Terrorism became discursively associated with social media posts, leaving the country, and even harboring negative feelings about the homeland. This expansive definition of terrorism was codified in Law No. 22, which collapsed all violent and nonviolent acts "against the homeland" as terroristic. This law coincided with the creation of a special Counter-Terrorism Court (CTC) to try state enemies. This kangaroo court tried tens of thousands of people in procedures that typically lasted a few minutes. All cases referred to the CTC (even those in abstention) automatically subjected citizens to state appropriation. To be rendered a terrorist in Syria was to effectively be cast out of the body politic as a disloyal subject.

The discursive and political processes for the transformation of enemies into friends and the bifurcation of loyal and disloyal subjects is the concern of chapter 3. The reconciliation process was a localized battlefield innovation that emerged during the stalemate period and then standardized and nationalized under Russian supervision beginning in late 2015. These agreements emerged out of battlefield sieges in which areas under rebel control were cut off from supply routes and encircled by regime forces. Once isolated, rebels and civilians under their control were given one of two bad options: either accept displacement to Idlib governorate or "reconcile" with the state and remain. Fighters were given the opportunity to be remobilized into the state's counterinsurgency apparatus. Anyone who wished to stay was allowed to do so. Those who left were effectively denationalized; their assets were appropriated, and they were forbidden from returning and living under state control. In physically and legally separating loyal and disloyal subjects, the reconciliation process allowed the state to control reconciled areas while minimizing threats from opposition politics.

Reconciliation was repurposed through the settlement process that citizens repatriating to reconciled areas or other areas under state control had to endure to be granted permission to return. In chapter 4, I show how the settlement process was constructed as a loyalty test in which returnees were required to perform the role of "loyal returnees" in order to formally "settle" their status with the state and return home. The settlement process involved the completion of a four-page questionnaire and an interview with a security official after which a determination of one's loyalty was rendered. Syrians outside of their country were permitted to apply through power of attorney. Applying for settlement was a complicated process for returnees who feared state punishment if they were *matloob* (wanted) or otherwise associated with denounced subjects. The settlement process was presented to the public as a return to the embrace of the homeland, where both repentant subjects and those "displaced by terrorism" would fulfill their national duty to rebuild their war-torn country. Much like the reconciliation process's alchemic transformation of fighters, the settlement process allowed citizens to reverse state categorizations that indexed them as disloyal. Settlement decisions were divorced from any restitution. People were allowed to return, but any punishments they incurred, such as property appropriation, could only be reversed through entirely different processes and applications filed with local civil committees.

Chapter 5 takes up the issue of the absent subject in Syria by inquiring into how the state categorized different forms of death, displacement, and absence. Some deaths were attributed to "terrorists" and thus conferred on the deceased's family the status of martyr and several (meager) economic benefits. Some forms of absence were due to terrorism, and still others because of a betrayal of the homeland. Half of Syria's population was displaced during the war, with hundreds of thousands of people killed, imprisoned, or missing. The state's resumption of control over reconciled areas allowed for the production of knowledge about absent populations and the implementation of measures to punish those deemed disloyal.

The circumstances surrounding the collapse of the regime and the creation of a transition authority in Syria in late 2024 form the subject of chapter 6. Here, I outline the military campaign that led to the overthrow of the regime before identifying some of the key transition challenges facing Syria's current and future authorities. In doing so, I highlight how political transition will occasion a series of encounters between different social and political forces inside and outside of Syria that will shape the country's transition trajectory. Encounters around reconstruction, refugee repatriation, transitional justice, governance, the constitution, and demilitarization will all shape how Syria's authorities are able to manage political transition.

Finally, the conclusion considers what the book's arguments mean in the context of a simmering conflict, continued territorial fragmentation, economic collapse, and continued global isolation.

1
The Astana Process and the Regional Context of Conflict Management

We reviewed our measures to create an atmosphere of peace and stability in Syria so that a political solution becomes feasible. The Astana process format is the most effective measure that facilitates a political solution in this regard.

—TURKISH PRESIDENT RECEP TAYYIP ERDOĞAN

Introduction

Syria's conflict created the conditions for widespread military intervention by several states who pursued competing political projects amid metastasizing violence. The United States established military bases in the country; Israel repeatedly bombed government and opposition sites; Iran, Russia, and Hizballah provided military support for the regime; and pro-opposition states like Qatar, Saudi Arabia, and Turkey funneled resources to various groups that contributed to their fragmentation. Meanwhile, the United Nations repeatedly tried to initiate a deliberative process to end the conflict. From the chaos of this landscape of widespread intervention emerged the Astana process, a tripartite model of conflict management led by Russia, Iran, and Turkey to manage the conflict. The Astana process was initially conceived as a model to manage various truces and reconciliation agreements between regime and rebel forces, but it eventually grew into a more complex mechanism to manage key aspects of the Syrian battlefield. This mechanism fostered cooperation by the tripartite powers and subjected major battlefield decisions to their consensus decision-making. The Astana process would also emerge as a space for the political negotiation of Syria's future after the regime declared "victory": A constitutional process, a repatriation program, and other political decisions were increasingly taking shape within the Astana framework. The norms, strategies, and practices associated with that framework emerged from the specificities of the battlefield and political landscape rather than through some grand design imposed by Russia, Iran, and Turkey. Astana thus more closely resembled a victor's vision for Syria than a negotiated solution.

United Nations–led interventions in the 1990s into conflict zones reflected a discursive and policy landscape imbued with the supposed triumph of liberalism after the collapse of the Soviet Union. The liberal peace interventions of the 1990s in Somalia, Bosnia, Liberia, Haiti, and elsewhere were stamped with a liberal optimism that external interventions could orient (post-)conflict societies around democracy and free markets. These interventions were intended to be total in their institutional and political reorganization of states: Constitutions were rewritten, markets were created, laws were enacted, and a culture of consumption was promoted through all corners of the globe that was captured in the language of "globalization" that pervaded the period. The total transformation of post-Soviet space that liberal interveners had attempted to effectuate had been transplanted into conflict resolution and peacebuilding.

Western euphoria that informed post–Cold War liberal peace interventions has recently given way to an acknowledgment that alternative methods of conflict resolution and conflict management, like the Astana process, have emerged from outside the West. These approaches are increasingly dominating the landscape of conflict interventions and shaping conflict trajectories.[1] China has taken on increasingly important roles in conflict resolution and peacebuilding around the world. A discernable Chinese "approach to peacebuilding" is rooted in hostility to liberal peace policy prescriptions that rejects norms and state roles advanced by the United Nations.[2] China's new role as a peacebuilder emphasizes a "development peace" that privileges economic growth over political transition.³ China is not the only country contributing to the rise of alternatives to liberal peace approaches. Turkey's peacebuilding efforts, for example, mimic liberal discourse without adopting most of the substantive policies of liberal peace.⁴ Russian intervention in places like Syria and Libya similarly reflects alternative norms, military strategies, and economic approaches to conflict zones. While these approaches have not collectively cohered into a discernable alternative to the United Nations framework for liberal peace interventions, they do represent approaches to the management, rather than resolution, of conflicts. Astana may have served as an alternative, but it was a highly contingent one whose trajectory was determined by the battlefield.

The failure of the United Nations to oversee a peace process for Syria should partly be understood in this context of alternative approaches to conflict management that have proliferated in recent years. These alternatives eschew conflict resolution in favor of conflict management that seeks political stability through the preservation of regime power. Unlike liberal interventions that seek power sharing and inclusion of oppositionists into government, illiberal approaches to conflict management seek to craft forms of peace that ensure the exclusion of state enemies from political power.⁵ This tension between liberal and illiberal approaches to conflict resolution/management inform the two questions I ask in this chapter: How was the United Nations–led Geneva process to resolve the Syrian conflict supplanted by the Russian-, Turkish-, and Iranian-designed Astana process to manage it? And how did the Astana design enable specific approaches to conflict management?

In asking these two questions I am interested in understanding how we conceptualize conflicts that do not end in liberal interventions and what this global trend meant for Syria. The Astana process's designs for Syria were born not out of universalist ideas about how conflicts should be managed or how they should end but rather the contextual negotiations between the tripartite powers. Successive rounds of negotiations between the powers reflected the ad hoc, contingent nature of deliberations. Astana's agenda, so to speak, was not the production of an ideal liberal society from the aftermath of conflict, but the management of Syria's conflict through a regional power structure that was itself born out of the trilateral relations between the Astana powers on other regional political issues.⁶ The circumstances surrounding how that structure emerged, how it supplanted the UN's efforts, and how it has enabled the regime's conflict management strategies is the concern of this chapter.

Managing Stalemate Until 2015

Conflicts are driven by macropolitical struggles (such as control over state power) and the localized conflicts that occur simultaneously. Lubkemann calls these localized conflicts "subplots" that have their own specificities, actors, issues, and forms of conflict resolution that are relational to the larger conflict but are nevertheless not solely defined by it.[7] Much of the literature on conflicts understands these subplots as fragments of war that reflect "local orders" or the "micro-dynamics of conflict."[8] Conflicts often give impetus toward the revival of dormant grievances and the emergence of war economies that produce their own logics of violence and "new" conflict elites. Conflict between Free Syrian Army (FSA) factions and Islamist fighters over control of the Bab al-Hawa crossing in 2012 was an early example in Syria's conflict of how local orders emerged outside of the broader struggle between the regime and its opponents.

The cumulative effect of Syria's local orders was to produce a military stalemate that was paralleled at the regional and international levels by a political stalemate. Metastasizing violence and the proliferation (and fragmentation) of armed groups created a fluid battlefield in which armed groups, often buttressed by rivaling state sponsors, were strong enough to remain militarily relevant but not strong enough to capture and control territory. Political efforts led by the United Nations and League of Arab States were unsuccessful in initiating a meaningful deliberative peace process or securing any political gains aside from a series of ceasefires and the opening of humanitarian corridors. While these gains reflect the complex interdependence between humanitarian and international peace negotiations,[9] the lack of tangible political outcomes preserved the stalemate. Syria's "war system" produced a protracted conflict in which actors calculated that the cost of continuing war was preferable to ending it.[10] The war was to be fought and won on the battlefield, and until then, a political process would not be a viable solution to ending the conflict.

The Syrian regime's management of the conflict occurred at the level of the battlefield and the international arena. On the latter front, Russia's support was central to the regime's ability to prevent an externally imposed negotiated solution to the conflict and the inclusion of the opposition and potentially the regime's enemies in any post-conflict government. During the 2011–2015 stalemate period Syria's local orders also contributed to the failure of efforts to resolve the conflict. Syria's stalemate was partly fueled by the competing interventions of regional states who erratically and inconsistently supported the political and armed opposition to the detriment of their consolidation. The FSA, for example, was rife with turf wars as Qatari-, Saudi-, or Turkish-backed officers jockeyed for control of the organization. Lacking any command hierarchy and with limited vertical coordination between the factions, the FSA quickly splintered into a series of localized groups incapable of forming a cohesive armed opposition. The Salafist-jihadist landscape was similarly fragmented as battalions, brigades, and fronts formed and contracted based on short-term battlefield needs. The cycle of external aggravation of battlefield fragmentation created fluid alliances and metastasizing local conflicts that fed into the larger stalemate. Qatari-Saudi competition in Syria occurred amid ongoing tension between the two countries' policies toward the Arab uprisings, culminating in a Saudi-led Arab Gulf isolation of Qatar.[11] Regional conflicts were thus shaping the nature of the Syrian battlefield as rivalries played out through the support of opposing groups.

The metastasizing battlefield produced fragmentation rather than consolidation of the armed groups who had differing perspectives on alliance building, governance, and political strategies. These conflicting visions created a fragmented battlefield in which nongovernment forces were often at odds with one another and not the government itself. By 2015, there were major pockets of armed group control, including the Islamic State of Iraq and al-Sham (ISIS), the Syrian Democratic Forces (SDF), Jabhat an-Nusra (JAN), the FSA, and other armed groups.[12] These groups were not strong enough to defeat each other, but they were strong enough to maintain a presence on the battlefield and create competing governance projects. The Rojava administration developed in the Northeast, ISIS created an administrative "state," JAN created governance structures in areas under its control, and cooperative administrative structures between violent and nonviolent opposition groups emerged in different locales.[13]

By 2013 violence in Syria was not only driven by the desire to overthrow the regime but out of a wish to control various territories under different administrative control. And while ideological differences and regional powers' interventions into Syria certainly fueled violence,[14] a political economy of war had emerged that provided further incentives to violence. Networks of violence emerged in relation to the conflict.[15] Lucrative trade routes were fought over by ostensibly allied groups, sieges took root throughout the country, supply chains providing weapons and food developed in the borderlands, and predatory behavior by armed groups in Syrian villages and towns further entrenched the stalemate as violence was no longer directed at simply overthrowing or defending the regime. Small groups of fighters would merge with larger ones, some brigades would merge to form fronts, which may collapse or change names, and fighters moved between different groups based on economic opportunities to capture the spoils of war. Such fluidity in the organizational structure of armed groups defined these networks of violence in relation to each other and Syria's war economies.

What was the nature of conflict that produced the stalemate? Richani has referred to the stalemate period as constituting a "war system" in which all actors were more incentivized to maintain conflict rather than negotiate peace.[16] For Richani, the war system emerges through three interrelated factors: the failure of the state to mediate social conflict, escalation into violent confrontation between different forces incapable of overcoming each other, and a political economy that sustains the war. In advancing a war systems argument about Syria, Richani critiques the civil wars literature on conflict duration for being overly prescriptive and focused on categorizations, coding, and generalizations that do not produce insight into how different parts of war systems interact. Richani points to the material elements driving violence, such as predatory economic activities and foreign sponsorship of armed groups, as constitutive of the stalemate. Underpinned by a political economy of war that fueled violence focused on territorial control of key economic rents, such as checkpoints and highways, control of predatory activity, sieges, and so on, the stalemate reflected both competing political projects and economic opportunities. Ultimately, the inertia of stalemate could not be broken by any major shift in Syria's local orders.

Breaking the Stalemate: Russian Intervention in 2015

Russia's military intervention in September 2015 set in motion battlefield shifts that disrupted patron-client relations and the organizational structure of violence that had produced the military stalemate. These battlefield shifts enabled the emergence of a Russian-designed process to mediate and manage the Syrian conflict. There are multiple domestic and geopolitical explanations for why Russia intervened into Syria,[17] but there is policy and academic consensus that the Syrian regime was at risk of collapse and that Russia's military intervention decisively shifted the conflict in the regime's favor. Shifting areas of territorial control between 2015 and 2022 certainly show this to be the case.[18]

The intervention began with air and naval strikes targeting armed groups in frontier areas with government forces, especially in Latakia, Homs, Hama, and Idlib. The initial strategy seemed to be aimed at alleviating battlefield pressure on government forces and their allies in preparation for more concentrated attacks later. Targeted attacks throughout the country were eventually supported by coordinated ground attacks that encircled key cities and supply routes. The first major city to fall under government control after Russian intervention was Sheikh Miskeen in Daraa Governorate.[19] Similar retaking of territory occurred in Latakia and Aleppo Governorates, and by early 2016 the intervention had been successful in cutting off major supply routes from Turkey to armed groups in Latakia and Aleppo Governorates. Throughout the year, rebel territorial control contracted while government control expanded. Palmyra fell to government forces, and armed groups in major towns in the southern and eastern parts of the country were cut off from each other and their supply routes.

In the context of a metastasizing, fragmented battlefield, the Russian military intervention did not initially concentrate on an enemy target or geographic area. All major governorates had pockets of armed group control, and these were duly targeted. Russia's strategic response to this battlefield was three-pronged: first, to concentrate aerial attacks on key sites of territorial control; second, to disrupt supply routes, effectively limiting the ability of armed groups to reproduce themselves; and third, provide aerial support for ground forces to besiege suffocated areas. Once an area was besieged, a reconciliation agreement (*musalaha*) was reached between government forces and the armed groups (see chapter 3). These reconciliations gave armed groups and civilians under their control two options: to leave and be guaranteed safe passage to Idlib Governorate (fighters would only be allowed to carry a handgun) or stay and pledge loyalty to the government, with fighters integrated into the state's counterinsurgency apparatus. In the aftermath of Russian military intervention these reconciliations became the mechanism to reestablish state control over rebel areas.

The Russian military advances and the imposition of reconciliation agreements were geographically uneven, occurring at an uneven pace throughout the country. The military success was dependent on the ground offensives led by the Syrian army and allied militias and the willingness of besieged armed groups to accept the terms of reconciliation. This radically changed the geography of the battlefield and reversed the processes of fragmentation that had defined Syria's geography since 2011. Smaller armed groups began to consolidate and retreat into Idlib while others simply vanished. Over time, elements of the FSA, Ahrar al-Sham, and other groups unaligned with JAN and its various iterations (Jabhat Fatah al-Sham, Hayat Tahrir al-Sham), fell under the loosely organized Syrian National Army (SNA), which was effectively under Turkish control if not command. The pockets of armed group control contracted, and a new geography of conflict emerged in the form of Astana's de-escalation zones (discussed below). The reconciliation agreements that were born out of the intervention became a mechanism for the external management of Syria's battlefield by Russia, Turkey, and Iran. These agreements legitimized battlefield gains and created new subjectivities and geographies that could be governed by the Syrian state in alignment with the tripartite powers.

The decisiveness of the Russian intervention in shifting the Syrian battlefield and the acquiescence of Turkey to these new realities contributed to the gradual withdrawal of support from Arab Gulf states and social networks for the armed groups. This withdrawal of support, coupled with the collapsing supply routes and the forced relocation of armed groups to Idlib, shifted the dynamics of stalemate and paradoxically made politics possible, beginning with the reconciliation agreements. Opposing sides to the conflict adopted maximalist political positions that were not subject to compromise amid a war system that produced stalemate.[20] Russia's intervention altered these dynamics and made politics possible. The question became, then, what kind of politics were now on offer given the new battlefield realities?

The United Nations and the Geneva Process

Until the Russian intervention the only serious attempts at a political solution to the Syrian conflict came from the United Nations special envoy. The envoy's efforts initially built on a short, ill-fated League of Arab States (LAS) mission in December 2011. More than a decade after the conflict began the United Nations' involvement in the Syrian crisis has produced no tangible movement toward a resolution. Bāli and Rana have argued that "the UN experience in Syria has been one of profound failure, either in offering an internationally mediated solution to the crisis or in safeguarding Syrian civilians."[21] This failure of the United Nations should also be understood within the framework of ongoing contestations of liberal international order,[22] as well as the limitations of liberal actors, ideas, and norms to guide post-conflict transitions toward a liberal peace. Universalist liberal ideas about how wars begin and end and how societies should transition to post-conflict peace are often imposed from outside conflict zones by actors such as the United Nations who take a lead role in designing and implementing post-conflict transitions. Liberal norms and practices never wholly translate into post-conflict spaces, and instead produce outcomes through interaction with local elites, ideas, national projects, and the many residues of conflict ontologies.[23] In the case of refugee repatriation, for example, Megan Bradley has shown how national politics and international norms clash to produce repatriation outcomes.[24] In this view, the interaction between competing ideas and norms produces outcomes that are specific to each given conflict. In Syria, the United Nations' failure has been defined precisely by its limited role in shaping how national politics responds to the conflict.

The internationalization of political efforts to resolve the Syrian conflict began with an LAS peace plan in September 2011 followed by a series of UN Security Council resolutions UNSCRs in late 2011 and early 2012 that condemned the regime's violence. The UN Supervision Mission in Syria was created by UNSCR 2043 to monitor ceasefires, but the Syrian regime and armed groups refused to recognize its authority. UN efforts to resolve the

Syrian crisis were bolstered by the February 2012 appointment of former Secretary-General Kofi Annan, whose specific vision for conflict resolution materialized in a six-point plan unveiled in March 2012. The plan embodied a liberal vision of how the war should end, with the cessation of hostilities and a power-sharing agreement as the cornerstones of peace: initiating a Syrian-led political process; implementing a UN-supervised cessation of violence; ensuring the provision of humanitarian assistance; facilitating the release of political prisoners; ensuring freedom of movement; and allowing for freedom of protest. By June, Annan had convened the first internationally organized deliberative forum aimed at resolving the conflict through the "Action Group on Syria" consisting of LAS and members of the UN Security Council (UNSC). The Geneva I conference produced a communiqué calling for a transitional government inclusive of both regime and opposition forces, which all states, including Russia, signed. Differences between the United States and Russia on the role that sitting President Bashar al-Assad would play in such a transitional government ultimately undermined any substantive follow-up efforts. Moreover, the battlefield in mid-2012 was witnessing the emergence of armed groups who were both opposed to any Geneva-type solution for Syria and were increasingly fighting each other over localized territorial disputes. Geneva I would not achieve any serious results because of these two factors.

The Geneva II talks were convened by Kofi Annan's successor (Annan resigned in August 2012), Lakhdar Brahimi, whose mediation efforts focused on generating US-Russian consensus on Syria that could serve as the basis for pressuring the regime and opposition (and their supporters) to negotiate a resolution. Brahimi's attempts to create a broad consensus under US-Russian auspices failed almost immediately when the United States objected to Iran's involvement in the talks, thus delaying the first formal Geneva II talks until 2014. Disagreements over who should represent the Syrian opposition also led to delays, and the Syrian National Council withdrew from the Syrian National Coalition over the latter's agreeing in principle to negotiate with the regime. Meanwhile, the battlefield began to resemble the competing power centers at the UN level as armed groups fought the regime and each other, and new governance projects emerged in areas outside of regime control. Battlefield fragmentation was aggravated by continued material support from the same outside actors who had ostensibly committed to the Geneva II talks, a remarkable undermining of the process before it had the opportunity to begin. The proliferation of armed groups with different views on the Geneva II talks, regional actors' continued commitment to a battlefield solution, factionalization within the political opposition, and the lack of US-Russian consensus proved to be insurmountable obstacles for Brahimi's vision for Geneva II. By May 2014, he had resigned.

Brahimi's tenure was marked not only by his failure to bring the United States and Russia together to formally negotiate a resolution to the Syrian conflict but also by these two states' negotiation of an agreement on Syria's chemical weapons program outside of the Geneva framework. On August 21, 2013, the Syrian army attacked Ghouta (a Damascus suburb) with chemical weapons, killing more than a thousand civilians. This was not the first suspected chemical attack by the army during the conflict, but it certainly gained the most international attention. The attack placed the Obama administration in a political bind. Up until that point, the administration had been content to let the conflict unfold and had resisted all calls for military intervention to topple the regime. The administration had publicly called for the ouster of Bashar al-Assad and willingly turned a blind eye to its allies' interventions into Syria, but it was unwilling to commit itself militarily or supply armed groups with heavy weaponry. This middle-ground position was compromised after the attacks because Obama had previously called the use of chemical weapons a "red line" that would trigger military intervention on the part of the United States. Interventionists from within the administration and the wider foreign policy establishment immediately called for a military response, echoed by many from within the Syrian opposition. Yet, what followed was a disarmament process that occurred without military intervention. Less than a month after the attacks, Syria had formally acceded to the Chemical Weapons Convention (CWC).

Syria's ascension to the CWC was the product of bilateral talks between Russia and the United States in September 2013 to formally negotiate Syria's disarmament within the framework of internationally accepted norms. Russia and the United States negotiated a framework agreement that was signed the same day Syria formally joined the CWC. Less than two weeks later, the Security Council adopted UNSCR 2118, obligating Syria to follow the implementation plan set out by the Organisation for the

Prohibition of Chemical Weapons (OPCW), which now had responsibility to oversee Syria's disarmament. The framework agreement allowed Russia to prevent American military intervention while allowing the United States to claim that it met its strategic disarmament objectives without military force. Makdisi and Hindawi have argued that both states adopted different narratives explaining the success of the agreement.[25] On the one hand, the United States saw it as a triumph of American coercion, arguing that disarmament would not have occurred without the threat of military intervention and diplomatic pressure. Russia, on the other hand, saw the agreement as the outcome of a deliberative, consensual process. By accommodating both narratives, the United Nations and OPCW were able to successfully oversee and implement disarmament. This process revealed two important realities that would structure the conflict's international dimensions moving forward: first, that the United States was unwilling to intervene militarily against the regime even when its own red lines were crossed, and second, that the United Nations, the United States, and Russia were indeed capable of joint diplomatic achievements when they so desired.

Brahimi's successor, Staffan de Mistura, inherited a very different conflict from his predecessors when he took over as special envoy. De Mistura convened Geneva III in April 2015, on the eve of the Russian military intervention. He adopted two principal strategies that distinguished his tenure from that of Annan and Brahimi. First, de Mistura sought to widen the deliberative tent, so to speak, by inviting multiple opposition groups and regional states to the negotiating table; and, second, he sought to insert the UN into the localized truce agreements that were occurring on the battlefield by throwing the organization's weight and authority behind them. On the first strategy, de Mistura was heavily criticized by the Syrian opposition for being deferential to Western interests, failing to exert any real pressure on the regime, and not advancing any international guarantees for the political process. Nevertheless, an October 2015 meeting among twenty countries, held barely a month after the Russian intervention, led to the creation of the International Syrian Support Group (ISSG). More momentum was given to Geneva III when UNSCR 2254 was adopted on December 18, 2015. The adoption of UNSCR 2254 was an important moment in the conflict because of how it was eventually interpreted by the Astana powers two years later. While reiterating the ISSG's commitment to the

Geneva process, UNSCR 2254 also advanced a ceasefire between the government and armed groups, excluding groups that all parties deemed "terrorist." The Astana powers would interpret UNSCR 2254 in ways that allowed for continued violence against "terrorist" groups while also allowing them to claim that Astana-designed political deliberations were consistent with the resolution.

Geneva III talks began on February 1, 2016, only to be suspended two days later when some opposition groups withdrew from the talks in response to regime violence in Aleppo. While this may have been the official reason for their withdrawal, many opposition groups represented in the High Negotiation Committee (HNC) were already reluctant to negotiate with the regime and under the terms set by de Mistura. Russia had insisted on inviting other opposition groups to the Geneva III talks that were outside of the HNC, a move seen by opposition groups as undermining the latter's legitimacy. This Russian strategy portended Moscow's approach to the Astana process; by legitimizing and inviting certain opposition groups and not others, Russia was able to provide serious claims that it was indeed negotiating and not imposing a solution. Western powers seemed content to let the process unfold accordingly. Akpinar argues that by the time of Geneva III, Western powers, including the United States, were content to have a deal on Syria no matter the design.[26] By 2016 these same powers had specific perspectives on the Syrian conflict that largely precluded them advocating for opposition demands: to halt the flow of refugees; to address the ISIS threat inside and outside of the region; a reluctance to engage in a large-scale military intervention; and concerns over jeopardizing the Iranian nuclear deal.[27] Opposition weakness and Western ambivalence paved the way for a Russian-led design for post-conflict Syria.

De Mistura had a decisively different vision for Syria than his predecessors, and he was successful in initiating a second major shift in the United Nations' role toward supporting ceasefires, which he labeled "freezes." Unlike his predecessors' attempts at creating a grand bargain for Syria between the major regional and international powers, de Mistura pursued an approach that expanded the number of states involved in Geneva deliberations while simultaneously contributing to the negotiation and implementation of battlefield freezes. This strategy directly involved the United Nations in the Syrian battlefield as a mediator between warring parties and sought to use freezes as building blocks for a wider, more comprehensive peace. The mechanisms for linking the two processes were never explicitly advanced by de Mistura, and it was never clear how the two strategies would eventually cohere to build the foundation for peace. Nevertheless, de Mistura continued to advocate for the possibility of reconciling the two processes.[28] De Mistura's first major initiative days after he was appointed as special envoy in October 2014 was to propose the "Aleppo Freeze" to the UNSC, a UN-mediated and -supervised "freeze zone" aimed at reducing violence to facilitate humanitarian corridors into Aleppo. His strategy was to try and capture an existing process and orient it toward the specific end of facilitating humanitarian corridors to break the sieges. In doing so, however, he mistakenly aligned the office of the envoy with what had essentially become surrender agreements. De Mistura referred to his efforts as "freezes" and distinguished them from the regime's ceasefires in recognition of the role that ceasefires played in the regime's battlefield management.[29] Nassar's analysis of the failure of de Mistura's approach is instructive here. He argues that his distinction between a "freeze" and a "ceasefire"—where the former involved a gradual reduction of violence and the latter a total cessation of violence—did not have any clear monitoring and supervision mechanisms to violence reduction.[30] Moreover, de Mistura had intentionally sought to localize freezes and decouple them from the larger political process, unlike his predecessor Annan, who called for national ceasefires and tied their monitoring to the Geneva talks. The de Mistura freezes delinking from the Geneva process further undermined their capacity to influence political deliberations. For all intents and purposes, de Mistura's strategic approach to the Syrian battlefield never threatened the regime's conflict management approach. By focusing on gradually reducing violence to enable humanitarian access, de Mistura's strategy never seriously threatened the regime or altered conflict management practices.

The "freeze" strategy was an attempt to insert the United Nations into ongoing battlefield processes and to reorient the UN's role around violence reduction and humanitarian access. De Mistura was aware of the regime's deployment of truces as surrender agreements and was consistent in his public declarations of this. He was also careful to refer to his strategies as "action plans," and not "peace plans" or "war plans" (the latter being how he referred to the regime's approach to ceasefires). This delicate balance between naming the UN's approach while distinguishing it from the regime's strategies suggested to many that de Mistura had adopted the regime's narrative of the conflict. How could de Mistura have recognized that reconciliations were surrender agreements but nevertheless promote policies that appeared to all parties to resemble them? His strategy seemed to shift the terms of local reconciliations around his ideas for freezes, thereby giving the United Nations a greater monitoring role and giving belligerents actionable (in his words) plans to assess success. At this point in the conflict, however, the reconciliation agreements were allowing the regime to depopulate enemy areas and reestablish control in large areas of the country. The regime's abandonment of these surrender agreements for freezes that did not serve their battlefield goals was an unlikely outcome of de Mistura's strategy. His failure to have the practice of freezes gain traction on the battlefield was also undermined by the ongoing ceasefire and monitoring process that Russia and Turkey had created through the Astana framework. The Syrian conflict's two most important regional actors were unlikely to jettison a conflict management strategy that was operable and limited the interference of outside powers like the United Nations.

By the time that de Mistura resigned and was replaced by Norwegian diplomat Geir Pederson in January 2019, the United Nations had been effectively relegated to observer status in the parallel Astana process, a forum that emerged in 2017 for the tripartite powers of Iran, Russia, and Turkey to collectively manage the Syrian conflict. The United Nations has assumed a role in contributing to the constitutional deliberations through Astana, but it has otherwise been a peripheral actor to the power politics shaping Syria's trajectory. There are many reasons for the United Nations' failure in Syria. There was never any serious commitment among the regime or opposition (and their allies) to ending the conflict through a deliberative process, let alone a liberal peace that focused on promoting human rights, parliamentary democracy, market reforms, and power sharing. A political solution could only be negotiated after one side gained military victory. Bâli and Rana argue that the narratives explaining the UN's failure relate to strategy and the fact that Geneva's design did not correspond to the battlefield interests of the major powers intervening into the Syrian conflict.[31] I have argued elsewhere that the Astana powers had actively undermined the Geneva process from the beginning because of their commitment to a military solution to the conflict.[32] Constantini and

Santini have explained the failure of the United Nations in terms most relevant to the overall argument I am making here. The UN had adopted the role of a mediator when the parties to the Syrian conflict had abandoned serious mediation efforts in favor of power politics and biased mediation. For them, the peripheralization of the United Nations in Syria was an intentional process aimed at reducing the power of mediators and liberal ideational frameworks in favor of power politics that privileged authoritarian stability over democratic political transition.[33]

The peace pursued by regional powers was focused on the stabilization of regime rule as the principal prerequisite for the management of conflict. The conflict could not be managed by the tripartite powers amid a liberal political process that sought inclusion, violence reduction, and power sharing as its principal goals. The basis for post-conflict order had to occur amid the elimination of enemies, not their inclusion in a political process. While this may explain how Iran, Russia, and Turkey came to undermine the United Nations, it does not explain why the three countries ultimately engaged in their own forms of cooperation and political deliberation outside of the Geneva framework in spite of their battlefield hostilities. Köstem has argued that Russian-Turkish security cooperation in Syria can best be explained through their increasing geopolitical alignment on key global issues.[34] Bilateral alignment has been the impetus toward military coordination and a commitment to a political settlement in Syria realized in the Astana process.

The Astana Process as Regional Conflict Management

The failure of the United Nations' efforts to resolve the Syrian conflict should be understood in relation to the success of the Astana process as a model for conflict management. The Astana process offered the Syrian regime, its allies Iran and Russia, and Turkey, the last remaining state sponsor of Syria's opposition, an alternative forum to the Geneva process for the management of Syria's conflict. The creation of this alternative process and the actors' sustained commitment to managing the conflict through its framework effectively supplanted the Geneva process. Yet, the Astana powers could not wholly abandon Geneva if they were to maintain a veneer of international legitimacy for Syria's political process. The Syrian Constitutional Committee (SCC), for example, was created by the Astana process and supervised by the UN, thus giving the world body a role (albeit minor) in Astana. The absorption of the UN into a secondary role through Astana suggests a new model for peacebuilding in which liberal actors may be on the periphery of peace efforts. In reference to Turkish peacebuilding efforts, Kocadal argues that while Western-led peacebuilding is no longer hegemonic, a non-Western alternative has yet to emerge.[35] New norms and practices around peacebuilding may not reflect universal liberal ideas, but they nevertheless reference them. For Kocadal, the absence of a clear alternative to liberal intervention contributes to the liminality of emerging, non-Western peacebuilding efforts and their discursive mimicry of the liberal peace.[36] Emergent powers emulate and mimic liberal values even when they do not actually adhere to them. As non-Western powers they are less invested in the perpetuation of a liberal international system but have not yet established an alternative that could wholly supplant the United Nations.

The Astana process began in January 2017 as a bilateral forum for Turkey and Russia to monitor ceasefires and reconciliation agreements negotiated between the Syrian state and armed groups. The reconciliation agreements (discussed in detail in chapter 3) created new subjectivities (e.g., reconciled fighters) and geographies (e.g., reconciled areas) that required monitoring by a military force. Battlefield developments that favored the Syrian state gradually involved the concentration of armed groups in Idlib Governorate and the demarcation of de-escalation zones in relation to Idlib and the Kurdish-dominated northeastern and northern parts of Syria. Turkish strategic interests in the country were increasingly focused on preventing Kurdish expansion regardless of whether the regime remained in place. On the issue of Kurdish autonomy, let alone sovereignty, there was agreement between Turkey and Syria. The Astana process provided a forum for the former to manage the Syrian battlefield in relation to its strategic interests and to provide a security umbrella for armed groups that were increasingly under its military influence. The FSA eventually collapsed into the SNA, an umbrella group controlled by Turkey that, by 2020, was the principal competitor to Hayat Tahrir al-Sham (HTS) in Idlib. As two of the three principal international actors involved in the Syrian conflict, Turkey and Russia found common strategic interest in managing the battlefield through Astana after the effects of the Russian intervention had so clearly shifted the trajectory of the conflict.

The Astana powers sought to design the political process to reflect the battlefield and not subject the conflict to any internationally supervised political transition. This new geography of conflict was the foundational block of Astana and the basis for the creation of "de-escalation zones" after the fourth round of talks in May 2017. These talks produced agreement on four de-escalation zones in Idlib Governorate (including parts of Hama, Aleppo, and Latakia), Homs Governorate, Eastern Ghouta (just outside of Damascus), and the Syrian-Jordanian border areas in Dar'aa and Quneitra Governorates. These were declared demilitarized zones where the tripartite powers guaranteed transit and humanitarian corridors through extensive monitoring and cooperation, including the sharing of patrols, ceasefire information, and military information. These agreements also gave certain groups freedom to operate in Idlib under Turkish protection. The SDF and HTS, however, were exempt from these stipulations, and their continued armament justified repeated Syrian and Russian aerial attacks into Idlib and a Turkish incursion into northern Syria under the banner of Operation Euphrates Shield. Importantly, there was consensus from within the Astana framework for these interventions.

Astana became a forum that reflected the battlefield and the strategic interests of the tripartite powers, who became the guarantors of a declared peace in Syria. The guarantors developed shared norms and practices that would be adhered to throughout the post-2015 period of conflict management despite major military operations such as the Turkish-led Operation Euphrates Shield and a series of sustained aerial attacks by Russian and Syrian forces in Idlib Governorate from 2018 to 2020. What, then, were the tripartite powers guaranteeing? The Astana powers sought to craft a peace that could sustain war and provide regional and international legitimacy to the regime's conflict management strategies.[37] The Astana guarantors eschewed any pretense to conflict resolution and instead produced a model for conflict management outside of the liberal epistemological and policy orbit. There were no promised World Bank funds, or bilateral funds for that matter. There were no serious, let alone coherent, ideas for how to reconstruct Syria coming from within the country.[38] And human rights norms were absent from any Astana discussions while humanitarian organizations remain largely outside of Syria. Organizations that did operate in the country were only allowed to do so under severe pressure and were often complicit in the regime's aid capture. I raise these contrasts to juxtapose Astana's designs for Syria with the promises of post–Cold War liberal imperialism to remake conflict societies along liberal lines through human rights, humanitarian, and neoliberal interventions that would sustain peace.[39] Astana's design was entirely about managing the battlefield according to the strategic interests of the tripartite powers while confining "big" political issues—such as a new constitution, the fate of Idlib and the Kurdish-held areas, political transition, and so on—to similar strategic deliberation. The Astana powers absolved themselves of any serious negotiations over implementing liberal norms.

When the Astana process began Turkish President Erdoğan proclaimed that the forum could potentially solve "one half" of the Syrian conflict, referring to the armed groups.[40] The "other half" to which he alluded was the Kurdish issue, which was initially not central to the Astana negotiations. This view of the "two halves" of the Syrian conflict aligned Turkish, Russian, and Iranian interests around preventing further fragmentation and the rise of new governance projects. Astana was created to manage the reduction of violence in ways consistent with the "two halves" of the conflict. The guarantor roles assumed by the tripartite powers ensured that the United Nations would remain a junior partner in any mediation efforts, which would mostly be negotiated around producing a "security peace."[41]

Astana's origins and design represent a unique form of conflict mediation. The tripartite powers are direct parties to the conflict and have tasked themselves with managing its trajectory. Two Russian international relations theorists have referred to Astana as an "international platform for Middle Eastern regional security" rather an explicitly political process aimed at achieving peace in the liberal sense.[42] This provided space for the tripartite powers to remain referential to the UN as a mediator and especially UNSCR 2254 as the basis for a political transition while ostensibly directing deliberations toward security matters. However, the clear delineation of a political track overseen by the United Nations (and consistent with Geneva) and a security track managed by the tripartite powers was a cosmetic distinction intended to provide international legitimacy to the Astana process. The United Nations has assumed a mostly observatory role in the Astana deliberations and has failed to substantively shift the nature of political deliberations between the tripartite powers. The consequence of such peripheralization was to reshape the nature of political deliberations in and about Syria, specifically, and to orient politics around regime stability rather than regime change.

The relationship between the Astana powers and the United Nations is exemplified in how the tripartite powers have both acknowledged and undermined UNSCR 2254. Although born out of the need to bilaterally manage the Syrian battlefield, the Astana process initially referred to UNSCR 2254 as the cornerstone of conflict management. UNSCR 2254 was passed in December 2015, when the effects of Russian military intervention were still unfolding, and while there was agreement then on its passing, there have been radically different interpretations of what 2254 means in the Syrian conflict. The Syrian regime and its allies have interpreted 2254 as legitimizing the regime's attacks against terrorists.[43]

The Astana process's success in fostering deliberation among the tripartite powers led to its eventual expansion into issues beyond the battlefield and ceasefires. This allowed the Astana powers to control the nature of international political deliberation over Syria and to ensure that the design, consideration, and eventual implementation of any agreed-upon political reforms would be consistent with the guarantor powers' strategic interests in Syria. As an observer to the Astana process, the United Nations had a limited role in directing deliberations. The one Astana-related space where the UN did have a more supervisory role was in the constitutional talks where the special envoy oversees constitutional deliberations. All other major political issues related to Syria's future had been confined to the Astana forum and to the addendum meetings held by the leaders of the tripartite powers.[44] The political effect of Astana's structure and relationship to the UN was to undermine liberal norms and ideas in shaping post-conflict Syria. The absence of an internationally agreed-upon role for the UN in Syria to ensure the implementation of liberal principles was one of the most important factors that has allowed the regime to orient the state around punishing enemies.

The emergence of Astana as the principal forum for the negotiation of regional power rivalries over Syria has had several important effects on the trajectory of the conflict and the state's ability to pursue a project aimed at enacting the social death of its enemies. Most importantly, Astana protected the Syrian regime from external pressure to initiate a political transition. Virtually all opposition demands made against the regime are ignored in the Astana framework. Key issues such as elections, judicial reforms, accountability and transparency, and a larger campaign against corruption are virtually absent from it. The Astana process thus provided a regional mechanism to manage the conflict trajectory outside of liberal pressures.

Astana's initial innovation was the creation of new geographies of conflict that could be managed by the tripartite powers. The de-escalation zones created in 2017 carved Syrian territory into areas both under and outside of state control. The four de-escalation zones were in Idlib Governorate (and included some parts of Latakia and Aleppo that were under armed opposition control), Homs Governorate, Eastern Ghouta in the Damascene suburbs, and parts of Daraa and Quinetra in southern Syria. The northwestern and northeastern areas under Turkish and SDF control, respectively, were not created as de-escalation zones. Each zone is patrolled by military forces from the tripartite powers to ensure that all reconciliation agreements are honored. The zones dramatically reduced the ability of armed groups to operate in Syria.

An important military achievement of Astana was the creation of collective enemies in the form of HTS and the SDF, whom the tripartite powers viewed as a collective threat. The strangling of armed groups on the battlefield paralleled their exclusion from Astana's political processes. Astana cast a wider net than Geneva in inviting a range of armed groups and regional states to the deliberations, but the largest, most powerful groups were always excluded. Participant invitations were determined by tripartite consensus, "decided by the sponsors of the process based on political criteria and preferences."[45] As expected, HTS and the SDF (and affiliated armed groups) were never invited to Astana. The tripartite powers had representatives on each committee, while heads of state met separately during sideline meetings, typically after one of the major battles initiated in Idlib or Operation Euphrates Shield. The choice to include some (weak) opposition groups while excluding others ensured the continued fragmentation of the Syrian opposition into several different camps without the requisite regional power support to influence Astana.

The one area where the Astana powers seemingly ceded to UN and opposition demands was around constitutional reforms. The SCC, proposed by

Russia, acknowledged one of the key demands of the Syrian opposition for constitutional reform while de-linking this process from political transition. Russia proposed a different approach to constitutional reform that allowed the Syrian government to control who it negotiated with and over what issues. In January 2018, Russia announced the formation of a Syrian Congress of National Dialogue (SCND) in Sochi, an attempt at narrowing the gap between Astana and Geneva.[46] The SCND did not include the existing Syrian Negotiation Committee (SNC) that had represented the Syrian opposition at the Geneva talks. In doing so, the SCND delegitimized the SNC and other existing opposition bodies while allowing Russia and Syria to create an opposition in their own vision. Similarly, the creation of the SCC in October 2019, after more than two years of discussions about its composition, was designed in a way to both exclude existing opposition bodies and ensure that the Syrian regime would not be forced into serious political concessions. In particular, the SCC would guarantee that any major power-sharing agreements or more comprehensive political transition that would undermine regime power would be prevented. Despite this, the SCC initially failed to make any meaningful progress, with the first round of negotiations ending in October 2019 with no agreements, and the second round in November not even taking place because the Syrian government withdrew on the first day. Meanwhile, de Mistura continued to show support for the initiative and to generate support throughout the United Nations.[47]

The SCND was an expression of the political will of the Astana powers and the Syrian regime to legitimize, yet also manage, a political transition process through the United Nations. The continued battlefield incursions during the first SCND meetings, the congress's heavily anti-Kurdish politics,[48] the regime's regular withdrawals, and the absence of any tangible results more than four years after its formation all reflected the incremental, managed approach to the SCND that Astana powers had deliberately designed. The composition, structure, and rules of procedure all effectively ensured a regime veto of any major changes. The SCND consisted of 150 members—with the government, the SNC, and "civil society" (determined in this case by the United Nations) each choosing 50—whose work was overseen by Geir Pederson in what the United Nations refers to as a "Syrian-owned and Syrian-led process."[49] The SCND was thus legitimized within the framework of UNSCR 2254's calls for a Syrian-led process. There were two bodies within the SCND: a "small body" consisting of 45 people (15 from each bloc) and responsible for drafting the constitution, and a "large body" responsible for approving the constitution. Decisions were supposed to be reached by consensus, and any approval required 75 percent of all members of either the small or large bodies.

By early 2023 the SCND had held nine meetings; Geir Pederson maintained de Mistura's support for the SCND while continuing to oversee meetings. Compared to the Geneva process, the SCND was relatively successful in creating dialogue between different Syrian actors. Progress and agreement were glacial, and it was always unclear what, if any, legal standing the SCND's final work had in Syria as the government representatives at the SCND often engage in intransigent tactics to prevent any meaningful progress on the constitutional talks. The SCND's inertia resembles the lack of progress in Geneva, but it is not an overall indication of the efficacy of the Astana process in reorienting post-conflict Syrian politics. Astana definitively emerged as the forum for the management of the battlefield and the negotiation of major political issues between the Syrian regime and the tripartite powers. In other words, there have been important political achievements born out of Astana that produced a military and political environment for the Syrian regime to engage in its own domestic reforms absent external pressure.

The Astana process sanctioned continued violence in the name of peacemaking by deciding which armed groups would be considered protected (such as the SNA) and which ones would be targets of tripartite state violence (such as the SDF and HTS). Contrary to liberal peace assumptions about the need to eliminate violence, especially state violence, Astana legitimized the continued violence against armed groups and civilian populations who were rendered enemies within Astana's framework. Armed groups that failed to reconcile with the state or who sat outside of the command structure of one of the tripartite powers were at risk of continued attacks. These provisions were specifically aimed at the HTS and SDF networks in northwestern and northeastern Syria, respectively. Russia and Iran had sanctioned Operation Euphrates Shield, Turkey's intervention against the SDF, while Turkey had consented to three sustained interventions in Idlib between 2017 and 2020. The Astana framework ensured that any armed groups or areas outside of the territorial control of the Syrian government would remain subject to military intervention by the tripartite powers, ensuring that violence would continue to be an endemic feature of post-conflict Syria.

The Astana process demonstrated how new norms of conflict management could emerge outside of liberal powers such as the UN. Astana's most enduring political effect will have been to preserve and stabilize the Syrian regime until its fall in December 2024. On the eve of Russia's military intervention, there were no possible pathways for the regime to survive, let alone rehabilitate its legitimacy within the region. By 2023, the Syrian government had been readmitted into the LAS. This was a remarkable outcome given the state of the conflict in mid-2015.

Conclusion

In the chapters that follow I argue that the Syrian state was oriented around the punishment of Syrians politically categorized as enemies for their supposed betrayal of the homeland. The absorption of the conflict logic of enmity into law and state practices was possible because of the absence of external liberal pressure guiding a post-conflict transition. This chapter has shown how the Astana process emerged to manage Syria's conflict at the expense of the UN and competing liberal approaches to peace and political transition. The regional process led by Russia, Turkey, and Iran created the international conditions for the state's marshaling of punishment against its enemies. The absence of an internationally mandated process that would have exerted pressure for a political transition, legal and institutional changes, and various other liberal policies to affect post-conflict resolution allowed the state to pursue a politics of punishment in parallel to the continued violence. The regional management of conflict by the tripartite powers was a cover that would allow, rather than check, the Syrian regime's continued ability to pursue political punishment.

Syria's conflict ontology and the Astana process's designs for managing it did not produce immediately legible population categories that the state could identify as punishable. The lines delineated between friends and enemies were confined to armed groups and the battlefield. And the country's territorial fragmentation produced very different pockets of opposition control that lacked contiguity or institutional continuity. Competing governance projects across disconnected territories made clear, legible identification of the state's enemies in the post-Russian intervention period virtually impossible. Moreover, blanket categorization of civilians living under opposition control as enemies would have been disastrous for the state's efforts to project itself as a legitimate political authority. This would have required banishment of millions of people under the pretext of guilt by association. Instead, as we will see in the coming chapters, the commonsense narrative was accommodating of these associations and allowed the state's categorization mechanisms to transform suspected or potential enemies into friends through the reconciliation and settlement processes. These processes for identifying legible populations and parsing out the loyal and disloyal were made possible by the Astana process.

The question remains as to how the state developed politically relevant categories that could be managed over the course of a simmering conflict. The description of these categories as part of the commonsense narrative would develop institutional and legal parallels that served to mete out punishment of state enemies. In the next chapter, I show how the state's discourse of terrorism as the cause of conflict created the enemy subject of the "spectral terrorist" that materialized in the Counter-Terrorism Court. In later chapters I show how categories of absent, unsettled, or deceived subjects would similarly be tethered to new laws aimed at bifurcating Syrian society and punishing those deemed disloyal. The conditions of possibility for such bifurcation among state-constructed political lines was the absence of an external intervention forcing a post-conflict transition toward an ideal liberal state.

2

The Spectral Terrorist as State Enemy

Distinguishing between friends and enemies is one thing; identifying the enemy with accuracy is quite another.

—ACHILLE MBEMBE

Most peoples of the world kill those they want to consider other than themselves: Hutus and Tutsis murder each other, as do Serbs and Croats. . . . There is another type of massacre, however, in which one kills those in one's own image.

—JAMES T. SIEGEL

Introduction

Syrian Minister of Foreign Affairs Walid Moallem held a press conference on the eve of the start of the Geneva I negotiations in 2014 at which he declared his country's willingness to engage in good faith deliberations to eliminate the scourge of terrorism that had penetrated Syrian society. Speaking alongside his Russian counterpart, Deputy Foreign Minister Gennady Gatilov, Moallem told reporters that both countries had agreed on the need for cooperation and coordination in the fight against terrorism and that the Geneva negotiations were one step in implementing their shared understanding. Naturally, opposition negotiators as well as United Nations facilitators were alarmed at Moallem's insistence on framing Geneva as a forum for deliberating how to combat terrorism rather than the several other political transition issues that others assumed would form the basis of negotiation. Moallem, however, made it clear that he refused to negotiate anything with people who "practice terrorism in Syria."[1]

Moallem's insistence that the Geneva negotiations focus on combatting terrorism was not simply a form of obstruction; rather, it reflected the state's commonsense narration of the war as a conflict between terrorists and the state. The deployment of the language of terrorism mirrored that of the global war on terror (GWOT) in its invocation of a spectral threat that required extraordinary measures to combat. For Moallem, negotiating with the very people and states who fomented terrorism in Syria, let alone engaging in deliberations with them over Syria's future, was a nonstarter. Syria's war was not with revolutionaries, protestors, or armed groups; the Syrian state was at war with terrorism itself. The commonsense narration of the Syrian conflict as a war initiated by terrorists necessarily framed state violence as counterterrorism. The terrorist subject (and their supporters) became the state's ultimate enemy and the cause of Syria's tragedy.

The language of terrorism was deployed not only to justify mass violence but also to identify, categorize, and punish state enemies who were far from the battlefield. In this chapter, I explore the construction of the spectral terrorist subject in relation to emergent regimes of punishment and argue that the bureaucratization of counterterrorism produced a politically relevant cleavage through which to bifurcate Syrian society. The spectral terrorist subject could easily be rendered as a state enemy through categorization that ignored specific ethnic, sectarian, or geographic markers. How, then, was the spectral terrorist subject identified, categorized, rendered into a punishable legal category, and acted upon? The answer to this question lies in an extraordinarily ambiguous and expansive definition of terrorism that assigned that label to a series of acts, non-acts, feelings, and ideas that Syrians were presumed to hold and that were said to constitute acts of harm against the homeland. The spectral terrorist subject was not simply someone who fought with arms against the state, but someone who posted anti-state thoughts on social media, someone who supported rebels with food or health supplies, or even someone who left the country.

Bifurcating Society Into Friends and Enemies

How do states decide who to punish for political transgression? Addressing this question requires us to think about how states render populations legible and governable. Scholarship on state repression inquires into the production of legible populations and the meting out of attendant rewards and punishments and how this provides insight into political behavior and actions.[2] Wedeen's argument that Syrians act "as if" they revere the president removes the question of intent or fealty and directs us to think about what behaviors are necessary and expected of subjects to sustain authoritarian governance.[3] The state does not care whether or not people believe; what matters is that they act as if they do. Political behavior in authoritarian contexts is not strictly conditioned by how state institutions seek to produce fear and docility among citizen subjects as much as how these subjects behave in relation to state violence.[4] Physical surveillance, discursive constructions of threats and enemies, or the carceral violence of authoritarian prison systems all produce variations in citizens' behavior relative to their own perceptions of fear and insecurity.[5] Citizens have agency and political maneuverability within the violent, securitized contexts of authoritarian state repression. The space for contestation, cooptation, or disassociation or association with state power, however, is shaped by the state's ever-evolving exercise of power and violence.

I focus in this chapter on how the state constructed an architecture of enmity that categorized Syrian society through the deployment of the spectral terrorist subject as state enemy. In the context of intensifying violence, the state's monitoring capacity is diminished, and punishment regimes may unnecessarily target groups in ways that impede state-building goals.[6] The decision by state authorities to mete out punishment to certain individuals or groups and not others depends on a "politically relevant cleavage structure,"[7] one that is malleable but nevertheless generative of legible populations upon which the state can act. While some arguments about state repression in Syria emphasize ethno-sectarian identity as the principal social cleavage that state authorities target for punishment,[8] and which Syrians respond to, I contend here that this is not a categorization that easily explains state repression. While sectarianism emerged as an important factor in Syria's conflict, reducing state repression to sectarian identity belies the myriad ways that the state seeks to create even deeper cleavages in society that allow for punishment against a wide range of Syrians, regardless of sect.

Bifurcating society by creating politically relevant cleavages created friend/enemy categories that are pliable and subject to changing state criteria for what constitutes threat. Ismail's work on the relationship between violence, subjectivity, and emotions is a productive entry point for thinking about how the Syrian regime bifurcated society, created and acted upon legible populations, and how this process was inherently destabilizing for citizens trying to navigate authoritarian governance.[9] For Ismail, the prison and the massacre form two apparatuses of government in Syria. They are not aberrations of otherwise liberal governance but rather central features of the system of governance and rule in Syria intended to induce feelings of humiliation and abjection in Syrians. These apparatuses of government seek to suppress political dissent and establish the affective conditions for a form of regime-society relations in which the exercise of state power and the threat of violence is always present for Syrians. To think of political violence as governmental is to understand the production of affect through violence as necessary for the creation of a particular kind of citizenry that is rendered docile, demobilized, fearful, and unlikely to engage in contestation:

> Understanding violence as a form of governmental power underlines practices and strategies that have as their objective and outcome not only to harm the body, the mind and the affect, but, also, to reconstruct, shape, discipline and normalize the subject of government. Practices of violence that generate the affects of humiliation, abjection and horror should not be dismissed as premodern or archaic, rather they should be examined in terms of rationalities aimed at making and unmaking political subjects.[10]

Violence forms subjects. And while Ismail takes the prison and the massacre as the ultimate forms of violence, she argues that the processes of subjectivization also work in everyday spaces in which pedagogies of rule are reinforced, such as schools and other social structures in which Syrians' social conditions and day-to-day lives were mediated through state power.[11] The state's biopolitics constitute what she calls a "civil war regime" in which the state is constantly at war with its population, where war exists as a permanent social relation upheld by a bifurcation of society into those deemed worthy of life and those deemed expendable.[12] The prison and the massacre were the sites where those deemed expendable were eliminated.

The bifurcation of society into "us" and "them," "friends" and "enemies," remained fluid through more than fifty years of Ba'athist rule, bending and reshaping according to Ba'athist ideological shifts and the emergence of new perceived threats. Permanent political emergency gave life to the civil war regime and slowly filtered through Syrian society and its institutions, co-opting social forces, such as tribes,[13] in the vague but never-ending war against state enemies. Such practices of co-optation alongside the deepening of infrastructures of violence contribute to subjectivization and the creation of enemies independent of their sectarian identity but rather tethered to politically relevant cleavages. Ismail argues that a pedagogy of fear has developed in Syria through practices of monitoring, surveillance, and the general disciplining of citizens, and that this pedagogy is tied to an infrastructure composed of prisons, detention facilities, and other spaces in which state violence is enacted against Syrian bodies.[14] Together, such practices constitute "affective technologies of government" in which fear and violence are intended to literally inflict horror "and to incite, in the subject, ways of feeling about and ways of understanding events, reality and her/his own positionality in the web of power."[15] To target enemies and maybe-enemies, to inflict violence and to not inflict violence, and to do so in ways that are governmental—that is, enacted throughout society and through the deployment of state institutions—is to rule through violence and to create subjects necessary to the maintenance of authoritarian rule.

To understand Syrian politics is in part to understand government through affect and the affective and cognitive states that formed Syrians' subjectivity. The principal aim of the Ba'athist system of rule remained a process of erasure, of elimination and eradication, in which Syrian society was bifurcated into friends and enemies and the latter acted upon with the full force of state power and violence in prisons, through massacres, and via everyday institutions that mediated the relationship between citizen and regime. For example, Ismail claims that Hama, as a site of regime massacre, haunts Syrians in different ways, first as an objective event of mass murder and destruction, second as a sort of specter, an imaginary of what has happened, and third as a fear of recurrence that the regime could "do Hama again."¹⁶ As such, "Hama was thus the prototype of an apparatus of government" as it exists as an objective fear (of death), a haunting fear (of the past), and a recurring fear (of massacre) for Syrians. In many ways, governance relies on fear and the actualities and threats of violence that induce fear in Syrians, and it is through these fears, through their recollection in prison memoirs, for example, that Ismail seeks to discern the rationalities of government in Syria. What I find most appealing about Ismail's argument is the juxtaposition of affective and violent technologies of government as producing political subjectivities. That is, actual violence, actual horror, and actual death exist alongside what Ismail calls "anticipated subjectivity," absent but anticipated state power, to produce affective states in Syrians.¹⁷

Ismail does not clearly identify a legible population that the Syrian regime acts upon because the point of the civil war regime is to create an ambient fear that shapes Syrians' subjectivity in relation to the state. There is no one group that is clearly targeted; everyone could be targeted. This is precisely how government through violence worked in Syria; the reality and threat of violence produced subjects that could be governed. I discuss this in more detail below, but suffice to say for now that the dividing line between who is protected from violence and who is a victim of it lacks clear definition. Blaydes suggests that problems of legibility may be due to a lack of information about populations on the part of the state.¹⁸ Social, political, and geographic proximity to the state increases a population's legibility to state authorities and makes it easier to distribute rewards and punishments.¹⁹ The Syrian civil war regime required a bifurcation of society into friends and enemies, but this bifurcation had to be flexible so that it could be extended to any individual or group deemed a threat to the state. Bifurcation also had to be flexible enough to maintain the threat of "anticipated subjectivity" on which state power depends.

Ismail's analysis of the pre-2011 period is instructive in turning our attention to the relationship between affect, violence, and government and to the importance of understanding how the state creates enemies and ambient fear and thus shapes citizens' subjectivity. In the post-2011 period the figure of the terrorist emerged as the spectral enemy through which the state's enemies could be discursively constructed and acted upon through violence and the law. This politically relevant cleavage structure gave the state discretion to act upon enemies, regardless of sect and ethnicity, as the terrorist target was the state itself. Defined broadly in legal terms to include anyone who writes a derogatory social media post, on one end, to someone who took up arms against the state, on the other, the figure of the terrorist has emerged as the Syrian state's principal enemy, as codified in Law No. 19 passed in July 2012. The terrorist embodied the disloyal subject who has "betrayed their homeland" and "worked in the interest of foreign enemies" to create a "state of panic." The spectral terrorist served to delegitimize anti-regime claims while creating a legible category for the state to inflict violence upon. I now turn to how the spectral figure of the terrorist was produced through narratives of disloyalty that presented acts of betrayal, abandonment, and treason as punishable and embodied in the terrorist subject.[20] The terrorist becomes the subjectivity through which a "politically relevant cleavage structure" could be organized.

Narrating Disloyalty and the Spectral Terrorist

State officials' narration of the conflict as a "crisis" imposed on Syria by outside enemies in collusion with internal saboteurs created the affective and political contexts for the discursive deployment of the spectral terrorist subject and the bifurcating of friends and enemies after 2011. Anyone who supported the actions of Syria's enemies to "harm the homeland" or "undermine the state" in words or deeds would be considered an enemy of the state. Disloyalty found expression in several themes that emerged in state officials' framing of the conflict, including abandonment, betrayal, and treason.[21] The deployment of such language had the intended effect of delegitimizing the state's opponents and undermining their political claims.[22] In Syria's case, disloyalty was narrated as a series of acts and non-acts committed by Syrians that ultimately harmed the homeland. Disloyalty found deeper discursive resonance in the spectral figure of the terrorist, allowing the state to portray the crisis as a counterterrorist struggle firmly situated within the wider GWOT. Once a clear discursive target of the GWOT rhetoric employed by the Bush administration, Bashar al-Assad's Syria "learned to stop worrying and love the 'War on Terror.' "[23]

Syria's embrace of the GWOT rhetoric and the discursive framing of the terrorist as the perpetrator of Syria's crisis provided both for the "commonsense" narration of the war (this is why the war is happening) as well as the subjectivization of enemies (this is who should be punished for starting this war).[24] In this section, I want to explore how disloyalty was narrated after 2011 through the prism of terrorism as a prelude to creating subjects that could be punished for betraying the homeland. Narrating disloyalty produced not only the victim/perpetrator binaries through which people could understand the war but also the political context for the identification and punishment of state enemies represented in the spectral figure of the terrorist. The "common sense" narration of the war required more than just state officials' infrequent speeches; it was also premised on an entire cultural and intellectual edifice that underpinned it.

The discursive construction of enemies and the narration of war through victim/perpetrator binaries is an important corollary to the actual violence that sustains conflict. Lewis and colleagues argue that state propaganda, information control, and knowledge production are three ways that discourse sustains conflict and creates commonsense narratives that explain to citizens why conflict is occurring while simultaneously delegitimizing state opponents.[25] Delegitimization occurs through the repression of alternative narratives and information and official statements that undermine opposition claims that serve to justify extreme state violence against enemies.[26] Syrian state officials marshaled several discursive frames to portray enemies as disloyal. These frames emphasized an individual's treasonous acts against the state through collusion with enemies and participation in acts that harm the homeland. To discursively produce the disloyal subject that would be acted upon by state violence, state officials, media, and cultural producers had to frame the conflict with reference to victim/perpetrator binaries that would undermine the legitimate claims of state opponents while portraying them as treasonous and disloyal. The official narration of the conflict as a crisis driven by terrorists and enemies of the homeland was buttressed by a cultural and intellectual edifice that reinforced this framing as the commonsense explanation for the war.[27] This edifice required a similar bifurcation of the conflict via victim/perpetrator binaries. After 2011, any act, feeling, emotion, or intention that could be loosely construed as against the state or homeland could be labeled terroristic. The fluid, expansive definition of terrorism that emerged from Law No. 19 allowed the state to target anyone—regardless of ethno-sectarian affiliation—deemed an enemy.

Terrorists and State Enemies

The categorization of enemies as terrorists reflected the regime's strategic instrumentalization of GWOT rhetoric both domestically and in international forums.[28] Even before the war in Iraq started, Bashar al-Assad loosely proclaimed a commitment to the war on terror while opposing its execution through violence and war, instead proposing that it be fought ideologically by spreading "moderation."[29] After 2011, Syrian officials made an abrupt and significant shift in their discursive and ideational approach to global terrorism by situating the conflict firmly within the logic of the GWOT. Whereas the war on terrorism was previously something to be criticized, by 2019 it was claimed that Syria's "fight against terrorism will lead to a political solution" to the conflict "and that any talk of a political solution while terrorism spreads is an illusion."[30] In a sign of how closely Syria aligned itself with the GWOT after 2011, a 2015 editorial published by the official Syrian Arab News Agency by Nasir Qandil argued that the United States had failed in its responsibility to eradicate terror and that it was now up to Vladimir Putin and Bashar al-Assad to assume the mantle as the only two leaders capable of "accomplishing the mission and bearing its costs."[31] Ironically, this sentiment resembled precisely what Syrian Intelligence Director Ali Mamlouk told his US counterparts in 2010.[32] This shift helps us understand how the spectral figure of the terrorist emerged as a state enemy after 2011.

The belief that Syria was a bulwark against global terrorism was widely held throughout the Arab world. Tunisian writer Toufiq al-Madani's 2018 book deftly captures how the Syrian regime situated itself within the war on terror without aligning with the policies of Western countries.[33] Al-Madani argues that the post-2011 Syrian crisis cannot be understood outside of Syria's opposition to the war on terror, which was ultimately an obstacle to the realization of the United States' imperial designs to remake the Middle East. For al-Madani, the Arab uprisings provided the context for the United States to destabilize Syria in concert with a pro-US business class and Salafi groups willing to take up arms against the state. This narrative about internal and external enemies cohered with the regime's framing of the conflict as a crisis stoked from the outside. The real war on terror for al-Madani was the one fought by Russia and Syria against these domestic and external enemies. Al-Madani saw Syria as a double victim of the war on terror, first because the country refused to acquiesce to American designs after 2001, and second because the United States unleashed terror on Syria to destabilize the country. Throughout the book, a host of external and internal enemies feature prominently.[34] The presence of spectral enemies prodded by their external clients was the most dominant framing of the conflict, on that presented the post-2011 period as a deliberate war against Syria. Faisal Mekdad, Syrian foreign minister, triumphantly said at the United Nations in 2022 that "the war on Syria has failed" because of the state's counterterrorism efforts.[35]

Framing state enemies as terrorists was a strategy to delegitimize them and collapse all opposition into the subject of the terrorist. The language of a "war on terror" came to saturate state and media narratives about the war, producing a spectral terrorist subject that was aided from outside by state sponsors of terror. A type of narrative emerged in which Syria was positioned as both a victim of the war on terror and (with Russia) the "only true force" (*al quwah al haqiyqah al wahdah*) capable of carrying this war to a full victory.[36] This distinction between Syria as a target of the GWOT, on the one hand, but also the only state capable of fulfilling the true mission of eradicating global terrorism, on the other, took on special salience after 2011.

The inherent fluidity of the definition of terrorism and the terrorist subject was a problem to be embraced rather than overcome by state officials. The creation of a spectral terrorist subject cast the net wide and allowed for the emergence of a range of subjects who would be forced to submit to a punishment regime linking terrorist criminality to legal status and socioeconomic rights (such as the right to work, own property, and so on). The spectrality of the terrorist was not confined to the fear of violence but encompassed a series of emotional and moral acts that constituted harm to the homeland. By collapsing terrorism into material, emotional, and moral elements, Syria's Law No. 19 sought to expand how state enemies were subjectivized and acted upon. This law operationalized terrorism as the basis for meting out punishment to state enemies, while the Counter-Terrorism Court (CTC) (al Mahkamah Aadaiya al Arhab), which was created to formally process these punishments, thereafter became a central pillar of the state's post-conflict state-building efforts to embed the logic of war in governance.

The CTC and Syria as a Counterterrorist State

Syria had been under a state of emergency since 1963. A cosmetic reform in 2011 to lift the state of emergency never resulted in any substantive change to the security apparatus's treatment of citizens. Emergency politics has relied on a sustained, always morphing narrative of state enemies. The construction of the spectral terrorist after 2011 and the materialization of a punishment regime through the CTC was the latest iteration of a form of statehood oriented toward targeting state enemies. After 2011, state enemies were represented in several consistently deployed discursive categories, but none became as powerful as the terrorist designation. The legal expansion of the crime of terrorism and the creation of the CTC deepened the violence of the state of emergency that had existed prior to 2011. The conflict gave rise to a renewed emergency politics aimed at the spectral figure of the terrorist. The CTC that emerged in 2012 as a replacement to the Supreme State Security Court (SSSC) was a much more comprehensive legal mechanism for the detention and prosecution of state enemies because of the remarkable powers it gave the state in the name of combatting terrorism.

On March 8, 1963, the Syrian authorities declared a formal state of emergency that remained in place until April 2011, when it was officially revoked during the early stages of the uprising. The state of emergency justified the simultaneous creation of the SSSC to prosecute state enemies. Rationalized through a discourse of imminent emergency and threat to the state, the SSSC sat wholly outside of any judicial norms, processes, or legal protections for defendants. Instead, the court became the space for the exceptional exercise of state violence against its enemies in the name of counterterrorism. Imprisonment, torture, indefinite detainment, and a range of other violent prohibitions that formally sat outside of the Syrian legal system, especially those pertaining to defendant rights, were sanctioned through the prison-court complex that acted upon state enemies. The exceptional nature of the SSSC constituted a major pillar in the Syrian regime's exercise of governmental violence, a form of acting upon the population in general, and enemies in particular, through violence that came to constitute the means of mediating social and state-citizen relations.[37] State violence was not some departure from everyday government but rather constitutive of it. The SSSC was a central structure in this governing logic. The SSSC kept no records of trials or decisions, allowed no observers into its premises, and effectively functioned to provide legal cover for the state's exercise of violence against its perceived enemies.

Over the decades since its creation, the SSSC had tried thousands of defendants from various social and political movements that were differentially constituted as threats to the state, from Kurdish political activists to Muslim Brothers to secular activists such as Nasserites and other Ba'ath Party members. There were, however, years during which the SSSC had not functioned at all, with at one point almost a decade passing without any trials.[38] Nevertheless, the SSSC existed as a mechanism for the state to extrajudicially prosecute enemies when needed in moments of perceived crisis. When protests began in 2011, one of the key demands was the abolition of the SSSC as part of broader calls for accountability. On April 21, 2011, the Syrian parliament passed Decree No. 53 formally abolishing the court. This measure, however, was largely cosmetic and did not moderate in any substantive way state and paramilitary forces' violent treatment of protestors or the role that courts played in legitimizing torture, imprisonment, and murder.

While state violence continued despite the cosmetic removal of emergency provisions, lawmakers and jurists were busy preparing a new law that would reproduce the emergency powers of the SSSC. The first manifestation of this was Law No. 19,[39] which redefined terrorism expansively and gave the state a wide range of powers to punish convicted terrorists through imprisonment, asset seizure, and execution. The new definition of terrorism included material and emotional acts and non-acts on the part of individuals that constituted harm to the homeland. The law defined terrorism as "Every act intended to create panic among people, disturb public security, damage the infrastructural or institutional foundations of the state, that is committed via the use of weapons, ammunition, explosives, flammable materials, poisonous products, or epidemiological or bacterial instruments . . . or by using any tool that achieves the same purpose." The expansion of the crime of "terrorism" through Law No. 19 provided the legal basis for the wide-ranging punishment of Syrians broadly categorized as terrorists. In practice, this definition opened a range of humanitarian and nonviolent acts to criminalization under the rubric of terrorism.

Hundreds of Syrians were arrested for providing medicine, serving food, posting on social media, and the like. Everyday acts that could be loosely construed as supporting terrorism were now subject to state prosecution.

On the same day that Law No. 19 was passed, the punishment regime for terrorists was expanded with the passing of Law No. 20 targeting public sector workers and pensioners for "dismissal from state services" if convicted of the crime of terrorism.[40] Any worker found guilty of terrorism would immediately lose their employment and any claims to a state pension. This provision would eventually be expanded to people convicted in absentia, with no recourse for reversing the court's decision available. The law reiterated Law No. 19's expansive definition of terrorism and deprived any worker or pensioner, as well as any of their accomplices, of their social insurance rights if convicted. This effectively cut off anyone convicted or suspected of engaging in or supporting terrorism from accessing state resources. Laws No. 20 (a different one from that cited above) and No. 21 were also passed to, respectively, criminalize kidnapping as an act of terrorism and deprive those convicted of social rights to state support.[41] These laws materialized punishment of the spectral terrorist and foundationalized the extension of punishment to other state enemies who were indexed as disloyal. In tethering punishment to absence these laws were opening new possibilities for the state to punish enemies whose non-actions (e.g., not showing up to work) allowed for their categorization as disloyal subjects through their designation as terrorists.

Detentions, prosecutions, trials (if they could even be called that), and the sentencing of those convicted of terrorism would be channeled through the newly created CTC. The CTC was created by Law No. 22 to prosecute terrorism cases less than a month after the new definition of terrorism, and a month prior to the passing of Decree No. 63, which empowered the Ministry of Finance to seize a suspect's assets or ban them from travel even before facing trial or being convicted of terrorism.[42] A person did not even have to suffer through the CTC's show trials before undergoing state punishment. Mere suspicion of terrorism was sufficient to invoke the state's intervention, and state incentives were created for citizens to denounce each other and to bring "cases" against their conationals.[43] Decree No. 63 was the first of a series of measures intended to provide legal justification for the reorganization of housing, land, and property rights, appropriation of assets, and erasure of Syrians' social identities under the guise of combatting terrorism. This became the formula for punishing enemies: categorize, identify, and appropriate. As the conflict dragged on, the state increased its capacity to engage in this process as it expanded the legible populations it targeted.

The CTC was part of the regime's carceral system that included civil and military courts that also tried people for various crimes. Cases were referred to the CTC by the security agencies after an individual was detained by one of the branches. Once they were detained, they were either released after an investigation by the branch (or payoff from the family) or referred to one of the three courts: military, civil, or CTC. The military court was designed to prosecute military members but was expanded to include civilian jurisdiction after 2011. Civil courts prosecuted most other civilian cases, and if convicted, someone would be transferred to one of the state prisons. Finally, there were CTC cases that handled various crimes of terrorism ranging from murder to association with armed groups. The expansion of the legal jurisdiction of these courts during the conflict reflected the large number of cases brought before them each month.

It is impossible to determine how many cases were referred to the CTC or how many people were convicted. Estimates about how many cases the CTC tried per month vary widely.[44] In 2014 leaked documents from the court showed that more than 100,000 people had files being processed by the CTC.[45] Many of these people had not been arrested but were simply wanted (*matlooben*) for terrorism. The expansion of the court and the public discussions that occurred thereafter suggest that the CTC was trying tens of thousands of cases a year in its three chambers. In a 2015 report on the working of the first chamber of the CTC, the Violations Documentation Center stated that "legal texts use general, vague words and expressions which may apply to anybody opposing the regime's repression of the people's uprising whether adults or minors, male or female, civil activists or armed rebels, or any other group that might form the slightest possible threat to the government. This accounts for the huge numbers and much diversified cases of the detainees who have been referred to the CTC."[46]

The trials themselves were hardly worthy of the label. They often took a few minutes and involved a defendant being brought in front of a judge who then quickly rendered a verdict without any presentation of evidence, deliberation, or any due process whatsoever. Virtually all defendants were prosecuted without any possibility of appeal. Upon conviction in the CTC, a defendant faced not only whatever penalty had been delivered by the judges (which could include hard labor, detention, or death) but was also immediately subject to a complete asset seizure and travel ban. Unsurprisingly, the evidence marshaled against defendants was often either fabricated or extracted under torture. Defendants had no opportunity to contest the charges against them, even when they were as minor as cooking or digging graves for terrorists.[47]

The CTC was so active in its first years that a second chamber was eventually added in Aleppo (the first chamber was in Damascus), followed by a third chamber in Homs.[48] Each chamber consisted of three presiding judges (one of whom served as president of the chamber), at least eight investigative judges, and a public prosecutor. Extreme corruption within the courts meant that defendants were often found innocent after paying bribes, a problem so rampant that the government regularly replaced judges (sometimes several at once). Judges and security officers openly solicited bribes from among the detained, with the price of a person's freedom often running into the millions of Syrian pounds. Decree No. 69 in 2020 and Decree No. 54 in 2021 are examples of the wholesale restructuring of judges in all three chambers of the court.[49] Defendants' lawyers existed only in name and were not able to see any information in their clients' files, including evidence, before the trials. In reality, there was no way to properly defend someone appearing before the CTC other than to try and bribe the judges.[50]

The courts' expansion accommodated the increases in cases and had not led to any changes in the trial structure. In 2015, prominent Syrian human rights lawyer Michel Shammas summarized the inner workings of the court and client-attorney relations within it:

> All work is conducted under the surveillance of cameras and security agents that do not allow attorneys to speak with their clients. Attorneys are not allowed to view files until after the detainee has been interrogated and they are not able to photocopy anything from the files. Judgments are based on evidence from the security branches, who usually extract confessions without any evidence. Court judges often use these security confessions ... [even] if they are not supported by other evidence.[51]

There was no due process in the court or independence from the security agencies, which monitored proceedings and placed officials in the court during all trials. Moreover, "the chairman and the other co-judges often declare their pro-regime views vocally while questioning the detainees. The court chairman openly and explicitly declares his support to the regime when he sarcastically taunts the detainees."[52] Farcical as this may seem, the CTC was an institutional innovation in Syrian emergency politics that served to tether punishment to categorizations that emerged after 2011.

The CTC created by Law No. 20 has been the subject of extensive analysis and critique by Syrian, Arab, and international organizations that see it as a continuation of the practices of the SSSC.[53] In fact, the CTC is a much more comprehensive legal structure underpinning state counterinsurgency than that provided by the SSSC. To substantiate this claim, I turn away from the critical approaches to Law No. 19 to an unlikely source, an article written by Manal Munjid, a supporter of the law and a member of Damascus University's Faculty of Law. Writing two years after the law passed, Professor Munjid provided a justification for the extraordinary conditions the new law and courts created to rid "this alien phenomenon [terrorism] from our society."[54] For Munjid, pre-2011 laws were simply insufficient for dealing with the violence and terrorism of the conflict period and thus required wholesale revision. She begins her paper by asking whether the new laws were necessary and why crimes after 2011 could not be punished through existing mechanisms. Her response revolves around the "state of panic" caused by terrorist violence and the comprehensive legal response needed to address it, effectively invoking the spectral quality of the terrorist subject. Munjid's analysis of the new law rests on three important distinctions: terrorism as a material act, terrorism as a moral act, and conspiracy to commit terrorism. The first understanding of terrorism is relatively straightforward and includes prosecution for any minor or major acts that cause damage to a person, building, or in the broader sense "the government" and thereby "creates a state of panic."[55] However, the nature of "panic" and the complexity of terroristic violence during wartime required the laws to have wide discretionary powers assigned to the judiciary. Munjid justifies the expansionary nature of the material definition of terrorism with reference to the extraordinary circumstances Syria faced at the time and the new threats posed by its internal and external enemies. As such, the law creates altogether new criminal categories associated with terrorism: terrorist organization; financing terrorism; terrorist training; terrorist methods; threatening terrorism; and promoting terrorism. These new legal provisions allow the state to prosecute terrorists who do not commit specific material acts but who may intend to, or who may facilitate such acts. These "moral" intentions overlap with and share the goals of material acts, which is to disrupt society and government and are punishable prior to an act being taken. This means that the establishment of intent to finance a terrorist organization is punishable as if someone materially supported an organization. Again, we see in these provisions the codification of the spectral fear of the terrorist. Munjid uses the example of the deserter to justify the death penalty against some terrorists: "A deserter, for example, who has been trained by the army and has left and perhaps went further and shared their military knowledge and experience, deserves the death penalty because he used this training against the homeland, so he is a traitor to his homeland."[56] Ultimately, for Munjid, terrorism is a "comprehensive problem" that requires a "comprehensive legal framework" with wide judicial discretionary authority to enact punishment. It is not simply acts of terrorism that are punishable, but desires to commit such acts, helping others to commit such acts, and having the "moral judgment" to harm the homeland. Law No. 19 enshrined spectrality and ensured that any citizen could be tried as a terrorist simply if their acts or non-acts constituted betrayal of the homeland. From here, the law expanded the definition of terrorism to include all threats made against the state. These threats could be made in any forum, including social media. The law's targeting of acts that create a "state of panic" invoked the spectral fear of the terrorist subject and those who enabled them. Indeed, the law was explicit in its targeting of anyone who aids and abets.

Munjid's endorsement of the law's broad powers mirrored state narratives about the necessity of emergency politics to respond to the spectral figure of the terrorist. I have less interest here in the legality of these measures than in how they functioned as wide-ranging punishments with legal rationalizations. The CTC was a key pillar in the emergent form of statehood in Syria that was discursively structured around counterterrorism and the need to punish state enemies. The CTC materialized the terrorist subject as state enemy and rendered them governable through a punishment regime that sanctioned imprisonment, murder, and asset appropriation. An expansive definition of terrorism rendered the exceptional the norm and held Syrians to subjective criteria for determining what side of the terrorist-counterterrorist divide they sat on.

Navigating Disloyalty

How did Syrians navigate ambient fear and the constant threats posed by emergency politics? Syrian writer Jad al-Karim al-Jabaae argued that parallel societies (*al mujtam'a al muazi*) exist in Syria, one that is loyal to the government and one that is loyal to the opposition.[57] For al-Jabaae, the lines demarcating both societies cross through sect, tribe, region, and family, creating a division that is "hard to explain," but which nevertheless saturates Syrian society and shaped individuals' relations with the state.[58] He calls these parallel societies a "government society" and a "civil or traditional society," with the former structurally penetrated by the state and loyal to it, and the latter acted upon by the state. The creation and aggravation of social cleavages, for al-Jabaae, constitutes the essence of government in Syria as something enacted outside of ministries. The state's creation of "objective enemies" (*al a'da al mudu'in*) produces a "generalized fear" (*t'mim al khuf*) in which "each citizen is condemned and wanted" (*kl muatn mdan wu taht al talab*).[59] These fears manifest in profound ways: fear of the state, neighbors, difference, associations, strangers, groups, political parties, and any other social formation captured in the creation of an enemy subject, the "objective enemy" who represents nongovernment society. For al-Jabaae, the "government society" is one driven by fear and the production of generalized fear to contain and act upon enemies.

What is the social basis of the "government society" al-Jabaae writes about? And how does the social differentiation underpinning loyalty reveal itself if both societies are not reducible to a specific social identity? He resists reducing loyalists to sect, family, clan, ethnicity, or regional identities, but rather insists on seeing loyalty as a product of a particular government (read: authoritarian) identity that citizens ascribe to that is grounded in masculinist and patriarchal notions of authority and legitimacy. While I see al-Jabaae's rejection of sectarian explanations for state violence, and his insights into the governmentality of fear and the division of Syrian society more broadly, as productive ways to understand bifurcation during conflict, I am less convinced that the dividing line is simply fealty to a patriarchal authority. What evidence could a Syrian marshal to prove such loyalty if they were, for example, being accused of conspiring with terrorists while they were stopped at a checkpoint? My point here is that demarcation is neither objective nor empirically verifiable and that the function of generalized fear was to precisely produce the conditions in which citizens have no clear strategies for proving loyalty to the regime. Al-Jabaae's contention that institutional mechanisms link state and citizen by fostering either fealty to or ostracism from the state similarly does not tell us how citizens can demonstrate loyalty and adherence to one society or another. In other words, how can someone prove they are loyal to the state? How can the state prove who its objective enemies are?

The Syrian civil war regime aimed not for clarity and legibility in defining enemies, but rather for the production of disorder that affectively and politically structured people's relationship to the state. Citizens may seek to gravitate toward identities or practices that confer loyalty, but these were insufficient to ensure protection from state violence. In Khaled Khalifa's *Death Is Hard Work*, Bolbol tries to perform loyalty by hanging the president's picture in his house, living in a loyalist area, and engaging in antiopposition conversations, but even these performances are insufficient to eliminate his neighbors' suspicions of his loyalties because of his birthplace.[60] Citizen behavior is structured around reward and punishment regimes, but this behavior may not always be legible to the state and thus renders people vulnerable to targeting.[61]

The spectral terrorist was the subject around which the Syrian state could begin to categorize state enemies. State officials' discursive construction of a disloyal citizenry required the bifurcation of Syrians into friend and enemy categories that could be materialized as a series of punishments through the legal system. The friend/enemy binary requires "a clear distinction between 'those who love this country' and 'those who do not'" that "becomes the fulcrum around which an enemy discourse revolves.... The discursive framing always permits the widening of this identification to include a much wider spectrum of possible enemies, both contemporary and historical, internal and external."[62] The pliability of enemy categories over the course of Syria's conflict meant an expanding categorization of enemies both inside and outside of the country. At certain times of the conflict, refugees were fleeing armed terrorists and were thus ostensibly allowed to return, while at others, refugees' choices not to return was said to indicate their disloyalty. Such contradictions between how and when Syrians were categorized and rendered friends or enemies points to the inherent instability of Schmittian friend/enemy distinctions. Binaries do not produce discrete, rigid categorizations that are politically clear and identifiable; rather, they function "as a continuing dynamic of political hatred" in relation to shifting ideas of who constitutes an enemy.[63]

The punishment of the spectral terrorist became the organizing principle of a new political order. The inherent instability of shifting friend/enemy categories fueled by collective political hatred produced chaos and mistrust masquerading as political order.[64] Indeed, friend/enemy categories were wielded as legal and political weapons by the state to create a climate of fear and chaos in which understandings of what it means to be a friend were constantly subject to change. Terrorist categorization has no objective logic, and the laws criminalizing terrorism were intentionally vague so as to apply to anyone the state deemed an enemy subject. The instability of friend/enemy categories functioned to affectively structure citizen behavior in relation to the security apparatus's various centers of power. Analogizing the situation to a metastasizing cancer, a Syrian doctor told me that "there is no demarcated line to say, 'Here is the oppressor and here is the oppressed, and if you are among the oppressors, you are safe,' because the attack, the violence, is not in one direction but . . . in every direction, and it grows from within."[65] State violence as a sort of metastasizing cancer speaks to the instability of multidirectional violence and the inability of citizens to avoid entrapment within an ecology of fear. The survival task, so to speak, was not to find a space on either line of the friend/enemy distinction, but to achieve extraction from the ecology altogether. The same interviewee relayed a story about their time in prison, despite having performed emergency medical procedures on regime soldiers and civilians in loyalist areas. Most of their cell mates were, ironically, lower-level soldiers and agents from within the intelligence services. Many of them were victims of denunciations and jealousy from within their own ranks. Over time, some of these prisoners would be released, at which time others would take their place, complaining that they had also been denounced by their comrades. The doctor shared these experiences as evidence of the inherent instability of what they referred to as multidirectional violence.

Under such conditions Syrians were unable to clearly situate themselves on the friend side of the bifurcation. There are no identifiable markers of loyalty that one can point to in order to ensure their personal safety. Similarly, behaviors and acts were not immediately understood as loyalist or oppositional, and compliance with the ever-changing criteria for what was and was not loyal was virtually impossible. Consider the case of the doctor again, who, after their release, was asked to testify at the trial of the person who had denounced them and was accused of stealing significant amounts of money from a state institution. They were being asked to denounce their own denouncer. The doctor refused to testify, not because they did not want revenge, but because "at that point, I didn't know who to trust."[66]

What does the multidirectionality of violence and punishment tell us about the state's attempts to render the population legible and manageable in relation to the conflict? Legibility is neither absolute nor objective. The subject of the spectral terrorist ensured that a key category that materialized into a punishment regime could be deployed against anyone. Most Syrians understood that their arrest, captivity, and possible torture and murder were not subject to the objective criteria of a legal case as much as the whims of the agent or intelligence agency dealing with them at any specific moment. Competition and paranoia between the security agencies, as well as the horizontal structure through which they communicate, encouraged agencies to look with suspicion on any Syrian transferred to their authority. For a Syrian to be formally released from detention, each agency had to provide a "security approval" for their release, meaning that the person in question was not on that agency's wanted list. In many cases, detainees were simply transferred to an agency without anyone knowing why. The terrorist subject provided a legal and political pretense to produce a chaotic political order in which all Syrians lived on the verge of being rendered terrorists.

Very few people were spared the burden of having to navigate multidirectional violence and the different security agencies' paranoid competition between each other. A Latakia-based Syrian writer and journalist named Hazem Mustafa (a pseudonym) recalls the story of a Mohammed Tatly (also a pseudonym), a service driver who worked in the State Security Branch (Fr' al Amn al Dualah) for five years before being arrested on charges of aiding armed men.[67] During his time as a driver, Tatly had discovered tunnels that armed groups had built underneath the branch building in Aleppo. His discovery led to a commendation, a reward of 400,000 Syrian pounds (about US$800), and certificates of appreciation from both the local offices of the Ba'ath Party and Colonel Suhail al-Hassan, a Russian protégé who headed the powerful Tiger Forces. When Tatly's neighborhood in Aleppo (al-Salaheen) was cleansed of armed groups he and his family returned and were immediately arrested by the Political Security Branch (Fr' al Amn al Siyasi) on suspicion of having relations with the armed groups. Even the presentation of the two certificates of commendation were not enough to quell suspicion. He spent months in prison and had been moved between different prisons and security branches in Aleppo, Damascus, Homs, and Latakia, before being put on trial under Law No. 19 for the crime of having "relations with armed groups" (al t'aml m'al mslhiyn). Tatly's status as a loyalist with high-level commendations was insufficient to protect him from being accused of terrorism.

The story of the Syrian doctor and Mohammed Tatly are just two of thousands of stories of how Syrians navigated the inherent instability and political chaos generated by categorizations grounded in the spectrality of state enemies. I am less interested in how people navigate spectrality and more in the production of political order out of the creation of spectral enemies and the materialization of punishment through the CTC.

The Spectral Terrorist as State Enemy

Syria's articulation of the war as a counterterrorism effort to an international audience paralleled the discursive creation of a spectral terrorist subject through which the conflict could be narrated. Presenting the state as a victim of terrorist perpetrators and their external supporters, Syrian officials created the conditions of possibility for the deployment of the terrorist as the subject around which political bifurcation could occur. This spectral terrorist subject was not simply one who exercised violence or purchased weapons for armed groups; they were also considered guilty of committing nonviolent acts of protest, posting social media posts, and even having certain feelings and thoughts. The identification, categorization, and punishment of the spectral terrorist subject effectively rendered all Syrians potential terrorists as any words, deeds, thoughts, or feelings that could be constructed as against the homeland were liable to be labeled terroristic. The point of this categorization, however, was not to create such blanket categorizations, but rather to produce disorder and chaos as governable order. The lack of any reasonable mechanism to prove or disprove one's political loyalty as a "non-terrorist" rendered everyone subject to state punishment.

The categorization of terrorism was accompanied by several exceptions, amendments, and mechanisms to reverse the state's suspicion. I am referring here not to the tried-and-true tactic of bribes but to official categories of subjects who were absolved of terrorist attribution through their recategorization as loyalists or repentant citizens. The transformation of a subject from a potential terrorist to a loyalist was facilitated through the narration of citizens as deceived or lost. Yes, they betrayed the homeland, but they would be forgiven because they were led astray by Syria's external enemies. Creating political and discursive space for the alchemy of potential terrorists only exacerbated the chaotic, disorderly management of the conflict.

In the absence of an externally imposed political transition the Syrian state was able to construct this alchemy within the counterterrorist framework. The implications of this for the trajectory of conflict management were profound, and the state's ability to maintain regimes of punishment was directed at the spectral terrorist. The conflict could be managed through a counterterrorism framework that demanded that repentant fighters and civilians express loyalty through various acts—returning to areas under state control, remobilization, fulfilling conscription orders, and the like—that did not require the state to concede wrongdoing for the violence after 2011. The conflict would be "resolved," and peace would emerge through a subjugation of citizens who had either taken up arms, left the country, or committed affective acts against the homeland. This meant that the political mechanisms for achieving peace and reconciliation in Syria lacked any deliberative form, but were instead defined, shaped, and implemented in accordance with the commonsense narrative of the war.

3

The Reconciliation Process

Transforming Enemies Into Friends

We have chosen two paths: the first and most important one is reconciliation. . . . The second path is to attack terrorists if they don't surrender and refuse to make peace.

—BASHAR AL-ASSAD

Introduction

In 2014 the United Nations' Economic and Social Commission for West Asia (ESCWA) convened the National Agenda for the Future of Syria project to bring together independent, opposition- and loyalist-affiliated Syrians over a series of workshops to articulate shared visions for Syria's future. More than eight hundred Syrians participated in these workshops over the subsequent years. The National Agenda's goal was to connect a vision of Syria's future with technical support for reconstruction to any post-conflict Syrian government.[1] The work of producing objective, technical goals for reconstruction was often interrupted by the ESCWA leadership's insistence on dialogue over key "nexus" post-conflict issues, including reconciliation. Naturally, nobody attending was opposed to reconciliation among Syrians, otherwise they would not have agreed to participate in this pluralist forum.

However, a major problem arose when the official United Nations translation of the word "reconciliation" (*tusaleeh* or *musalaha*) was found in the workshop literature.[2] These words have been used by the Syrian regime to describe a series of reconciliation agreements (*musalahat*) between the government and various armed forces. Rather than serving as actual deliberative agreements that provided anything resembling a reconciliation between two belligerent parties, the *musalahat* were a feature of the regime's counterinsurgency strategy to bifurcate fighters, displace civilians, and erase the vestiges of conflict in formerly "liberated" areas. The ESCWA's insistence that a shared vision for Syria be filtered through the liberal language of reconciliation created serious confusion. Were participants there to discuss actual reconciliation among Syrians, or reconciliation in the way that the regime had presented it?

The state's approach to articulating and materializing a specific version of reconciliation was a conflict management strategy that legitimized violence, displacement, and erasure in the name of producing a "social solution" (*hal ajtma'ee*) to Syria's conflict. The vision of a social solution quickly emerged as one in which only certain Syrians were allowed to participate. In this chapter, I am interested in how a specific version of reconciliation was constructed as a political value and then materialized as a conflict management strategy. As a political value, reconciliation eschewed dialogue between belligerents in favor of an approach that shifted culpability for Syria's conflict onto the regime's enemies. To reconcile, then, was not to engage in deliberation, but rather to accept the restoration of regime rule. Reconciliation presumed a victim-perpetrator delineation that absolved the state and its allies of any accountability for the war. The politics of Syria's reconciliation was oriented toward the restoration of regime power rather than the emergence of a new, inclusive "we."

The reconciliation agreements materialized this version of reconciliation as a political process that created new conflict subjectivities and categorizations that were acted upon violently by the state. The "reconciled area," along with the "reconciled fighter" and their "reconciled factions," became important categories around which conflict management unfolded. A reconciled area was targeted for purification of opposition vestiges, most obviously through the forced displacement of armed and unarmed people and through the bureaucratic absorption of legal provisions that nullified property transfers and other forms of certification that occurred outside of state institutional recognition. The spectral terrorist subject was definitively embodied in the armed opposition fighter, so the question of how to "return them to the embrace of the homeland" (*t'ud ala hadn al watan*) required some form of alchemy that was compatible with the commonsense narrative. A "reconciled fighter" was only permitted to reconcile if they or their "reconciled faction" accepted remobilization into the regime's counterinsurgency apparatus. This remobilization transformed an enemy fighter into a friend of the state. These designations created corresponding categories worthy of punishment: the unreconciled area, the unreconciled fighter, and the unreconciled faction. The politics of reconciliation that emerged in Syria allowed the state to bifurcate and act upon armed fighters and the areas under their control. It is no wonder, then, that the participants in the National Agenda had reservations about discussing reconciliation.

As a political process reconciliation also revealed the limits of institutional state reach and the importance of new conglomerations of notable power rooted in Syrian locales. These new forms of power emerged in the form of local reconciliation or civil committees who served as intermediaries between the state and the fighters they were seeking to reconcile. As intermediaries these groups materialized reconciliation by overseeing its bifurcating processes and conferring legitimacy upon it. Working with the local security apparatus these committees were responsible for negotiating the terms of reconciliation and displacement among fighters and civilians in besieged areas. Devolving state power to these committees proved to be a useful institutional innovation in managing the conflict. By the time these committees took on similar roles for settling civilians (explored in the next chapter) they had ceased to become mere negotiators and had instead become mechanisms for producing knowledge about the population that allowed state institutions to decide who fought, who stayed or left, whose house was destroyed or damaged, and, most importantly, who could be considered a loyal or disloyal citizen.

Regime-Style Reconciliation

The absence of a deliberative process to end Syria's conflict made possible the imposition of a battlefield solution after the Russian military intervention in 2015. Absolved of any responsibility to offer concessions to its opponents the Syrian regime was able to craft peace through a vision of reconciliation that cast out fighters and civilians who were unwilling to accept state authority.[3] The language and implementation of peace, in other words, become a way to sustain war.[4] What role did the commonsense narrative play in advancing a politics of reconciliation that was institutionalized at the state level and enacted through local intermediaries? Reconciliation is a common political goal of all societies emerging from conflict, so there is nothing novel about the adoption of this language in Syria. What is perhaps novel in the Syrian example is how reconciliation was deployed as a mechanism to manage rather than resolve conflict. In most contexts mired by extreme social divisions or armed conflict reconciliation is pursued as a mechanism to overcome violent, exclusionary pasts and to restructure politics around the prevention of further conflict.[5] The normative goals of reconciliation are tied to political visions of the past and present. Thus, reconciliation was enacted as part of the infrastructure of punishment against state enemies.

The politics of reconciliation are inherently exclusionary and tied to political processes that emerge in the wake, or at the least in the simmering, of violent conflict. Syria's conflict trajectory unfolded along the spectrum of a victor's peace, resembling countries such as Rwanda and Sri Lanka where post-conflict reconstruction projects were openly defiant of liberal norms.[6] The forms of reconciliation pursued in Syria eschewed deliberation and abandoned any pretense to liberal compromise and dialogue by framing reconciliation as a restoration of political order. Syria's reconciliation project more closely resembled that pursued in Algeria, where the Charter for National Reconciliation and Peace was created to provide immunity to state officials while absolving them of responsibility for the civil conflict. Joffé's skepticism about "whether [the Algerian charter] should be considered as an example of 'reconciliation' at all, particularly as it is based on the concept of submission to the authority of the state,"[7] is aptly applied to Syria's own reconciliation process, which in both design and effect discarded a national deliberative process in favor of a politics of reconciliation that demanded citizen regret, responsibility, and repentance as the criteria for inclusion in the body politic and the basis for the restoration of political order.

National reconciliation was conceived as the submission of the citizen to the authority of the state. The Syrian state's reconciliation process was thus premised on the denial of regret and responsibility by the state and the expectation that individual "deceived" (*mghrur*) citizens would express political regret for the wrongs they committed during the conflict. The expressed political outcome of citizen regret and their patriotic "return" from a deceived path was not the creation of a new collective, an inclusive "we" that builds the foundations for post-conflict community through a shared understanding of what it means to be Syrian after the war.[8] The demand for citizen regret and repentance as the basis for reconciliation absolved loyalists and the state for responsibility for the conflict, and was repeated in official announcements, curricular changes, policy reforms, and a climate that promoted state absolution. The "social solution" to the conflict was framed as returning people to political order, not creating a new one. The fighters who were offered reconciliation, and the citizens who were offered settlement after them, were required to profess regret at their betrayal of the homeland as a condition for their inclusion back into Syria.

Regret as one pillar of reconciliation mirrored the state's victim-perpetrator narration of the conflict in which citizens were deceived by Syria's enemies into betraying their country. The regretful citizen was required to demonstrate repentance and absolution upon their return to the embrace of the homeland. This demand reinforced the reconciliation process as one that prevented dialogue or contestation of opposing narratives. The normative goal of reconciliation was not to negotiate the commonsense narrative or provide space for state concessions; submission to state authority was the normative and political goal of reconciliation and would be achieved through the parsing out of loyal and disloyal citizens and the latter's repentance. This is precisely the offer that fighters were given when approached for reconciliation: Either accept disarmament and displacement to Idlib or repent and accept remobilization in the state's counterinsurgency apparatus.

As a political value reconciliation materialized as a bifurcating tool to separate loyal and disloyal fighters. Reconciliation did not emerge as a process in the temporal sense that people and societies build toward something over time, but as a single moment in which people are forced into accepting regret and performing repentance as the basis for reconciliation. Reconciliation represented restoration of the self, community, and country in the aftermath of conflict.[9] The South African Truth and Reconciliation Commission is an excellent example of the importance of reconciliation as a distinct political value in post-conflict (in this case, post-apartheid) societies. Much like the South African example, political reconciliation assumes an expression of collective regret and responsibility from those associated with perpetuating conflict, most often state officials. The principle of "amnesty for truth" established the ethical context for individuals to express regret and responsibility within a state-sanctioned forum. Reconciliation processes, however, can also be deployed by states to suppress responsibility, establish specific "truths" about a conflict, and to advance novel post-conflict identities. Rwanda's National Unity and Reconciliation Commission, for example, seeks unity "through the creation of a meta-'Banyarwanda' identity that transcends ethnic cleavages."[10] This denial of ethnicity in favor of a broader "Rwandanness" "is belied by the fact that only Hutus are being prosecuted for their crimes."[11] In each case how reconciliation is institutionalized shapes the forms of political order that emerge in its wake.

Syria's state-led reconciliation process lacked any of the institutional, ethical, or identity-based aspirations present in either the South African or Rwandan examples, and was driven by the normative goals of restoring political order rather than creating something altogether new. The emergence of a post-conflict "truth" follows from the regime's narration of the conflict as a crisis imposed by domestic and external terrorists who sought to harm the homeland. An editorial by May Hamidouche succinctly summarized the state's position on how to achieve national reconciliation through a "social solution" by arguing that the first condition for reconciliation was to settle (see chapter 4) the files of "those who were deceived" and to turn them away from those who "ordered them from the outside" and toward their true patriotism.[12] The political project behind reconciliation was the alchemic transformation of the "lost" citizen into the "patriotic" citizen. Undergirding this transformation was an ideal loyalist subject who had remained steadfast and committed to defending the state. In reality, however, loyalist subjects were indexed as such and remained largely uncommitted to preserving regime power.

Narrating reconciliation as the transformation of the "lost" citizen subject into a patriotic one established the basis for pursing reconciliation as a political project of repentance outside of deliberation. The responsibility for reconciliation was thus firmly placed on the shoulders of the fighter and citizen who was required to demonstrate their absolution and return to the patriotic fold. Responsibility through repentance would occur for fighters through their acceptance of remobilization into the regime's counterinsurgency apparatus. Thus, although the state was heavily invested in framing enemies as terrorists the discourse of reconciliation carried the possibility, even for armed fighters, of absolution and repentance for state enemies. As a political value reconciliation was conceived through the assumption of regret, repentance, and responsibility by the armed fighter who had betrayed their homeland. This materialized in reconciliation agreements that eschewed process in favor of fighters (and civilians in areas under their control) being forced to decide between displacement to Idlib or formally pledging loyalty to the state and remobilizing under the authority of the military.

Such a narrow materialization of the state's vision of reconciliation tacitly rejected most of the mechanisms associated with reconciliation. There was no transitional justice process as state officials refused to accept any responsibility for violence. There was no formal need to declare immunity for state-affiliated fighters since they had done nothing wrong. Fighters' repentance was enough to constitute the dispensing of justice. There was no dialogue between belligerents. Contesting the state's narrative about the conflict or reconciliation itself was strictly off-limits at the moment of reconciliation. And there was certainly no attempt to produce a shared "truth" about the war or to provide compensation for its victims. The absence of a reconciliation pact that could serve as a reference for how to construct post-conflict order further narrowed the scope of the state's reconciliation project.

Reducing reconciliation to a choice that fighters had to make nevertheless required a legal and bureaucratic infrastructure to manage the process as it unfolded in different Syrian locales. Reconciliation depended on its being framed as a political process that moved the country from war to peace even if the process for doing so did not involve any deliberation between belligerents. The choice was, of course, never about some commitment to the regime, but was instead driven by political calculations. It was incumbent on the state's commonsense narrative, however, to equate loyalty with commitment. In the next section, I outline how a state ministry was created to implement a vision of reconciliation and how its structural limitations produced the conditions of possibility for the emergence of localized conglomerations of notables who intermediated between the state and the reconciled areas.

Institutionalizing Reconciliation

State officials' narrowly constructed view of how reconciliation should occur did not prevent the institutionalization of reconciliation through the creation of a new ministry. In June 2012 the Ministry of National Reconciliation (Wzrat al Dulah Lshun al Musalahat al Wataniyah) was created as a new state body to facilitate reconciliation in Syria under the leadership of Ali Haidar (head of the Syrian Socialist National Party). At the same time, a National Reconciliation Commission was created as a special parliamentary body that would report directly to the People's Assembly. As the conflict progressed and the Syrian army recaptured areas from armed groups, National Reconciliation Committees (Ljnah al Musalahat al Wataniyah) were formed in areas to oversee the reconciliation process and to collect information about the missing, kidnapped, displaced, and murdered. The creation of these committees formalized an ad hoc process linking notables, armed groups, and the state in direct negotiations over loan truces. The committees reported to the commission, which in turn reported to the parliament, leaving the ministry itself mostly outside of the day-to-day affairs of the committees. On November 26, 2018, Decree No. 361 terminated the Ministry of National Reconciliation, and a subsequent decree on the same day (No. 19) recreated the National Reconciliation Commission as a body under the authority of the prime minister and accountable to the Council of Ministers. Ali Haidar was made president of the new commission. A year later, the commission was terminated on October 22, 2020, through Decree No. 22,[13] because, as parliamentarian Ammar Bakdash claimed, the commission was "no longer useful."[14] Bakdash was speaking a particular truth about the ministry itself, if not the national reconciliation project, which had by 2020 become almost entirely driven by (now more or less autonomous) local civil reconciliation committees that were under the oversight of the security apparatus.

The Ministry of National Reconciliation had an inflated public role in the narration of the conflict as a terrorist war against the homeland and in advancing a "social solution" to Syria's crisis, but very little actual political power to oversees reconciliation processes. The ministry was mostly confined to promoting cultural events in the name of reconciliation. One example is that of the four-day poetry marathon organized by the "We Are All for the Homeland" (*kulna lil watan*) group formed by the ministry. The poets Farqad Al-Salloum, Ali Suleiman, Zainab Ibrahim, and Latifa Khadouj, under the supervision of the poet Suleiman Sheikh Hussein, recited poems for four days without interruption.[15] Such events took place throughout the country and gave the appearance of a cultural shift toward reconciliation. While the ministry was propagating a culture of reconciliation it was publicly tasked with overseeing the work of local reconciliation commissions. Such bureaucratic oversight would have been impossible for a ministry that was never seriously staffed. In 2016, Minister Haider complained to the parliament that the ministry only had twenty-five employees—simply not enough to conduct the work of any national ministry, let alone one of such importance during a war.[16] Haider would continue to agitate publicly for more resources in the years to come to no avail.

The Haider-led ministry maintained a public commitment to peace, forgiveness, and unity as the path toward reconciliation, while the legal infrastructure for bifurcating and punishing disloyal Syrians slowly took root in the background. The ministry was tasked with collecting information about the missing and deceased, particularly abductees, the kidnapped, and the "martyred," a specific legal designation for those who died while fighting with the army or state-affiliated militias, and which carried with it specific state benefits for their kin. Much of this information was being relayed to the ministry through civil initiatives that linked local notables, armed groups, and state-affiliated fighters in shared local truce negotiations that were occurring with relative frequency in the period prior to Russian intervention.[17] These ad hoc initiatives were eventually institutionalized in 2016, first as the National Reconciliation Committees and then as the Civil Initiative Committees (al Llijnah al Ahliyah). The committees were ostensibly under the authority of the ministry. In reality, however, these new institutional designs reflected emergent power centers in Syrian locales where notables and elites had assumed important roles in managing the conflict on behalf of the state.

The institutionalization of these localized power centers took place through a deployment of local elites and notables through the structure of the reconciliation committee to ostensibly strengthen the "social dimension" (Ib'ad al ajtma'ee) of reconciliation.[18] Recruitment of elites and notables was an important step in the process of socializing reconciliation and creating a political process for the transformation of enemies into friends. Socialization can broadly be understood as the process through which "actors adopt the norms of the community," and is thus relevant to understanding how ideas about violence, peace, and reconciliation are transmitted in societies.[19] The targets for socialization were those state enemies that had betrayed the homeland. Two parallel processes of socialization were occurring around the time of the Russian military intervention. On the one hand, the Haider-led ministry took on a prominent public role in promoting a culture of reconciliation that equated peace and harmony with a restoration of political order. On the other hand, local elites and notables were coalescing into committees that enacted the regime's politics of reconciliation by specifically negotiating displacement agreements with armed fighters. These agreements became the basis for bifurcating fighters and civilians into friends and enemies and creating new conflict management practices for organizing state power in areas that fell back under state control.

The substantive political work of reconciliation as a conflict management practice shifted to the local committees while the Haider-led ministry lacked sufficient resources and a clearly defined mandate. On September 5, 2016, Minister Haider launched an altogether new initiative that was essentially a cosmetic restructuring of the National Reconciliation Committees, which remained formally under state authority. The Civil Initiative for Local Reconciliation (al Mbadrah al Ahliyah lil Musalahat al Mhliyah) was created under the authority of Sheikh Dr. Jaber Mahmoud Issa as a "parallel" project to support the work of the National Reconciliation Committees, which had, in Haidar's words, become "defective in some places due to corruption."[20] Framing the new initiative as a "restructuring" of reconciliation efforts, Haidar commented on the necessity of civil society involvement alongside the state in achieving reconciliation. Speeches at the launch for the Civil Initiative at a conference aptly called "National Reconciliation for the Good of the Homeland" affirmed both the role of the state in achieving reconciliation and the necessity for "independent," civil society involvement in reconciling the warring sides. Much like the National Reconciliation Committees, the civil committees would have local branches in specific cities and locales. The creation of the new initiative occurred amid growing frustration within the ministry about the limited role it was playing in the reconciliation process and the slow pace of reconciliations.

These committees lacked any horizontal integration and therefore also national character and reach. As conglomerations of local notable, clerical, and elite power they were loosely organized bodies created to mediate between the state and fighters and civilians in formerly rebel-held areas. They coordinated almost exclusively with the local branches of the security apparatus and the Ministry of Finance, where information about disloyal citizens targeted for asset and property confiscation was sent, and not the Ministry of National Reconciliation. The individual and collective authority of the committees was both localized and dependent on the good graces of the security apparatus, which had the authority to pick and choose who would sit on these committees. Their collective power in the conflict must be understood within the limitations of their localized relationships with the security apparatus and the lack of a horizontal mechanism to connect different centers of power.

The civil committees were state-sanctioned constellations of local power composed of notables, clerics, and elites whose political loyalty was a prerequisite for inclusion. As constellations of state power these local intermediaries were agents of conflict management who were sutured to the Russian presence as much as they were to the Syrian security apparatus. They had tenuous linkages with state institutions and mostly coordinated with local security actors. Reina has referred to the arrangements between the state and local power brokers in the Colombian context (such as paramilitaries and landowners) as "coalitions" that formed to dispossess peasant landowners coercively and illegally during periods of conflict.[21] A similar process unfolded in Syria as the state devolved power to these civil committees, which then became embedded in strategic relationships with the security apparatus, militias, and other elites. These coalitions gave their members access to the necessary resources and processes to undertake substantial land appropriations under the guise of reconciliation. The committees' work was a form of indirect rule that socialized new power centers into an emergent political order from which they financially benefited. Membership on a committee became an opportunity for local elites and notables to accumulate assets and property under state-sanctioned processes. As a form of indirect state rule, the committees were tasked with identifying loyal and disloyal populations in reconciled areas once agreements were reached with oppositionists.

The ineffectiveness of the ministry and the devolution of power to local coalitions occurred alongside changes on the battlefield stemming from the Russian intervention. The gradual retaking of territory accelerated the demand for reconciliation agreements and created new possibilities for these local coalitions to categorize and act upon state enemies. Questions about how to organize and govern areas that fell back under state control were filtered institutionally through the local committees, who formally took up the necessary bureaucratic tasks.

Reconciliations as Conflict Management

The changing battlefield after September 2015 contributed to the expansion of the reconciliation agreements and the state's legal infrastructure to identify, categorize, and punish different kinds of enemies. Siege warfare was an especially prevalent strategy that "allowed the regime to keep its enemies isolated in place and to prevent their advance without having to commit or divert combat resources from other theaters."[22] Prior to 2015 Syrian territorial fragmentation among differing, often competing armed groups was a key feature of the conflict along with local agreements between these armed groups that addressed issues of civilian mobility, governance, authority, cooperation, or humanitarian aid.[23] These local agreements were narrow and focused on immanent issues between different parties.[24] The reconciliation agreements that were forced on armed groups after 2015 were thus not novel features of Syria's conflict when first introduced. Over time, however, these agreements became standardized and less about managing the here and now and more about managing the fighters, civilians, and properties in areas formerly outside state control.

Reconciliations negotiated between armed groups, civil committees, and Russian and Syrian security forces were tactical battlefield agreements best understood as "surrender agreements" as they occurred between asymmetrical powers and required armed groups to withdraw from areas they formally controlled.[25] The principal function of surrender agreements was to expel armed groups and manage their surrender through a formal process that consolidated territorial gains.[26] Siege warfare made reconciliation agreements possible. The main impact of sieges was to suffocate supply routes and inflict a slow stranglehold on besieged areas through pacification and deprivation.[27] Dwindling supplies threatened armed groups' material capacity to reproduce themselves or govern the areas under their control. After a prolonged siege, representatives from the civil committees would approach commanders to negotiate a reconciliation on behalf of the state. Here, residents and fighters would be asked to accept two conditions. The first was the return of the territory to state authority, and the second was the requirement that anyone remaining in the area reconcile their status with the state. In many cases civil committees would also present forcible expulsion orders for known oppositionists. Those who refused reconciliation were guaranteed safe passage to Idlib, the last major rebel stronghold in northwestern Syria. In effect, the second condition was a mechanism to bifurcate friends and enemies in areas about which the state had very little information. The process asked people to self-select whether they were loyalists or not. Those who left were required to notify the state and were rendered non grata along with fighters who went to Idlib.

These reconciliation agreements were antithetical to any serious dialogue and reflected the state's narrow understanding of reconciliation as a reestablishment of state control. Sosnowski refers to these as "highly one-sided agreement[s] where the party in the position of power essentially imposes terms on a party that has little ability to refuse them."[28] By offering people the choice to stay or leave, reconciliation agreements "necessitate people calling themselves out as either collaborators or defectors."[29] Anyone involved in opposition politics was unlikely to choose to remain in their city or town as doing so would subject them to arrest and imprisonment. Should they choose to stay they would be subject to a settlement process (detailed in the next chapter) that would determine whether they would be subjected to state punishment for subversive behavior during the conflict. The demonstration of loyalty was a political act that sought to collapse loyalty and political commitment into the state project.

As a conflict management strategy, the reconciliation agreements allowed the state to create new categories of bifurcation aimed at isolating potentially loyalist fighters from opposition ones. Reconciliation agreements provided an answer to the question of how the state would manage armed fighters since designated fighters in opposition areas were not offered the opportunity to return to civilian life. If fighters refused displacement to Idlib they were forcibly remobilized into the state's counterinsurgency apparatus. The latter process came to be known as the settlement (*tswiyah*) of fighters' status. The initial political and legal basis for the settlement of former fighters was Administrative Order No. 5136 (2014), issued by the head of the army's Security and Military Committee to legalize the rehabilitation of former fighters with the aim of remobilizing them. Until the reconciliation agreements these efforts at remobilization were rather limited. A shifting battlefield, however, changed this, and Decree No. 14, passed in July 2016, provided a more comprehensive legal structure for fighters to reconcile with the state. The decree offered fighters amnesty from punishment if they turned themselves in and accepted remobilization in the army or National Defense Forces (NDF).

In February 2016, less than six months after the Russian intervention began, the Center for Reconciliation of Opposing Sides and Refugee Migration Monitoring in the Syrian Arab Republic (hereafter Russian Reconciliation Center) was founded to monitor the implementation of reconciliation agreements. Just over a year later, in March 2017, the center ceased its daily bulletins about the progress of reconciliations and claimed to have recorded and overseen close to 1,600 separate agreements. Many deprived areas that fell back under state control did not see any serious improvement in their living conditions.[30] The rapid pace of reconciliation agreements allowed both Russia and Syria to describe them as a substitute for a disarmament, demobilization, and reintegration (DDR) campaign. In each case, the reconciliation committees would negotiate with the opposition on behalf of the state. These agreements did not simply return state control to formerly rebel-held territories; they created new geographies to manage (reconciled areas) and new individual (reconciled fighters) and collective subjectivities (reconciled factions).[31] The rapid reintegration of reconciled areas into the state over the course of just over a year raised questions about how these areas would be governed and managed within the larger conflict.

State strategy for how to manage reconciled areas involved completely erasing the vestiges of non-state authority. A patchwork of competing governance models emerged in Syria during the conflict that provided alternatives to the state.[32] This erasure first targeted all organized forms of alternative governance that had emerged after 2011, including opposition councils, courts, civil administration bodies, and civil society organizations. These governance models, even more so than the armed fighters, represented the most serious threat to the reassertion of state authority in reconciled areas. One of the many tasks of the local committees present in these reconciled areas was to identify these governance projects and terminate them.

The policy of erasing vestiges of non-state authority was enacted through the expulsion of known oppositionists and the dismantling of opposition institutions. Known members of governance bodies and even medical staff were forcibly expelled as part of the reconciliation agreements.[33] Expulsion was also a practice of bifurcation because it allowed local committees to identify, document, and initiate appropriation measures against known oppositionists. Forced expulsion was typically followed by legal measures that appropriated the individual's assets and withdrew the legal rights that allowed them to live and work in Syria. These laws included Law No. 23 (2015), which expedited property expropriation; Law No. 11 (2016), which suspended property transfers in non-regime areas; Law No. 33 (2017), which completely transformed the issuance and management of property documentation; and Law No. 4 (2017), which altered the Civil Status Code, among many others. Their expulsion was both physical and social.

In the early stages of the conflict legal measures such as these were passed at the local level before being scaled to the national level after the Russian intervention. The nationalization of appropriation laws and measures to nullify property transfers was part of state efforts to both punish enemies and erase the residual effects of oppositionist rule. Law No. 11, for example, erased all property transfers and automatically restored ownership to previous owners, who were required to submit documentation and present themselves in person (or through power of attorney) to reclaim their land. Since many of these transfers occurred because people were leaving the country, very few did so. Documentation requirements laid out in Law No. 33 also made this process difficult. In many cases, properties went without being reclaimed and were eventually confiscated by the state. All of this occurred under the guise of a narrative about displacement and property transfer that portrayed property owners as victims of oppositionists.

The expulsion and erasure of known oppositions paralleled the state's erasure of all alternative governance institutions. There was no pretense toward integrating state and opposition bodies after reconciliation. Any existing governance institutions were simply dismantled. This erasure extended into the past. All decisions, certifications, regulations, and property exchanges sanctioned by these authorities were rendered null and void, creating havoc among people whose life events now lacked documentation. I return to this issue in the final chapter, but for now suffice to say that the state's approach to erasing vestiges of opposition rule in reconciled areas had profound effects on people's ability to return to their homes and how elites were able to accumulate property assets in the aftermath of reconciliation. Both processes were intertwined. In identifying the assets of disloyal subjects, the civil committees were creating new war spoils that could be confiscated by the state and redistributed. These processes were formalized and legalized through an infrastructure of appropriation. The committees' ability to identify and initiate appropriation measures against disloyal subjects made them lucrative, powerful spaces for local notables to enter.

The return of Eastern Ghouta to state control illustrates the state's approach to reconciled areas. When government forces took control of Eastern Ghouta in April 2018 they immediately annulled all sales contracts that had been approved and documented by local authorities between 2011 and 2018, essentially the entire time that the area was outside of state control. This was immediately followed by a decree targeting Eastern Ghouta from the Central Real Estate Directorate in Damascus to the effect that all property transferred in this period be restored to its original owners. Although this was presented as a form of restitution the original ownership was not in fact immediately restored; that would require the owners—many of whom no longer lived in Syria—to physically present themselves in Eastern Ghouta.[34] Instead, former property owners were given only thirty days to present themselves before the property would be considered unclaimed and then auctioned off (national laws dictated that people had one year to claim their property). To return, however, former property owners would first be required to settle their status with the state. Many people were unwilling to return and risk imprisonment and thus knowingly allowed their properties to be confiscated.

By rendering all property transactions documented outside of state institutions invalid local authorities could acquire cheap land in newly reconciled areas. As a conflict management strategy, the project of restitution created an infrastructure for further bifurcation of Syrians. Those who returned and claimed (or tried to claim) their property were reintegrated into the commonsense narrative of the war as loyalists, while those who did not return were categorized as absentee and unsettled subjects. The process of reinscribing state power in reconciled areas through invalidation of opposition documentation was also a process of differentiation and subject-making through the reorganization of property rights. Those who were able to make state-approved claims on property would be spared categorization as absentee or unsettled subjects. The dichotomies of absent/present and unsettled/settled subjects provided clear indices of loyalty and disloyalty.

Managing property in reconciled areas fell under the jurisdiction of a special directorate within the Ministry of Finance called the Directorate for Managing Seized Funds and Confiscated Property (Mudeerat al Amwal al Masdrah wu al Mistuli 'Lihah), which was responsible for documenting, processing, and distributing all assets and properties acquired in reconciled areas.[35] By creating legal ambiguities around ownership and restitution these authorities were able to take advantage of a legal infrastructure of appropriation that emerged to manage reconciled areas. This included specific ministerial decrees targeting individuals for appropriation, absentee property provisions, annulling all property transfers, and implementing appropriation orders if an individual was convicted by the CTC.

The Directorate for Managing Seized Funds and Confiscated Property is an example of how a new state institution oriented around the punishment of disloyal subjects through appropriation was created. This body was specifically created to manage assets in newly reconciled areas. Doing so allowed the local committees and security apparatus to develop a system of appropriation and cleansing. On the one hand, appropriation measures initiated against an absent or displaced subject would block their return. On the other hand, the displacement and prevention of return would reduce any contestation of state power. The reorientation of ministerial, judicial, and executive power around the punishment of opponents through property appropriation had its roots in state practices aimed at managing reconciled areas. This legal infrastructure was strengthened and expanded in late 2023 when a new law on "Managing and Investing Transferable and Non-Transferrable Seized Property Confiscated Through Unappealable Judicial Ruling" passed the People's Assembly. This law nationalized local practices that took root in reconciled areas by providing legal cover for the appropriation of properties owned by state enemies. Judicial seizure in reconciled areas thus became the basis for a national approach to appropriating properties owned by state-designated terrorists and absentee subjects. Under the pretext of reestablishing state control authorities created new categories of presence and absence that allowed them to legally categorize property for confiscation.

The bureaucratization of property appropriation provides perhaps some of the only serious evidence for state institutional capacity in reconciled areas. By the time the Russian Reconciliation Center was dissolved more than 1,600 reconciliation agreements had been reached. The territory covered by these agreements was vast, and in each case the structure of civil committee and security appropriation was implemented and funneled through the Ministry of Finance. The civil committees in these areas were not only tasked with facilitating reconciliation but also with generating information about the whereabouts of residents and the status of property. This information would be circulated through the Ministry of Finance, which, after receiving the consent of the security apparatus, issued circulars detailing property confiscation. Auctions for confiscated property were intended to benefit loyalist elites. For example, in areas around Damascus confiscated homes were being auctioned to loyalist elites for as low as US$3 in 2015.[36] Adleh and Favier summarize the post-reconciliation state of governance by noting that "ties with security services and loyalty to the regime are the main determinants for reshaping the dynamics of local governance that emerge in post agreements localities."[37] Ironically, years later the security apparatus in reconciled areas began encouraging residents to self-organize, collect taxes, and govern towns.[38]

Reconciled and Unreconciled Subjects

The terms of the reconciliation agreements clearly delineated friends from enemies while creating altogether new conflict subjectivities that were created under the banner of reconciliation. The "reconciled fighter" was an armed fighter who had effectively repented and joined the patriotic ranks of the army. They were narrated as lost loyalists who have recommitted to the state. The "reconciliation factions" (*fasaeel al musalahat*) were battalions who chose amnesty and integration into the state's counterinsurgency apparatus over disarmament and displacement. The "reconciled area" was a new geography targeted for resocialization and cleansing of opposition remnants. The transformation of former fighters and battalions from enemies into friends occurred through a discursive rehabilitation that presented them as returning to the patriotic fold and a legal settlement structure that ostensibly gave them immunity from state retribution. These new subject categories had counter-subjects who would be punished: unreconciled fighters and unsettled civilians (those who chose displacement to Idlib). Unlike the spectral terrorist, who lacked any immediate loyalist counter-subject, the implementation of reconciliation produced loyalist subjects alongside disloyal ones. As loyalism also indexed political commitment the reconciled fighters and reconciled factions were presumed defenders of the state. Their total withdrawal ahead of HTS advances in December 2024 demonstrate the weakness of the link between reconciliation as a political process and reconciliation as a political reality.

Regime-style reconciliation materialized forms of individual and collective subjectivity that could serve as the political-legal basis for punishing enemies. Reconciliation was an important process in the subject-making of Syrians who had been categorized as enemies (the unreconciled fighter) and friends (the reconciled fighter). The latter subject was produced through repentance and state forgiveness that conferred loyalty back onto the person. In this way, the subject's transformation from enemy to friend could be narrated by emphasizing their deception and psychological state as initially driving them to betray the homeland. The bifurcation of reconciled and unreconciled fighters indexed loyalty and disloyalty as subjectivities to be managed by the state. The reconciled fighter would express their loyalty through remobilization into the state's counterinsurgency apparatus. Remobilization required a parallel discourse concerning the rehabilitation of former fighters that allowed for their re-embrace into the homeland. The reconciled subject was made through a language of rehabilitation that emphasized, but forgave, their betrayal of the homeland.

Reconciliation and amnesty were mechanisms to transform repentant fighters into friends and to preserve their social and legal connection to Syria, whereas fighters and civilians who chose displacement over reconciliation were divested of their properties through ministerial fiat. As part of the reconciliation agreements all fighters and civilians who chose displacement were forced to surrender their names and other family information (e.g., address, other family members). The Ministries of Finance and Justice would cosign circulars stating that the displaced had forfeited all rights to property, bank accounts, assets, and work in Syria.[39] Once these circulars were produced the targeted subject would be forbidden from claiming or transferring their assets. These punishments were often extended to the kin of unreconciled subjects.

Soon after the reconciliation agreements came into effect these circulars were limited owing to the lack of information security officials and civil committees had about state-categorized subversives. However, while reconciliation agreements accelerated as the battlefield shifted, several thousand unreconciled fighters and civilians who had accepted displacement were subject to asset forfeiture. The pace of displacement and forfeiture corresponded to the success of the sieges in forcing surrender and creating "reconciled areas." What had been mostly ad hoc and localized forms of punishment directed against known fighters and opposition sympathizers were then slowly scaled up and deployed against other fighters using a common language and legal justification for punishment after reconciliation.

Bifurcating fighters into reconciled and unreconciled and acting upon them accordingly represented the closest thing to a DDR campaign pursued by the state. DDR aims at facilitating the transition from war to peace through the reduction (or elimination) of combatant weapons and combatants' integration into the post-conflict polity. By reducing the means of violence, DDR programs seek to shift contestation to the political arena and away from the battlefield. Power-sharing agreements shore up DDR programs and provide a political corollary to battlefield alchemy in which former belligerents are expected to share power in a new post-conflict political arrangement. Remobilization in the wake of reconciliation was delinked from any broader national power-sharing agreement and was negotiated on a locale-by-locale basis. By treating armed fighters as the fragmented groups they were the state and the Russian supervisors of reconciliation could simultaneously present reconciliations as a national project while refusing concessions on any opposition demands, such as a political transition or transitional justice.

Remobilization was mostly an unstructured process in which reconciled factions were absorbed into different army divisions or the NDF or expected to engage in combat independently of a central command structure. Reconciled factions from the southern governorates of Dar'aa and Quneitra were mostly conscripted into Syrian Arab Army units and deployed throughout the country, while those from Homs and Hama remained in their areas as part of the NDF.[40] Most of the conscripted fighters were divided between the Fourth and Fifth Divisions of the army, which were controlled by Maher al-Assad and Russian ally Suhail al-Hassan, respectively. But in general remobilization occurred according to battlefield needs. One reconciled faction, the Golan Regiment, had spent more than a year after reconciliation fighting in Palmyra, Homs, Jobar, Damascus, and Hama before settling into Quneitra as the main pro-government force in the area.[41] These factions often fought under the command of a division or the local security apparatus and were never fully integrated into an existing unit. They were a part of the military apparatus but also separate from it. This also helps explain why so much of the military apparatus withdrew during the HTS advances in December 2024.

Remobilization did not provide safety guarantees for reconciled fighters and their factions. Such was the nature of the state's arbitrary exercise of power against both friends and enemies and the structure of remobilization that forced reconciled factions to serve as moveable pawns that were isolated from other elements of the security apparatus but nevertheless accountable to them. Many of these factions were viewed with disdain by other state-affiliated fighters for their previous betrayal.[42] Separating reconciled factions from existing military units while forcing them under military and security command enabled the violent retribution campaigns that state-aligned forces engaged in against them. Invoking a loophole in the reconciliation agreements that allowed the state to arrest reconciled fighters for civil crimes, a campaign of arrest and retribution began around 2018 that targeted the commanders and fighters of reconciled factions. In one case, an entire brigade of reconciled fighters operating in Barzah was killed or imprisoned.[43] Retributions against reconciled factions remained common for years after their reconciliation.[44] These factions were treated as dispensable and, despite the legal amnesty extended to them by the state, were still punishable through arrest or murder. Unsurprisingly, the local security apparatus in reconciled areas failed to abide by the terms of reconciliation in several cases.

The campaign of retribution against reconciled factions was instructive in terms of how state violence was arbitrarily and indiscriminately deployed against even those deemed friends. Distinguishing between reconciled and unreconciled fighters as surrogate categories for loyal and disloyal subjects was an important innovation in the state's management of conflict. Here, the armed population was categorized based on their relationship to the state and whether they were willing to accept remobilization. Parsing out fighters in this way allowed the Syrian state and its Russian military overseers to distinguish between friends and enemies. Unlike liberal counterinsurgencies where the goal is ostensibly to separate fighters from civilians, the Syrian counterinsurgency campaign was oriented toward separating fighters from their factions based on their willingness to accept remobilization or displacement. Yet, the bifurcating effects of reconciliation were not enough to address the lingering perception of betrayal and abandonment that remained attached to most reconciled fighters. The ambiguity of state categorization ensured that no reconciled fighters were ever safe from retribution. Political commitment to the state was demanded of them but never reciprocated.

Subjective transformation through the reconciliation process was not a guarantee that one could claim loyalty to the state. Categorization was inherently unstable and subject to the arbitrary violence of the battlefield. In chapter 2, I introduced the story of a Syrian doctor who described the line between oppressor and oppressed as being essentially unknown. Formally reconciling with the state was insufficient to ensure one's security and protection from state violence. Nevertheless, the transformation of fighters from enemies into friends was an important conflict management strategy to secure reconciled areas and to provide the fighters needed for battles elsewhere. By undergoing subjective transformation, the reconciled fighters and their factions helped materialize an imposed political solution that substituted for a deliberative political process. These new subjects provided categories around which newly created power centers and state bodies could concretize the state's conflict narrative.

Categorizing reconciled and unreconciled fighters was also one of the first pillars of the state's expropriation infrastructure, and it began by targeting fighters and civilians who accepted displacement to Idlib. This was an important feature of the legal infrastructure of punishment that emerged initially, unevenly, throughout the conflict before being essentially nationalized as part of the reconciliation agreement process. In each of the hundreds of reconciliation agreements, those who accepted displacement forfeited their rights as Syrians. A legal infrastructure had to be erected to punish them through both de facto denationalization and confiscation of assets. This ensured that their attempts to return to Syria or control their assets from afar would be virtually guaranteed to fail. Some Syrians who also accepted temporary displacement while awaiting settlement and guaranteed return after reconciliation have been denied such opportunities,[45] with the result that they have effectively been stripped of their citizenship rights as well. These newly reconciled areas were cleansed of disloyal elements, and a legal infrastructure of appropriation buttressed these efforts and ensured that they would be unlikely to ever return to their villages, let alone exercise civil and social rights.

To accept reconciliation was therefore to retain some connection, no matter how tenuous, to the state, while to reject reconciliation was to accept that one had no prospects for living in Syria under state control. This process was self-selecting except in cases where expulsion lists were part of reconciliation agreements. This bifurcation made rendering punishment easy as the names on expulsion lists—as a condition of accepting passage to Idlib people had to provide their family information—could easily be transferred to the Ministry of Finance for the purpose of issuing appropriation measures and relevant orders.

By May 2017, when the Russian Reconciliation Center ceased issuing daily reports about reconciliation progress, more than 1,600 reconciliation agreements had been documented. Thousands of fighters had either been reconciled or deemed unreconciled and subject to appropriation. Hinnebusch and Imady estimate that between 2011 and 2016 more than 20,000 fighters took advantage of state amnesty and were transformed into reconciled fighters.[46] The categorization and punishment of unreconciled subjects through reconciliation agreements was an important step in bureaucratizing enmity as a durable feature of post-conflict statehood. Whereas the spectral terrorist exists as a ghostly figure with no specific loyalist counterpart, the unreconciled subject contrasts politically and ethically with the reconciled subject. This binary is important insofar as it serves as a surrogate for loyal and disloyal subjects. We also see in this specific categorization the embedding of the state's narrow view of reconciliation as it was absorbed in conflict management practices. Rather than offering all fighters some form of amnesty, the state has constructed reconciliation around fealty to the regime. Fighters who accepted the restoration of political order and remobilization under state command were categorized as loyal, in contrast to those who refused to do so and were cast out of Syrian society. Reconciliation agreements thus materialized the state's notion of reconciliation quite literally as restoration.

Illiberal Reconciliation

The state's conception of reconciliation as a political value was narrowly defined as the restoration of political order. Efforts at reconciliation would naturally be structured around the erasure of the legacies of opposition governance and armed group presence throughout the country. This is a rather uncommon occurrence in the trajectory of conflicts in which former belligerents engage in deliberations and dialogue to construct a new order that seeks to prevent the outbreak of further violence. Syria's trajectory sits somewhere on the spectrum of the victor's peace where an incumbent regime can claim some form of victory in the conflict. Notwithstanding the unresolved territorial issues in the Northeast and Northwest of the country, this is precisely how the Syrian state had approached reconciliation. As proclaimed victor, the regime sought to design a reconciliation process that buttressed rather than undermined state power. These designs, however, concealed deeper changes to political order that took place despite the proclamation of victory.

The reconciliation agreements that emerged out of the local truces prior to 2015 would not have been politically feasible without the decisive Russian military intervention. The rapid establishment of state control over opposition areas between 2015 and 2017 posed the problem of how the state would deal with areas that had been outside of its authority for years. The answer to this question was found in the materialization of the narrow view of reconciliation as restoration. This occurred, first, through categorizing subjects as reconciled or unreconciled, and second, by acting upon the former through laws that punished their disloyalty to the state. The failure to reconcile was an admission of one's disloyalty and immediately rendered one vulnerable to punishment.

Reconciliation agreements were governed outside of the state Ministry of National Reconciliation because of the highly localized and fragmented nature of the armed groups. There was, by design, no larger national process through which social and political reconciliation could be negotiated between different parties. The ministry was thus relegated to the role of promoting a "culture" of reconciliation, while the substantive political work was assumed by the civil committees and security apparatus. Indeed, the ministry's brief tenure and relative lack of authority—it had no more than twenty-five employees and virtually no capacity to initiate reconciliation processes—indicates where the actual power constellations that drove "reconciliation" throughout Syria were. These constellations represented coalitions of local interests whose work as intermediaries of state power positioned them to reap the material benefits of punishment through appropriation. These coalitions were able to collectively identify property for appropriation and acquire it in auctions that were often closed to the broader public. Reconciliation agreements as counterinsurgency were thus also a mechanism for the state to reward elites it deemed loyal.

Armed fighters and the areas that they operated in posed only one of many conflict management conundrums for the state. Fighters were easy to parse out from one another, especially when they were given the choice of self-selecting. Determining which civilians or internally or externally displaced populations could be similarly categorized as loyal or disloyal would prove to be much more difficult. The state would have to rely on its newly created intermediaries in the form of civil committees, whose roles had slowly morphed from negotiating truces and reconciliations to supplying the security apparatus and state institutions with information about locals and their political allegiances. The infrastructure that emerged in response to the expansion of reconciliation agreements from 2015 to 2017 implicated civil committees and local coalitions in the exercise of state punishment. These coalitions not only managed the negotiating process as intermediaries but played the crucial role of collecting and sharing information about locals: who was aligned with the opposition, who accepted displacement to Idlib, who was a loyalist, where people lived, and so on. This process of information gathering was honed by the civil committees through the reconciliation process, where the simple task of delineating between loyal and disloyal subjects was aided by the latter's acceptance of displacement to Idlib. In this case all the civil committees had to do was document names. As we will see in subsequent chapters, these committees' ability to categorize subjects according to a different set of criteria, such as settlement status and absence, would extend the state's infrastructure of punishment to more than just fighters in reconciled areas.

4

Settling Friends, Unsettling Enemies
The Settlement Process and Civilian Subjectivity

> *The homeland is the only guarantor of our lives, and the Syrian Arab Army is the one that preserves the dignity of the Syrian citizen, and every person who has lost his way must benefit from the amnesty decree and return dear to the embrace of his homeland.*
>
> —RADWAN SULEIMAN (AFTER RECEIVING HIS SETTLEMENT DECISION)

Introduction

A mostly unremarkable story published in April 2022 by the Syrian Arab News Agency (SANA) captures much of the performative nature and generative work of the settlement process in transforming state enemies into friends. The April 17 story mostly revolves around three *matlobeen* (wanted) named Adnan al-Saadeh, Louay al-Faraj, and Bahir al-Hawas who had applied for settlement in the Dayr ez-Zor Governorate.[1] As in almost all regime media stories about the settlement, this report briefly detailed the lives of the three men and their excitement about finally settling their status with the state. The story explained that the three men were wanted for desertion, a punishable crime in wartime. Why did the officers present that day settle their status rather than arrest them? The (plausible) explanation given was that the three men were in areas controlled by the Syrian Democratic Forces (SDF), who had prevented them from reporting to their military units when summoned. Once they were allowed to move out of SDF areas, they "seized the opportunity" to appear in Dayr ez-Zor and settle their status. Their settlement was described in terms familiar to anyone who had been following reports of the process. The men were happy to "return to their normal lives" despite being "late to join the ranks of the army." Another interviewed man, Mounir al-Abbar, reiterated the same version of this story as well as his excitement about joining the army. A fifth settled man, Abdel Basset al-Arayb, was quoted as encouraging all wanted people to settle their status and "ignore the lies being told" about the process.

The glee that the five men were said to feel after their settlement was reproduced in several years' worth of state media reports about the progress of the "settlement of status' (*taswiyah al wad'*) program that emerged out of the reconciliation agreements. The settlement process was a vital part of the state's infrastructure of bifurcation and punishment. The state deployed settlement as a technology of governance to separate loyal and disloyal citizens through the status of the settled and unsettled. As in the previous discussion of the reconciliation agreements, settlement sought to erase the vestiges of conflict, transform subjects (in this case, civilians) from enemies into friends, and to clearly delineate people who were loyal (settled citizens) and those who were not (the unsettled). Settlement status thus indexed a subject as either loyal or disloyal. Similarly, a settled citizen was deemed a loyal one who was committed to the state. Categorizing the displaced, deceived, and deserters as settled or unsettled became a tool to stratify citizenship and distribute or withhold rights.

Settlement substituted for a repatriation program in which all Syrians would be encouraged to return to their country; the alternative was a process that only permitted the repatriation what I have elsewhere called "loyal returnees."[2] A loyal returnee is someone who must narrate their life during the conflict in loyalist terms consistent with the state's narration of the war. The settlement process was predicated on a victim-perpetrator framing in which an applicant must fit their story. There is no space for contesting state narratives at the point of applying for settlement. Instead, applicants were expected to construct a "genealogy of loyalty" that positioned them as victims in the conflict even if they did confess to affective or psychological betrayals.³ The latter point is important because the state had so heavily invested in discursively producing enemies and in framing absence as a surrogate category for the disloyal. Creating categories of subjects who could be settled and transformed into loyal subjects was necessary for the process. Settlement absorbed enmity into a mechanism to bifurcate citizens and prevent those deemed disloyal from ever returning to the country.

Who Can Settle Their Status?

The state's conception of reconciliation focused more on the repentance and absolution of the citizen subject and less so on a deliberative process in which opposing narratives and experiences would be reconciled. The emergence of a post-conflict "truth" followed from the regime's narration of the conflict as a crisis imposed by domestic and external terrorists who sought to harm the homeland. The insistence on a specific victim/perpetrator narration of "truth" served to absolve the state of responsibility for the conflict and shift regret, guilt, and responsibility onto individual citizens for their political transgressions during the war. The subject of the "lost," "confused," or "misdirected" citizen became the subject that needed to be transformed and led back to a "normal life" and away from the sources of their deception. Enemies could be transformed back into friends if they acknowledged their deception and accepted a return to the homeland and state authority. Such a return was not only physical but political as well. Settled citizens were indexed as loyal subjects committed to the state.

The settlement of the deceived or psychologically unstable citizen was an important part of the state's narration of conflict because it allowed for the articulation of certain citizens as worthy of redemption. Deceived citizens could be forgiven if they had not committed acts of violent terrorism against the state, and their redemption could only be realized through state forgiveness and benevolence. Those who harbored "bad thoughts" or who aided the opposition had been deceived, but ultimately their hands were not "stained in blood." Situating the deceived citizen as both perpetrator and victim facilitated their subjective transformation through the settlement process. An editorial by May Hamidouche succinctly summarized the state's position on how to achieve national reconciliation through a "social solution" by arguing that the first condition for reconciliation was to settle the files of "those who were deceived," removing them from the influence of those who "ordered them from the outside" and returning them to their true patriotism.[4] The political project behind reconciliation was the alchemic transformation of the "lost" citizen into the "patriotic" citizen. Narrating reconciliation as the transformation of the lost citizen subject into a patriotic one established the basis for pursuing reconciliation as a political project of repentance and not deliberation. It is more accurate in the Syrian case to see the state's approach to reconciliation as an attempt at restoring an existing political order rather than ensuring one emerged out of the ashes of conflict.

The question of who could or could not be settled and thus return to "normal life" (*hayat taba'iyah*) in Syria was determined by the specific state categorizations ascribed to each applicant. Several of these categorizations are relational to the conflict and the specific victim-perpetrator framing of the commonsense narrative. For example, someone who has knowingly fought with armed groups has hands "stained in blood" and is not permitted to settle. At the very least, if they tried, they would be immediately arrested. Someone who was "deceived but does not have hands stained in blood" was, however, a candidate for settlement as their betrayal or disloyalty in this case was affective and psychological, not material or political. In the case of the affective-psychological disloyalty, a subject can be transformed from a deceived subject (a catch-all category for people who emotionally betrayed the homeland) back into a loyal, national subject. A third category, that of the *matloob* (wanted), typically refers to subjects whose crimes include desertion from the army, failure to respond to a conscription call, or leaving a public sector post, but can also refer to anyone whose name appears on a security blacklist for perceived nonviolent crimes.

If the absent were categorized as disloyal, how could they return? The state's categorization of different forms of physical and affective absence was loose enough to provide space for the alchemic transformation of certain citizens from enemies into friends. The subject of settlement is thus either criminalized as *matloob*, rendered emotionally unstable as a deceived or "mentally ill" subject, or viewed as someone whose displacement is attributed to terrorism rather than a betrayal of the homeland. In the latter case a determination of the subject's status is dependent on their performance of repentance through the settlement process. Demonstrating such affective and psychological states requires the performance of loyalty through regret, remorse, and repentance that reaffirms one's loyalty to the state through the disavowal of previously harmful feelings and actions. A subject's repentance coheres with state narratives about victims and perpetrators in the conflict. Someone who was emotionally weak enough to be deceived into hating their country demands pity and salvation from the "life of chaos" (*hayat al fudah*) toward which Syria's enemies turned them. They, too, become victims in Syria's conflict because they were turned away from their homeland and deceived into fighting against it or, at the very least, harboring "bad feelings" toward their country. The benevolence of the state (and specifically the president) offered rescue from this affective state and a secure return to the "embrace of the homeland."

The emotionally unstable subject's transformation from enemy into friend relied precisely on their articulation as misguided, deceived citizens who were permitted to return after demonstrating regret for their affective and psychological transgressions. A person's deception should not have led them to commit or aid acts of violence against the state. The category of "the deceived whose hands are not stained in Syrians' blood" (*mmn gharar bhm wa lam ttltakh aydiyhm bdm al suriyyeen*) is a more specific archetype for the deceived as it indicates that they were not involved in committing violence. This subject could be articulated as a victim of the conflict because they were deceived by the state's enemies but did not hurt loyal Syrians. The deceived subject's crimes were affective and not material.

The *matloob* and *matloobeen* form a specific legal categorization that refers to someone having been convicted or suspected of committing a crime. The fear of being wanted by the security apparatus pervades Syrian society. To be wanted is to be criminalized and marked for potential imprisonment, torture, and death. The category of *matloob* is a much more precarious subjectivity from which one applies for settlement. One's status as *matloob* could result from anything from a single denunciation to a formal criminal charge or even a case of mistaken identity. In these cases, settlement requires some formal legal resolution of the person's wanted status. The most common cases in this respect are military deserters.

The "displaced by terrorism" (*al mahajriyn bf'l al irhab*) subject was someone whose departure could be easily explained by their having been victimized by terrorism. Settlement applicants could almost always reasonably explain that they left Syria because they feared armed groups operating in or near their areas. Victimhood here was easy to narrate and bureaucratize. Both domestically and internationally the regime's main explanation for such horrific waves of displacement referenced the "wars of takfiri terrorism and economic terrorism."[5] Terrorist perpetrators and their de facto international allies had been the principal agents of Syrian suffering. In this narration of the war, Syrians outside of the country were similarly victimized alongside people inside of the country. This entextualization of victimhood made settlement compatible with the narration of a genealogy of loyalty.

The Council of Ministers created a coordination body (*hiyah tnsiyq l'udah al mhjriyn fi al kharaj*) for the return of displaced people from abroad in 2018 to coordinate repatriation. This was part of the state's declared repatriation program after proclaiming "victory" in the war. The question of how to repatriate absent, unsettled subjects who had otherwise been categorized as disloyal and targeted for punishment was addressed through an altogether new categorization of the displaced as victims of terrorism. The "displaced by terrorism" categorization provided the state with a plausible discursive explanation for absence that remained consistent with the commonsense narration of the war as a terrorist project against the state. Framing potential returnees as victims of terrorism sutured their fates to that of the state and aligned with state discourses about the "return to normal life" for the misguided, mentally ill, and deceived, who were similarly being invited to restore their relationship with the state.

Framing the unsettled as misguided and deceived was important to distinguish them from people whose hands are "stained in blood" (*mmn lam ttltakh aydiyhm baldma*). This is a broad categorization that captures not only people who took up arms but those who aided them, such as doctors or drivers. Those whose hands are stained in blood are distinguished from the *matlobeen*, who are typically wanted (and are aware that they are wanted) for crimes of absence and desertion rather than specific acts against the state. For example, someone who has not responded to a conscription call immediately knows that they are wanted by the state authorities for desertion. Desertion does not immediately equate to defection or the assumption that someone took up arms against the state because they ignored their conscription call. This distinction is important as far as settlement goes. Desertion could be explained in different ways. For example, someone could claim that armed groups in their area prevented them from answering the conscription call. This was the kind of crime that "was not an exclusive marker of political opposition,"[6] but nevertheless posed informational problems for the regime. The ambiguities around desertion, a crime of betrayal of the highest order, could be explained away during the settlement process.

There are significant variations in how the state categorized people who were applying for settlement. Together, these categories suggested both the presence of betrayal and the possibility of repentance. The narratives that these categories weave remains consistent with the dominant narration of the war as imposed from without by Syria's enemies. The deceived subject, for example, was someone who was weak and pliable but who should nevertheless be welcomed back to the homeland. They, too, were victims of the conspiracy against Syria. There had to be palatable reasons for the *matloob* not to have followed conscription orders, and the displaced subject would need to narrate their displacement as resulting from the actions of opposition, and not state, forces. These ambiguous categories allowed state officials to present the settlement process in terms consistent with the commonsense narrative of the war.

By forcing Syrians to settle their status before they could return to their homes (or remain in them in reconciled areas) the state was also able to develop knowledge about the population that could be marshaled in the punishment of perceived opponents. This occurred through both a simple ledger of who returned and who did not (thus creating the opposite categories of the settled and unsettled subject) as well as the knowledge gleaned from settlement application interviews. These interviews provided information about the war and about citizens that allowed the state to act against people whose political status and whereabouts were unknown. Forcing citizens to denounce others also served to resocialize settled citizens vis-à-vis emergency politics and to demonstrate commitment to the state. These moments of actual contact with the state produced anxiety and worry among people who feared the consequences of denouncing friends, relatives, or acquaintances. In some cases, people would simply conjure up generic names to share with the authorities or otherwise invent stories about people they knew were deceased.[7] I am less interested here in political behavior and the forms of dissimulation the settlement engenders than in how the process forced public fealty to the regime and socialization into a post-conflict order.

The Settlement Process as Authoritarian Alchemy

The settlement process served the state's conflict management strategies through the transformation of citizen subjects from enemies into friends, by providing bifurcating categories that reinforce friend/enemy distinctions, and through the production of knowledge about the population and its activities during the conflict. Settlement served as a substitute for a national political settlement insofar as it allowed the state to decide who is loyal and disloyal and who can and cannot return. As such, the settlement process absolved the state and its officials for any wrongdoing during the conflict and placed responsibility for the war on the shoulders of deceived Syrians. The process was presented as initiating a transformation of the subject through the state's acceptance of their repentance. How did the state discursively and institutionally frame these transformations?

The Syrian state's reconciliation process was premised on the denial of regret and responsibility by the state and the expectation that individual "deceived" citizens would express political regret for the wrongs they committed during the conflict. Importantly, the expressed political outcome of citizens' regret and their patriotic "return" from a deceived path was not the creation of a new collective, an inclusive "we" that built the foundations for post-conflict community through a shared understanding of what it means to be Syrian.[8] The need for citizen regret and repentance as the basis for reconciliation absolved loyalists and the state for responsibility for the conflict, and was buttressed by official announcements, curricular changes, policy reforms, and a climate that promoted state absolution. The "social solution" to the conflict was framed as returning people to political order, not creating a new one. The "deceived" citizen was often portrayed as morally and psychologically weak because they were so easily manipulated by external enemies. The return of the deceived citizen to the homeland paralleled a discourse of psychological (re)stabilization in which the citizen would return to their senses and support the homeland. The language of psychological stability (*al stqrar al nfsee*) was regularly used to describe the affective and emotional states of Syrians who were settling their status at settlement centers. News reports and television clips regularly carried stories about people who regained their psychological stability and returned to the homeland. Reconciliation with the state "restored psychological stability," "returned them to normal lives" and "relieved them of the burden of regret."[9] The subjective transformation of the deceived subject was always about a restoration or stabilization of the self that indexed loyalty and a commitment to the state.

Settlement sought to reconstruct a moral-political order founded on subservience to the state rather than one that was negotiated out of the remnants of conflict. The settlement process in Syria similarly sought to generate a subjective transformation of the citizen from an enemy to a friend and thus served as an alternative mechanism for transitioning subjects from conflict to peace. This alchemy, however, occurred within a narrow framework that produced the criteria for inclusion and exclusion based on perceived loyalty to the state. The question of who does and does not get to apply for settlement, how the settled are to politically and affectively demonstrate their loyalty, and what happens to those who are rejected, or who do not apply at all, were generative of a political order in which the basis of inclusion remained loyalty to the state. Disloyalty, as demonstrated by one's rejection of settlement or failure to apply, opened someone to a range of punishments targeting them and their kin. Settling one's legal status with the state involved both a resolution of outstanding legal issues (such as desertion) and an affective restoration of the link between citizen and state through the former's repentance. Until this can occur, a citizen was presumed disloyal and subject to punishment.

The settlement process was also articulated as a restoration of the self and as a political mechanism to restore the wanted, misguided, deceived, and "mentally ill" and to allow them to "return to the embrace of the homeland." Restoration, rather than reconciliation, was the principal political goal of settlement. The settlement process should thus be understood as a project to reinscribe the polity into the pre-2011 political order that was disrupted by conflict through the restoration of the deceived citizen. Here, the "return" of the deceived subject to the homeland becomes an important narrative tool to deny state culpability and shift responsibility to Syrians while also providing them a veneer of loyalty and political commitment. According to state officials, security and stability could only be maintained through the expression of an affective and political repentance in the form of the deceived subject pledging loyalty to the homeland. Political order would be based not on the creation of something new, but rather on the affirmation of something old in which its cancerous elements have been cleansed.

The settlement process was also a mechanism for the state to performatively erase the affective and psychological vestiges of conflict through the transformation of citizen subjectivity. In Rwanda, mediation efforts sought to rid people of "bad ideology,"[10] which post-genocide leaders articulated as having given rise to genocide. By ridding themselves of "bad ideology" through mediation processes Rwandans were supposed to be engaging in a form of cleansing that freed them from the ideas that produced the conditions for genocide. The mediation processes established to affect this transformation were highly contested spaces in which naturalized binaries of victims (Tutsi) and perpetrators (Hutu) were challenged by participants who rejected the state's categorization and narration of the conflict in simple good/bad terms.[11] In Syria the settlement process provided an opportunity for citizens to similarly express their cleansing of "bad ideas," but without a comparable opportunity to challenge the state's commonsense narrative. There is no process of admission, a clear construction of guilt and innocence, and no formal restitution for any (bloodless) "crimes" settlement applicants have committed. Ridding oneself of "bad ideas" that led to deception and disloyalty positioned the settlement applicant as a perpetrator cum victim, and one who was worthy of state empathy.

Producing the settlement process as one in which citizens return to the embrace of the homeland after acknowledging their deception and disloyalty initiates the subjective transformation of the citizen required to act as a substitute for an actual political settlement process in which the state and its adversaries are forced into political negotiations. Settlement is a process of social repair, to be sure. But it is a process of explicitly exclusionary social repair in which some (the loyal) get to participate, and others (the disloyal) are forbidden from participating. It is also a process in which the norms and ideas shaping post-conflict order are forcibly restricted to cohere with the state's commonsense narrative. Even in Rwanda, where mediation sought to similarly restrict victim-perpetrator framings, the dialogical nature of mediation processes produced opportunities for contestation. In contrast, Syria's settlement process foreclosed possibilities for contestation and required applicants to situate their return within a loyalist genealogy.[12] Settlement, thus, did not share political, moral, or processual characteristics with other transitional justice mechanisms that seek a break from a past, one that is presumed to have created the conditions for the initial outbreak of conflict, or the construction of an altogether new post-conflict identity, to move society past presumably violent ethnic identity categories that produced war. Rather than create something new, settlement helped to reinscribe a specific moral-political order. The political aim was not the construction of something new, but rather the return of something old—fealty to the regime.

The settlement process located the solution to the conflict in the conversion of the unsettled citizen, characterized by their backwardness, deception, and disloyalty, into a full citizen. Settlement as alchemy and authoritarian social repair means that the solution to the conflict was articulated in terms distant from the demands of the protestors or any of the subsequent forms of violence and destruction enacted by the state since 2011. Victimhood's entextualizaton demanded that Syrians enact silences while they were constructing genealogies of loyalty. The settlement process thus required citizens to maintain secrecy. Secrets and stories must be suppressed to fit the commonsense narrative. People know what to say and what not to say in specific moments.[13] To paraphrase Buckley-Zistel, Syrians must "pretend" reconciliation and repair.[14]

Settlement was nestled within a discourse of a "return to normal life" that framed the state's post-2016 repatriation program. A return to normalcy emphasized the restorative aims of the settlement process. This language of a return to normalcy was repeated throughout state and civil committee officials' pronouncements about the goals of the settlement process. It was also, not unintentionally, incorporated into the language of forced gratitude that settled citizens espoused in the dozens of television and newspaper reports about the success of settlement. News reports about settlement centers and the processing of cases tended to repeat the same language and framing of the settlement discourse as well. As a discourse about settlement and return, the language of normalcy also served as a repatriation discourse intended to show Syrians and the world that Syria was "safe" for return.

A settled citizen's return to the embrace of the homeland is both a return to normalcy and part of an imagined mobilization to join the state in reconstructing the country and fighting terrorism. There is a repetitive language here of "partnering to reconstruct our country" (*nsharak bi 'mr baladna*) and seizing "a new opportunity for them to participate in that which was destroyed by terrorists" (*frsah jdiydah lhm llmsharkah a'dah bna' dmrah alarhabiyun*). Returning with "one hand" (*'iyd wahda*) to the embrace of the homeland portrays the citizen's return in relation to the conflict. They are not simply returning home; they are returning to rebuild their country and protect it from terrorism. Return, then, was not objectively framed as a process of repatriation, but rather as one of loyalist repatriation where the citizen must commit to the defense of the homeland alongside the state.

Amnesty thus provided an important mechanism for the state to encourage deserters to settle. State amnesty had been consistently framed as a gift bestowed upon citizens by an enlightened and benevolent leader. Ahmed Hamadeh's May 2022 editorial in SANA exaggerates the praise for President Assad after the issuing of Decree No. 7 in April 2022 by referring to his "tolerance" and "morals" as driving his desire to forgive state enemies. This forgiveness is a victor's forgiveness: the pardoned had "made mistakes and were exploited by aggressors who wanted to break up our country and destroy it," but could now "return to normalcy and live with values of reform and tolerance, not terrorism and hatred." Moreover, the extension of amnesty to include some "terrorist crimes" meant that "the large number of people who were deceived" to create chaos could, along with Syrians outside of the country, safely "return to their homeland and participate in its reconstruction." Hamadeh's editorial reflects a consistent public position advanced by the state and affiliated media in which amnesty is portrayed as a benevolent gift intended to secure the alchemic transformation of the deceived back into citizens.[15] State forgiveness "represents a valuable opportunity for the deceived to return to the embrace of the homeland" and "to adopt dialogue as a way to eliminate the effects of war."

The imagined dialogue between state and citizen took the form of the latter submitting their status for "settlement" by the state as determined by the civil committees and the security apparatus. Decree No. 7 (2022) was an especially unique amnesty decree because it was the first to pardon crimes and not specific individuals. However, for someone to receive amnesty they would have to formally settle their status. Amnesty was an invitation for citizens to "return to practicing their normal lives" after settling their status with the state.[16] State media regularly celebrated the amnesties and settlements that have occurred since 2015. Images of citizens sitting across from soldiers engaged in conversation or document exchanges repeatedly appeared in newscasts and as interludes between programming on Syrian television. They showed state officials or civil committee members discussing the settlement process, settlement centers, and often several snippets of "settled" citizens showing gratitude and praise for their settlement with the state. One such "settled" citizen, referred to as Yazan Ayoub, told reporters that he "submitted my settlement documents and received a settlement card, and this is thanks to the sacred opportunity the state gave us, based on the amnesty decree, to correct the path of our lives." Other "settled" citizens told state media that settlement was "the beginning of a stable life." State and citizen narratives of settlement mirrored each other perfectly across hundreds of Syrian settlement centers and were repeated in the dozens of news and television reports of citizen settlement. The repetition of the return to a "stable" or "normal life" also served to naturalize reconciliation as a rehabilitative process.

The public performance of state forgiveness and citizen repentance after each decree reinforced amnesty as a gift bestowed upon people rather than the outcome of a deliberative process between state and citizen. Deliberation was eschewed in favor of a reconciliation that emphasized correction, repentance, and a return to the homeland. Cultural producers played an important role in propagating such a vision, especially after Decree No. 7 (2022). The head of the Aleppo Artists Syndicates, Abdel Halim Hariri, publicly stated in May 2022 that the "amnesty decree is a step toward forgiveness and restoring national cohesion" and provides "young people . . . a new opportunity to return to a normal life after they learned their lesson and understood that they were tools in the hands of those who wanted to destroy the country."[17] An important element here of reconciliation and amnesty is the deceived subject—sometimes young, always criminal, temporarily treasonous—whose illegal actions against the homeland were engineered without their knowledge. The deceived citizen became an important metaphor for the state to explain conflict and to enact the alchemy of large swaths of society it once deemed criminal and treasonous.

By framing citizens' actions through the deceived subject, the state could articulate unilateral forgiveness, and not dialogue, as the basis of reconciliation. Forgiveness was a form of restoration that absolved the state for any wrongdoing during the conduct of the war. The problem, so to speak, was the deceived citizen who betrayed their homeland. By forgiving this subject through the settlement process the state was restoring their connection to the homeland and offering them absolution for their crimes. As a process rhetorically aimed at restoring the citizen-state relationship, settlement also served to produce the conditions for future security and stability through the preservation of the regime. Restoration should be understood here as both a "return" of the citizen and a reinscription of a political order governed by the regime. The bifurcation of society into the settled and unsettled creates a legible population from which to govern through enmity and punishment. The unsettled are a source of insecurity and instability, as are those whose absence threatens the state in other ways (such as deserters, who deprive the army of soldiers). To control and manage the population in this way is to render the citizenry legible only in relation to the conflict and to create categories of life and belonging that correspond to the regime's commonsense narrative of the conflict. The process of "composing" an enemy does not refer strictly to the composition of an identifiably ethnic or sectarian subject (such as Muslims in Hindu-majority India, or Hutus and Tutsis in pre-genocide Rwanda), but rather to the production of an enemy subject who is composed differentially in relation to state narratives around affect, psychology, and violence. Composing a "minority" in this sense has little to do with the threat one supposedly presents to an imagined nation, ethnicity, or religion, but rather through their threat to the state. To restore security and stability, this unsettled subject must be carved out of the body politic, deprived of rights, and refused entry (settlement) into the country.

Settlement frames social repair as occurring through a citizen's repentance and legitimization of the state rather than a process of dialogue that emerges among different segments of society. The state's desire to absorb citizens seeks to "normalize" their lives and have them contribute to the reconstruction of the country. Settlement as restoration of the social fabric foreclosed any possibilities for citizens to contest the moral-political order at the moment of return and/or settlement during the application submission or interview process. Unlike in Rwanda's various remediation spaces, in Syria settlement foreclosed contestation over the meanings of the terms "victimhood," "absence," and "perpetrators" in favor of a politics of repentance and compliance in which fealty is performed. Instead, contestation and dispute were routed through the civil committees as intermediaries of state power in front of whom Syrians contest issues of restitution. By shifting contestation of the commonsense narrative and its material effects (property appropriation, subsidy withdrawal, and so on) to the civil committees, the state positioned these bodies as intermediaries. The effect was to suppress any deliberation or dialogue with the state over socialization, integration, or wartime divisions that emerged between those who stayed and those who left.[18] Citizens' performative (and, it must be added, instantaneous) resocialization at the moment of the settlement interview is reminiscent of the several ways that Syrians navigate fear and the threat of regime violence and act "as if" they accept the state's legitimacy.[19]

The settlement process sought the restoration of political order through the legal (and violent) parsing of society into the settled and unsettled, which served as legal categories delimiting loyal and disloyal subjects. Settlement was not only constitutive of this bifurcating process; it was also part of the larger edifice of enmity and punishment that "frames, absorbs, and repackages political violence" through legal, bureaucratic processes.[20] What was presented as a process to facilitate the return of Syrians to their homeland should be understood as the legal, bureaucratic, and political production of disloyal subjects and subjectivities that can be punished through the state's legal infrastructure. Settlement became an integral component in the durability of the conflict and the absorption of enmity into the state apparatus.

Settling the Unsettled: From Enemy to "Loyal Returnee"

How did the settlement process transform Syrians from potential enemies to "loyal returnees"? Settlement was a repatriation program intended to facilitate the return of Syrians from internal or external displacement. This process sought to construct a "loyal returnee" out of a subject previously categorized as an enemy.[21] Settlement occurred through a bureaucratic process whereby a Syrian applied for settlement at one of the dozens of settlements centers (*markaz al tasaweeah*) throughout the country that operated mostly on a daily basis. The applicant typically submitted an application in person on behalf of himself and his family, while in some cases a recognized power of attorney could submit the application for someone outside of the country. Settlement centers were also located at the Syrian borders with Lebanon and Jordan, allowing returnees to submit them directly upon arrival. Otherwise, Syrians were expected to submit their settlement applications in settlement centers located in their home governorate (some exceptions were made for those residing outside of their governorate). Applications were almost always submitted by men acting as representatives of their families.

Physical return to Syria and political restoration was not simply the result of a bureaucratic process where one registers a desire to return and was then permitted to do so. Settlement required a narration of return that was consistent with the commonsense narration of the war. If those who were absent were demonstrably disloyal through their departure from Syria, how could they be restored to the national fold? How could Syrians be rendered worthy of return? Syrians wishing to return had to reverse the state's suspicion and demonstrate that they were politically loyal to the state. The settlement process can be understood as a loyalty test that the state administered to would-be returnees to determine whether they posed a threat. The application and process thus served to create new categories of bifurcation between settled and unsettled subjects. To return, Syrians had to demonstrate that they are what I have called elsewhere "loyal returnees."[22] This began with the settlement application and was followed by an interview with a security official and then a decision rendered by a settlement committee (*lijanah al tasaweeah*).

The settlement process required a returnee to complete a four-page application and submit to an interview at one of the many settlement centers throughout the country. Once the application and interview were completed the returnee was subject to "security approval" before they were formally given settlement papers and allowed to return. Here, the application was circulated among the security apparatuses to ensure that an applicant was not *matloob* and that their return would not pose a threat to state security. The application itself began with a formal pledge that the applicant has not engaged (and has no plans to engage) in any acts of violent or nonviolent harm, including attacks against army and security personnel, participating in protests, or any form of public disruption. The first section of the application required the applicant to provide personal information, such as place of birth, relatives, education, and so on. This information could be checked against the civil registry and potentially other sources of government information about applicants (such as state employment).

The subsequent section of the settlement application inquired into an applicant's political activity since 2011 and aimed at identifying any potentially subversive behavior on the part of the prospective returnee. In this and subsequent sections, an applicant was required to narrate their lives as victims of terrorism and to construct a genealogy of loyalty that aligned them with the state and the commonsense narration of war.[23] The perpetrator-victim relationship narrated through the application process was clear: A returnee had to present themselves as a victim of terrorist violence, explaining away their absence as the result of having been either "displaced by terrorism" or in a state of "psychological weakness." In the latter case, subjects had some room to demonstrate a disloyal past if there was no evidence or indication of violence against the military or citizens. The categories of the deceived and mentally ill were important here in facilitating alchemy as such subjects were presumed to have committed affective disloyalty without a serious materialization (i.e., violence).

The deceived or weak citizen was offered forgiveness by the state and the opportunity to return to their "normal lives." Regular SANA reports regurgitated official accounts of the state's compassion in allowing people to return after their deception. These reports regularly described the "great opportunity" the state afforded citizens to "return to their cities and villages and contribute to the homeland's reconstruction."[24] Acknowledging one's deception or weakness permitted them to apply for settlement and receive state forgiveness because their deception was consistent with the commonsense narrative of the conflict—namely, that Syria was infiltrated by external enemies who poisoned the population. State demands that settlement applicants construct a genealogy of loyalty were inclusive of those who were willing to admit to affective betrayals of the homeland. As deceived citizens, they were also victims of the conflict.

The expectation that applicants would construct a genealogy of loyalty required them to narrate their experience of conflict from the perspective of one of its victims and to explicitly identify how Syria's enemies perpetrated crimes against the homeland. There was no space in the application to contest state notions of victimhood. For example, questions such as "Have you carried arms against the Syrian Arab army? or "Are your hands stained in the blood of Syrians?" could never be answered in the affirmative if an applicant wished to return. These questions pointed the applicant toward a narration of the conflict as one of its victims and enforced the state's abdication of responsibility while forcing applicants to narrate their situation through a specific victim-perpetrator framing. The second section of the application then transitioned from asking about an applicant's actions during the conflict to their knowledge about others.

Questions about what applicants knew about other Syrians' subversive behavior generated new knowledge for the state to act upon unsettled, absent, or otherwise "criminal" Syrians. Any names that produced through this process almost certainly found their way to a blacklist of *matloobeen*. These blacklists functioned as informal warrants for arrest and have had a profound effect on the lives of people both inside and outside of Syria, effecting the latter's ability to return. Applicants' responses vary widely from those who fabricate information to those who explicitly denounce people they know. This section of the application was thus extremely important for the state's knowledge about society and aided future efforts to determine who was loyal, who was a threat, and what kinds of subversive activities people were engaged in during the conflict. Providing this information about people allowed Syrians to demonstrate loyalty and align themselves politically with the state.

The settlement application was also structured to produce information about the conflict and the Syrian citizenry that could be acted upon by the security apparatus. The third section of the application asked about an applicant's knowledge of the war, the battlefield, and the armed groups fighting the state. These were very granular questions that had nothing at all to do with the settlement of one's legal status. Questions about what applicants knew about armed groups, their members and leaders, the locations of their activities, bases, and ammunition depots, and even their knowledge of chemical weapons were not intended to determine an applicant's connection to armed groups, but rather to produce information about them that could be mobilized to produce more *matloobeen*. The settlement process filled major information gaps for the state in its population by producing information about the whereabouts, activities, and political affinities of Syrians. This information was filtered through local committees and the security apparatus. Syrians' awareness of how the state extracted information about citizens through this process was a major obstacle to return as information provided about someone was often the basis for their inclusion on a list of *matloobeen*.[25]

The fourth section of the application extended the information-gathering function of the process by inviting applicants to denounce relatives, friends, acquaintances, coworkers, neighbors, and even people outside of Syria by providing information related to any violent or non-violent acts directed against the interests of the homeland. All names registered here were added to the long list of *matloobeen*. This section broadly aimed at producing knowledge of any nonviolent acts directed against the state, including financing armed groups, posting on social media, and the like. Through this sharing of information, applicants were able to dissociate themselves from the identified people and their activities even though they were expressing knowledge about them. Much like the third section of the application, this section filled in information gaps for the state. Narrating a genealogy of loyalty through the settlement application required applicants to demonstrate specific forms of association and dissociation. They had to denounce others and share information about subversive activities while also avoiding association with these individuals or activities. Distinguishing between friends and enemies required applicants to position themselves as victims of the conflict as well, and this portrayal of victimization was aided by a commonsense narration that emphasized that supposedly weak citizens had been deceived into betraying their homeland.

Collective victimhood is a political construction that is sometimes, but not always, tethered to objective physical and emotional wounds experienced by a group. There is no doubt that in Syria everyone has suffered regardless of their locale, sect, ethnicity, or political affinities. The settlement process effectively limited collective victimhood to a loyalist framing tethered to the commonsense narration of the war. The transformation from unsettled to settled subject revolved around this notion of a collective loyalist victimhood. Anyone who stayed in the country and who was never categorized as settled or unsettled was part of the large swath of Syrian society constructed as a loyalist victim. In this case, one's sustained presence in Syria equated to loyalty with the state. These are the broader conditions in which applicants claimed victimhood and the state constructed an archetypal victim. The unsettled or absent subject had, conversely, identified with Syria's enemies and are thus perpetrators. Here, leaving Syria, failing to fulfill conscription duties, posting anti-state messages on social media, and so on, are all expressions of disloyalty that manifest in a subject's categorization as unsettled or *matloob*. The person being settled is twice victimized: first, through the deception of hostile, outside forces that turned them against the homeland, and second, as a member of the homeland that was ripped asunder by outside forces. Settlement was a way for people to transform their status from perpetrator to victim.

The settlement process, however, provided an opportunity for people to align themselves with a loyalist victimhood through the construction of a loyalist genealogy consistent with the commonsense narration of the war. Collective victimhood was narrowly constructed in relation to the regime's narration of conflict, which allowed some subjects to acknowledge that they may have contributed to harming the homeland, and thus to collective victimhood, but that they, too, were victims of the same emotional and political forces that seek to harm Syria. As deceived subjects, they were also victims. Settlement provided them an opportunity to acknowledge this deception and their "wrong acts" as constituting harm to the homeland. The process has therefore emerged as a technology not only for repatriating Syrians, but also for loyalist victimhood to gain materiality and act as a space for people to formally express their loyalty to the state. Victimhood was not debated or contested throughout the settlement process; rather, it is reinforced through the application process and the oft-repeated celebrations of successful settlement applicants.

The settlement process thus entextualized victimhood as both a process and a transformation of citizen subjectivity. As a process, settlement provided a mechanism for the state to bureaucratize victimhood and subject citizens to what is effectively a loyalty test. Syrians could only successfully pass the test once they had sufficiently repented for their own deception and constructed a genealogy of loyalty that demonstrated alignment with state-constructed notions of collective victimhood. They profess themselves to also be victims as a condition for their return. In this way, settlement also entextualized victimhood through the transformation of one's subjectivity from an enemy into a friend. Whether categorized as *matloob* or deceived, a Syrian could reverse state suspicion through the settlement process. Settlement allowed Syrians an opportunity to be recognized as victims only if they are narrowly recounted their lives within the commonsense narrative. To not settle, then, was treated as a de facto expression of disloyalty that aligned an unsettled subject with perpetrators.

Adjudicating Settlement: Categorizing Loyalty and Creating Citizens

The adjudication of settlement applications took the form of an opaque process that reinforced the arbitrary exercise of state power. There are no public records of the deliberations and no clear criteria for how someone secured settlement. A necessary process of "security approval" for each decision rendered by the settlement committees further clouded the decision-making process. Nevertheless, there was a very public portrayal of the process in media reports that celebrated the widespread settlement of Syrians. Each governorate had its own settlement centers composed of local notables who formally processed the applications in tandem with the security apparatus. These centers processed applications for people in person and through delegated legal representatives (although receiving power-of-attorney permission was difficult). They would also process applications for people who intended to return or lived elsewhere. Finally, settlement centers also existed at Lebanese and Jordanian border crossings to immediately process returnee applications. There were no clear guidelines for how long adjudication should take. In the case of in-person applicants the whole process could last several hours, whereas someone applying through a legal representative could take days or weeks. There were no public records of the number of applications that were either approved or denied.

The adjudication of a settlement application culminated with a decision not just about whether someone could return to the country, but also about what kind of person gets to return. Settlement sought to bifurcate the loyal and disloyal by forcing returnees to present themselves as "loyalist returnees,"[26] those who have returned to the embrace of the homeland and will commit to protecting it. Here, again, loyalty was equated with a political commitment to the state. Settlement was presented as holding the promise of restoring life and normalcy to the deceived subject. Publicly, settlement was also framed as a restoration of citizenship through the rehabilitation of the deceived subject. (Re)socialization into Syria's political order required citizens to demonstrate loyalty to the state through an acknowledgment of their betrayal. While restoration was presented as the normative and political goal of the settlement process the collective effect was to create new stratifications within the citizenship regime.

Settling one's status became an important mechanism to separate the loyal from the disloyal and to produce new forms of citizenship in relation to the conflict. There were three gradations of Syrian citizenship generated by the settlement process. The first was the unsettled present citizen, a person who never left their village or city and resided in areas that remained under state control. These citizens were presumed to be loyalist by virtue of their having remained in Syria throughout the conflict. The second was the settled citizen, who I have described throughout this chapter as someone constructed as deceived or treasonous who was offered repentance by the state once they could demonstrate a genealogy of loyalty. These settled citizens, however, often forfeited the right to have their property or assets restored upon their return. Finally, the unsettled absent citizen was a subject who lived outside of state control and refused to return to their homeland. This refusal cast these Syrians outside of citizenship and political community.

Citizenship is marked in relation to the conflict by separating citizens into loyal and disloyal. Stratified citizenship was an outcome of the subjugating and subject-making practices of the settlement process that categorized loyal and disloyal citizens. Settlement created social and political differentiations that corresponded to legal regimes that prohibited the full exercise of one's rights as a Syrian, including controlling property. What emerged were competing regimes of citizenship that were directly tethered to the state's conceptualization of the conflict. A stratified citizenship regime was created that privileged the rights of the unsettled present citizen. The politics of enmity and punishment had been translated into legal practices that created several citizenship regimes whose stratification and interaction directly corresponded to a political vision of Syria's future that foreclosed the existence of disloyal subjects.[27]

The settlement process and its attendant citizenship regimes were tools of inclusion and exclusion. In this way, Syria's citizenship regimes share certain commonalities with those that emerged in post-Yugoslav spaces where the potential return of refugees and internally displaced persons generated a discourse promoting unequal citizenship and seeking to prevent the return of "undesireables."[28] Differentiation is one of the constitutive elements of the Syrian citizenship regime. Another element is the de facto denationalization of the unsettled absent citizen.[29] To be denied settlement, or even to fear applying for settlement, was akin to forfeiting all rights as a citizen and being cast out of political community. This was not an unintended effect but a deliberate feature of the settlement process that sought to categorize, distinguish, and stratify citizens through a political process aimed at differentiating between loyal and disloyal subjects. It is here again that the absence of an internationally supervised process of return allowed the state to construct repatriation practices outside of liberal norms.

Successful settlement did not guarantee that settled citizens would receive restitution. A legal regime to manage property inside and outside of areas of government control was created that was de-linked from repatriation. Settled citizens were required to make legal claims for restitution that often involved long, costly bureaucratic processes to establish ownership. Since many settled citizens were unable to receive state-sanctioned documentation for life events the transfer of property within families was also extremely difficult. Moreover, many damaged or destroyed properties were placed under the guardianship of civil committees tasked with deciding whether homes were safe enough for their inhabitants to return. This also required settled citizens to make legal claims on property and forced committees to make decisions about the livability of homes and buildings. In some specific cases, settled citizens had to apply for security approval to enter their villages. This application was separate from the settlement process and required families to demonstrate evidence of ownership. As documentation laws changed during the conflict, which made demonstrating ownership more difficult, families were often forced to remain outside of their villages and homes because they were unable to provide proof of ownership. Finally, squatters often moved into abandoned homes and apartments. Many of these squatters were categorized as loyal by virtue of having stayed in the country, and they often enjoy some protection from the security apparatus.[30]

Settlement and Repatriation as Conflict Management

State categorization of citizens as deceived, mentally ill, or psychologically unstable both cast them as enemies and allowed for them to be transformed back into friends. This transformation occurred through the settlement process, a project of social and political differentiation that grew out of the reconciliation agreements. Settlement extended differentiation to civilians who were either outside of the country or in areas outside of government control. Indeed, this category of "outside of state control" was an important designation applied to both people and property in areas where the vestiges of opposition control had to be eliminated. People were asked to settle their status by constructing a genealogy of loyalty in which they were able to present themselves in politically palatable ways that facilitated their transformation. This meant presenting oneself as deceived or as a victim of terrorism. Each category allowed applicants to situate themselves within state-constructed notions of victimhood.

The question of whether and why someone would choose to apply for settlement is an important one that provides insight into how Syrians lived in fear of state violence. Many people since 2011 have engaged in what can broadly be called anti-regime activity (e.g., by posting on social media). Still others feared that their absence from Syria would be considered too suspicious.[31] Some feared that they would be denounced upon returning to the country, or that they had already been the subject of such a denunciation.[32] There are simply no good answers to the question of whether and why someone would try to return. What we do know is that these decisions to return were certainly informed by calculations about how the state's arbitrary exercise of power could affect them. Some people choose not to take any risks.

Settlement created subject categories tied to the commonsense narration of the conflict that were indexed as either loyal or disloyal. To be settled was to formally demonstrate loyalty, while to remain unsettled was to take on a disloyal subjectivity. Those who remained in state-held territory throughout the conflict were already indexed as loyal and did not have to demonstrate their loyalty or pursue property restitution. These categories foundationalized a citizenship regime in which the bifurcating line through Syrian society was the settled and unsettled. Much like the reconciliation agreements, settlement allowed for the rehabilitation of the deceived subject and their re-embrace of the homeland. Settlement was thus oriented toward the restoration of state rule rather than the creation of an inclusive political order out of the ashes of conflict. Settled citizens were expected to legitimize this order by returning to work, responding to conscription calls, and performing other acts that demonstrated their loyalty to the state.

The number of unsettled Syrians remained extraordinarily high until December 2024, when the regime collapsed. More than half of the Syrian population has been displaced since 2011, and many of those people remained in parts of the country (the Northeast or Northwest), neighboring countries (such as Lebanon, Turkey, and Jordan), or immigrated elsewhere. How did the state construct and categorize these people in relation to settlement? These absent unsettled subjects had been explicitly targeted by the state for punishment, even if the settlement process presented an opportunity for their alchemic transformation. The political project to categorize absent subjects gave specific meaning to the various forms of absence experienced throughout the conflict that allowed the state to distribute rewards and punishments. Importantly, absence became the pretext for the reorganization of housing, land, and property rights and large-scale property appropriation in the name of punishing the absent.

5
Absence as Disloyalty

A Syria with 10 million trustworthy people obedient to the leadership is better than a Syria with 30 million vandals ... after 8 years, Syria will not accept the presence of cancerous cells and they will be removed completely.
—BRIGADIER GENERAL JAMIL AL-HASSAN

We encourage every Syrian to come back to Syria.
—BASHAR AL-ASSAD

Introduction

How could the Syrian state categorize citizens who were no longer in the country or in areas under its control? The response to this problem was to treat absence as an act of disloyalty that warranted state punishment. Much like the settlement process's structured alchemy, according to which displaced Syrians were transformed from enemies into friends, categorizations and laws around absence contained the possibility for subjects to reverse state suspicion. In previous chapters I considered how reconciled and unreconciled as well as settled and unsettled subjects materialized a commonsense narration of the conflict and indexed loyalty and disloyalty. In this chapter, I asked how categories of absence provided new subjects around which punishment could be distributed. Throughout the conflict, absence was largely framed as an act of disloyalty that could only be explained if someone was fleeing armed groups. As the conflict progressed the possible explanations for someone's absence expanded. An army deserter may have failed to answer their conscription call because they were imprisoned by an armed group. Whether plausible or not the commonsense narration of conflict became inclusive of these explanations for absence.

Three principal categories emerged from the state's politics of absence. The first is the *matloob*, or wanted, subject. These subjects were blacklisted for a range of possible crimes. They were absent in the sense that the state had not settled their status and their whereabouts were unknown. Anyone who was *matloob* could not claim property rights as these were subject to the approval of the security apparatus. The second category is that of the *ghayab*, or absent subject. These subjects generally included people who were outside of the country or whose whereabouts were unknown. The absent subject could thus refer to anyone who was missing, imprisoned, or displaced. The final category was the "absent from state territory" subject, typically used to refer to people who were living in Syria but in areas outside of state control. This subjectivity corresponded to legal designations of land and property transfers outside of state territory that were targeted for nullification.

The enactment of punishment against the wanted, absent, and absent from state territory subjects took many forms in Syria but were mostly directed toward the restriction of housing, land, and property rights and the appropriation of property. In this chapter, I explore how a politics of absence took shape around the state's narration of absence as an act of disloyalty. I begin by exploring the complexity of absence in Syria through a discussion of displacement, death, and the missing. From here, I ask how absence was differentially categorized and how these categorizations created new subjects indexed as disloyal or loyal. I conclude the chapter by asking how the state distributed punishment to wanted and absent subjects (and their kin) through various measures.

Displacement, Death, and the Missing

In the summer of 2022 I interviewed someone outside of Syria about the possibility of returning.[1] When I asked them bluntly, "Can you return to Syria?," they paused and made a *tsk* sound while raising their chin; "absolutely not," they seemed to be saying. I asked again and received the same response. "What happened to the land, homes, and other physical property you owned?" I asked. "Was property destroyed?" They went on to explain that everything remained standing with minimal damage. The homes were habitable, and the properties could function as businesses. The problem, this person explained, was that it would be impossible to return after being outside of the country for so long and feel safe in resuming any sort of life there. It would be dangerous, if not impossible, to explain their absence in ways that would allow them to simply return and resume ownership of their properties. To their knowledge they had not been blacklisted, nor had their properties been formally confiscated. The problem of returning and reclaiming their land was thus not tied to damaged property, having *matloob* status, or loss of formal ownership; it stemmed, rather, from fear and insecurity. There was simply too much at risk for them to return. How this person perceived those risks is an interesting question in and of itself, one that has been explored in the scholarship around refugee repatriation.[2] What is important for my purposes here is how this person understood their absence from Syria as shaping their opportunities for return and restitution.

Absence took many forms in Syria. The state defined an absent person in strict geographic terms as someone who not living in areas under state control. Refugees, the internally displaced, those living in the Northwest and Northeast all formally counted as "absent" subjects. The deceased, kidnapped, imprisoned, and those whose whereabouts were either unknown or concealed were similarly classified as absent until a determination by a civil committee declared otherwise. Both inside and outside of Syria problems with registering life events (e.g., births, deaths, marriages) with the state created altogether new categories of unregistered people who were not identified in family registries. Deserters and people who left their public sector jobs were also considered absent. Some people were simply considered "missing." This chapter is interested in how the regime constructed a politics of absence through specific categorizations that absolve some citizens of absence while punishing others.

The interrelated and cascading effects of violence have displaced millions of Syrians and left hundreds of thousands missing. Identifying these missing and deceased and determining the circumstances surrounding their absence informed the regime's political projects around absence. Categorizations in one place have no bearing on categorizations in another. For example, someone granted refugee status in Germany will be categorized as simply "absent" in Syria. The question that I am most interested in here is how the state developed knowledge and political strategies concerning the millions of "absent" Syrians. Denunciations and intelligence agencies' blacklists provided specific information about individuals' political loyalties and anti-regime activities that created the subject category of the *matloob*. Most absent Syrians' political affinities, however, were unknown to the state. In much the same way that the crime of terrorism codified acts, non-acts, attitudes, and beliefs, the state's response to the deficit of official knowledge about absent populations was to wholly designate them as disloyal. Anyone categorized as *matloob* was presumed to be disloyal regardless of where they were. Presence in state territory became a proxy for loyalty, absence a proxy for disloyalty. The kin of either the absent or the *matloobeen* were not spared from being labeled disloyal. In the subsequent section, I turn to how absence was differentially categorized and how disloyalty was tethered to different forms of absence. Later sections deal with how the state created mechanisms for absent citizens to reverse their status.

Categorizing Absence

How did the state differentiate between forms of absence? What indexed some forms of absence as loyal and others disloyal? State categorizations of absence followed from the commonsense narration of the conflict. Some forms of absence were considered evidence of betrayal; others, however, were not because it was understood that some Syrians left out of fear of armed groups. Likewise, some forms of desertion amounted to betrayal, while others did not because Syrians could not escape areas under armed group control. The distinctions between "good" and "bad" absence corresponded to a politics of categorization that indexed loyal and disloyal subjects. The process of categorization was made possible through the coalitions of local committees and the security apparatus that generated information about the population through the settlement process and other forms of knowledge extracted from loyalist citizens.

Absence as disloyalty materialized through a series of categorizations that tied someone's physical status outside of Syria to subjectivities that could be punished. The relationship between absence and disloyalty reflected the regime's repatriation discourse, which emphasized the goal of repatriating loyal citizens while disregarding those who were considered enemies, traitors, or part of some potential fifth column. Much like the distinction between settled and unsettled citizens, how someone narrated their absence from Syria in terms consistent with the state's narration of conflict would determine their categorization and possibilities for return. The principal question then is how the state determined why a given person was absent and what knowledge about the population informed that determination and what the consequences were for someone's categorization. For example, someone could reasonably explain their displacement to Lebanon by referring to "terrorist" actions in their village. In this case, absence was understood and rationalized through the commonsense narration of the conflict. One could not, however, explain one's absence by pointing to a refusal to serve in the military or an escape from an area under state control. The politics of absence rendered certain forms of absence punishable and others forgivable.

The state's rendering of absence as a proxy for disloyalty created new spectral categories that required punishment. Chapter 2 argued that the spectral figure of the terrorist undergirded antiterrorism policies that framed specific acts—from violence to social media posts—as terroristic harms against the state. The antiterror infrastructure that emerged rendered any acts that challenged the status quo to be subversive and the perpetrators of such acts—no matter their profession, ethnicity, sect, or class status—as subversives whose killing or imprisonment was rationalized to protect the status quo.[3] The use of state terror against opponents was extended to people whose crimes could have included thoughts, associations, or emotional attachments (to a loved one) that could harm the homeland. In such an expansive rendering of state enemies, nobody is/was safe. An enemy designation was only made possible through someone's physical presence in

Syria. An interaction with the state at a checkpoint, workplace, or anywhere else could immediately trigger a person's arrest.

An altogether different form of enemy categorization was produced by Syrians' absence. I am interested here in how the state categorized different forms of absence and rendered these categorizations actionable through its violent and bureaucratic apparatus of appropriation. Officially, the state constructed absence as referring to anyone "outside of state territory," which broadly referred to the externally displaced and anyone living in areas under opposition control. However, I take absence here to extend to a range of other categorizations that include people whose whereabouts may be unknown (the kidnapped, deserters, those who left work, and the internally displaced) and those who died during the war (such as "martyrs"). The categorization of absence corresponded to reward and punishment regimes extended to subjects while also providing the basis for the creation of a political process to transform the absent (such as a deserter) from an enemy back into a friend through the settlement process. The production of knowledge about "absent" subjects relied on a network of denouncers, informants, imprisoned people, civil committees, and the security apparatus that produced bureaucratic knowledge about absent people who could then be acted upon. In many cases, state institutions would act upon absent subjects without any evidence or formal conviction.[4] The ultimate arbiter of who was absent and how to categorize that absence was the security apparatus, which had to render approval for the state to officially categorize absence. Once a decision was approved, the machinations of the state punishment apparatus—courts, ministries, civil committees—could set in motion appropriation against absentees and their families.

Categorizing absence was not an objective process of simply counting who was and was not in state territory; it was, rather, a political process whereby absence and disappearance was given political meaning in relation to the conflict. I wish to understand forced and involuntary disappearances through "the political projects that produce disappearances in the first place."[5] While the questions of who the disappeared are, how they can be identified, and what caused their disappearance are important, I am interested here in "the kinds of politics that their disappearances produce and are produced by."[6] The politics of disappearance in Syria is inscribed with the regime's commonsense narrative of the war. The disappeared and the deceased are subject to categorizations that correspond to different forms of rewards (e.g., if one's death is classified as a martyrdom) and punishments (e.g., deserter). Inquiring into how the Syrian state manages death, disappearance, and absence is a productive entry point for thinking about how population management occurred during the conflict.

The categorization of death, disappearance, and absence are important indicators of how the conflict was narrated and how the state managed populations "here" (i.e., inside Syria) and "there" (i.e., outside of Syria or in nongovernment areas). The narration of absence in relation to the conflict helps us understand its bureaucratization and effects on everyday life. The act of creating victims and perpetrators through narratives of absence was materialized in the knowledge practices of civil committees and the appropriation politics of the state.[7] I seek to trace the subjective political construction of absence through specific categorizations of acts that acquire materiality through conflict management strategies. The requirement that all decisions related to categorizing missing or deceased people obtain security approval ensured that any state categorizations of absence contained in them a moral condemnation;[8] one cannot be a "real" victim if they have affectively or physically abandoned the homeland or materially aided terrorists.

The state's blanket categorization of absence as disloyalty belies the complexity of people's displacement and their relationship to family, home, and place in Syria. The effect of criminalizing absence was to render millions of people fearful of returning or making claims on property from outside of the country. Absent subjects were forced to follow a moving target of rules and laws to claim their property or transfer it. Power-of-attorney provisions were complicated as anyone who was *matloob* or otherwise under suspicion was unable to legally delegate a power of attorney. Returnees similarly had difficulty making claims on property in areas that suffered heavy destruction. The effect of such bureaucratic regulations was to disincentivize the making of property claims, thus letting legally imposed restrictions lapse and formalizing the state's appropriation of property.

The genealogy of the state's marshaling of absenteeism as both a legal category for punishment and a political identity can be traced to the state's manner of dealing with detained Muslim Brotherhood members in the late 1970s and early 1980s. At that time, the state passed laws forbidding the transfer of property from "absentee" subjects to their families that targeted Muslim Brotherhood members and their families. All absentees' assets were frozen and any familial claim to property would require security approval. Identical practices of categorizing and punishing absenteeism were revived in 2016 with the passage of Decree No. 11 (discussed below), nullifying property transactions in areas outside of government control and creating new legal categories of absence. Much like other articulations of absence and absenteeism during the conflict, property owners who sold their assets and left the country were automatically deemed disloyal for abandoning their homeland. Their inscription as disloyal subjects who harmed the homeland through their absence created altogether new categories of exclusion that tethered loyalty to presence and disloyalty to absence.

Compounding the association of absence with disloyalty was individual and familial issues related to formal documentation of life events and property ownership. In the case of property ownership, Syria's complicated legal structure for land ownership included formally registered and informally transferred lands. The customary system of land transfer accounts for about half of all land in Syria, effectively placing it out of formal registration and documentation. Each governorate in Syria maintains separate land and civil registries, further complicating documentation requirements. The customary system of transferring land ownership through families without documentation posed serious problems for absentees who wished to return and reclaim their property rights as the state's laws around property documentation, transfer, and restitution privileged formal documentation as the evidentiary basis of ownership.[9] These legal changes to how Syrians could demonstrate ownership became part of the bureaucratic apparatus of appropriation, creating loopholes, ambiguities, and documentation gaps that facilitated state confiscation of land.

Many displaced people lost or had their property documentation destroyed altogether. The effects of missing documentation on the ability of Syrians to gain residency outside of Syria, return to the country, or restore their property rights was profound. A study of Syrian refugees by the Norwegian Refugee Council found that 70 percent of Syrians over the age of fourteen did not have a national ID card proving their Syrian nationality, while around 24 percent of refugees were not even included in the family booklet registered with the Civil Registries Division of the Syrian

Ministry of Interior.[10] There are cumulative effects to so many Syrians not being registered within the civil registries. First, because life events are registered in the family booklet and not as individual events tied to the person, the registration of subsequent life events was not possible. For example, if someone divorced their spouse and could register this life event in the family booklet, they were unable to register a subsequent marriage. Similarly, births and deaths were formally registered not through the issuance of certificates but via registration in the family booklet. Civil Status Law No. 13 (2021) forbid recognition of any documents not registered in the Syrian state's official records. Second, missing or unrecognized documentation negatively affected property transfers and inheritance as family members or their life situations (e.g., marriage) may be unrecognized by the Syrian state. For example, "If refugees do not have copies of those documents when fleeing their homes, their ability to reclaim their property depends on the survival of these documents in the registries,"[11] but accessing these requires costly bribes in many cases. Third, the effects of registration and documentation gaps disproportionately affected Syrian women, who have difficulty making claims on property if their husband is deceased, missing, or outside of the country.[12] These problems were exacerbated by the cascading effects of the conflict on women-led households. The gaps caused by the reorganization of documentation and registration inside of Syria created a form of generational punishment that prevented spouses and their children from claiming ownership of assets.

The state's reorganization of documentation requirements in parallel with a punishment regime that eased the state's ability to appropriate assets caused hundreds of thousands of Syrians to lose property rights. Stubblefield and Joireman succinctly capture how the state has taken advantage of absenteeism to undermine property rights:

> The Syrian regime has carefully and bureaucratically enacted a series of legislative decrees over the course of the conflict, each of which undermines the property rights of certain Syrian citizens. Since this has occurred in a context in which people are already displaced, it follows, rather than forces, the displacement of people, yet prevents the restitution of the property of those who have been displaced, also potentially preventing their return. Unlike specific acts of violence that are tied to a moment in time, laws endure long after a conflict is over.[13]

The inability to register life events produced the conditions for similar generational effects. All life events documented by authorities other than the Syrian state, such as ISIS, the Syrian Salvation Government, Rojava / Autonomous Administration of North and East Syria, or neighboring countries where Syrians reside, are not recognized by Syrian authorities. This is an especially acute problem for Syrians in areas such as Idlib or the Northeast as their residency made it difficult to travel back and forth to government areas to have life events documented. Consequently, many Syrians were forced to purchase forged documents or pay brokers (*samasir*) to obtain life-event documentation. The passing of Civil Status Law No. 13 formalized the nonrecognition of documents not registered in official Syrian state records.[14] Any civil event involving a Syrian citizen had to be submitted within a defined time frame to the relevant registration unit connected to the Ministry of Interior. Anyone outside of state territory was thus forced to return to register any life events. While this was certainly possible, and people did move between areas outside of government control and those under it, the risks were substantial, and most people were discouraged from doing so. After more than a decade of conflict and displacement there are entire families whose life events remain unrecognized by the Syrian state.

The passing of Civil Status Law No. 13 (2021) was aimed at digitizing the national registry and providing an administrative framework for Syrians to record life events with the state from outside of the country, replacing a similar from 2007. The law called for the creation of a Single Syrian Registry (al-Amanah al-Suriah al-Wahidah) to digitize all Syrian records and create a single database for citizens with national numbers. The new registry system also led to changes in how Syrians registered life events. Syrians were no longer required to travel with paper documentation back to their local registry offices (the *noufous*, often located in villages where they no longer reside), but could do so through newly created Civil Registry Centers (CRC) throughout the country. The new law itself was, on the surface, intended to streamline the registration of life events and to ease the registration process for Syrians both inside and outside of the country. In practice, however, Law No. 13 created significant obstacles for documentation that could have generational impacts on Syrian families. Syrians in areas in Idlib under the control of the Syrian Salvation Government (SSG), for example, had no access to CRC and could not move freely between SSG and state areas to register events. Once the ninety-day window for registration closed families would require special permission from the governor to establish a committee to adjudicate the claim. The law was also intended to create a population database for the government. However, if someone was not registered, they were simply not able to exercise property rights.

The state's production of information about a fragmented population paralleled attempts to bifurcate society into the loyal and disloyal and ensure that those in the latter category would be prevented from exercising any rights as Syrians. The effort to generate knowledge about the population brought together civil committees, individual denouncers, registries, the security apparatus, and the Ministries or Interior and Finance to produce the *matloobeen* as a subject and to categorize the absence of those who were not formally wanted by the security apparatus. These categorizations intimately reflected the conflict's narration. Only certain kinds of victims were martyred; others were killed while betraying the state. Some of the displaced fled terrorists, while others turned their backs on the homeland. Creating these categories out of the narration of conflict allowed the state to justify appropriations as punishment for betrayal of the homeland.

CATEGORIZING THE DECEASED

The ubiquity of death during the conflict has had profound effects on Syrian cultural production. The corpse has become an especially important subject as a means of highlighting how violence in Syria targets the dead as much as the living.[15] These forms of "necroviolence" include erasing the individual's identity, denying burial, mutilation, mistreatment, and erasure from memory. Since 2011, a body of Syrian cultural production has taken the corpse as the subject through which war stories and experiences are narrated. The corpse serves to frame victims and perpetrators and can also serve an agentive role through "postmortem resistance."[16] The movement of corpses to burial sites has been a central theme in Syrian cultural production. Joud Said's *A Man and Three Days* tells the story of a vain, cowardly theater director who fails to muster the courage to return his cousin's corpse to the village for burial.[17] The cousin, Bairam, had died fighting as a soldier, and his life and death in service of his country are contrasted with Majd's cowardice and opportunism. Eventually, Majd is able to return Bairam's corpse for burial and in the process is redeemed for his betrayal of his homeland. This moral story about sacrifice and redemption contrasts with the brutal journey described in Khalid Khalifa's *Almawt aml shaf* (published in English as *Death Is Hard Work*). Khalifa's novel centers around the character of Bolbol, another cowardly figure whose origins in an opposition village never quite endear him to his loyalist Damascene neighbors, despite his hanging of the president's picture and adoption of a loyalist persona. Bolbol's father, Abdel Latif al-Salim, is a revered opposition figure whose illness forced him to leave the village and seek treatment with sympathetic doctors in Damascus. Right before his death, Abdel Latif asks his son to make sure he is returned to his village for burial alongside his sister, who died by suicide in protest of a forced marriage decades earlier. Bolbol calls his siblings, Fatima and Hussein, from whom he is estranged, and asks that they fulfill their father's request together. They oblige.

The painful, absurd journey that Abdel Latif's children embark on with the corpse evidences the necroviolence inflicted on the deceased during the conflict. Although he is dead, Abdel Latif remains *matloob*, and at one point in the journey regime soldiers attempt to have the corpse arrested. Such absurdities continue throughout the story. In one scene, the siblings are unable to pass through a checkpoint because the soldier overseeing it is unsure whether the corpse of a wanted man can pass. Each new encounter with the state brings with it new humiliations and bribes. The siblings' situation does not radically improve once they reach opposition territory. By then their father's body has become badly decomposed, and an encounter with Islamists leads to Bolbol's arrest before being rescued by his uncle. The body is eventually buried in the village, but nowhere near Abdel Latif's sister. Their journey back to Damascus is much smoother without a corpse that happens to always be *matloob*. Death, it seems, is indeed hard work.

The absurdity of Khalifa's story highlights the necroviolence inflicted on corpses and the power of the *matloob* category. Literature on the politics of the dead in conflict contexts tends to be framed around questions of accountability (when there is some form of transitional justice) and memory making. Identifying who died, how they died, and what the political projects behind their deaths were, are important processes in the establishment of truth, memory, and justice. The deceased can also serve as subjects of categorization that allow the state to extend rewards and punishments to families through kin punishment. Death and its categorization become a mechanism for the state to extend the politics of enmity.

State categorizations of death and martyrdom were important practices that created loyal and disloyal deceased. The Martyrdom Law No. 1 (2017) was the first to require the categorization of death through a martyrdom certificate. This certificate conferred status on the deceased and their families and allowed them to make claims on the state. The process of obtaining a certificate required security approval and the issuing of a document certifying the deceased's status as a martyr and their connection to the family. The law was made retroactive to March 15, 2011, the unofficial date of the start of the conflict. The martyrdom law had been buttressed by other laws delineating loyal and disloyal injured or deceased. The Military Service and Security Personnel Law Decree No. 15 (2019) created definitions of soldiers, officers, and other security personnel who were martyred or missing during conflict. These categorizations became the basis of a reward regime for those deemed martyrs, a proxy category for loyalty. The state's use of death and martyrdom as a bifurcating category to extend rewards and punishments to deceased Syrians and their families had a multiplier effect on the social and civil rights of millions of Syrians.[18] Legal claims to martyrdom by soldiers, aligned militia fighters (such as the National Defense Forces), and members of the security apparatus could only be made by families in cases where the death was proven to be "a result of war, military operations, or at the hands of hostile elements or terrorist gangs" (*bsbb al harb aw al'mliyat al harbiyah aw 'al iyd 'nsar m'adiyah aw 'sabat arhabiyah*). Categorization as a martyr extends to the deceased's family certain economic benefits beyond a pension, such as a monthly payment for children enrolled in university (Decree No. 11, 2020), building permit exemptions (Decree No. 9, 2019), preference in state employment (Decree No. 1, 2018), including a provision that half of public sector job vacancies should go to martyrs' families (Decree No. 22, 2017), and free medical treatment and discounted public transport (Decree No. 20, 2015). The categorization of a death as a martyrdom was an important state practice that determines loyalty and tethers martyrs' families to the state through a reward regime.

DESERTERS, EVADERS, AND STATE EMPLOYEES

State officials' vitriol for absentees was especially intense toward deserters and conscript evaders. A July 2015 speech by Bashar al-Assad, at that point his first public speech in more than a year, directly addressed the issue of desertion and evasion and blamed the problem for the Syrian army's inability to maintain control over territory. Claiming that Syria was experiencing a shortage of manpower, and that the army was gutted because of deaths, deserters, and evaders, al-Assad touted a general amnesty that the government had passed the day before. There was a tension between how state officials denounced desertion and evasion while simultaneously offering amnesties for such crimes. Evasion and desertion became a major problem for the state as the conflict dragged on and the need for soldiers increased. The creation of the highly localized National Defense Forces (NDF) was one way for the state to recruit and retain soldiers, who were, officially, state employees operating under the umbrella of the NDF. Conscripted soldiers in Syria were deployed in governorates outside of their home areas, a long-standing practice dating back to the 1970s. The NDF structure allowed conscripts to stay "at home" and fight alongside loyalist militias as a fulfillment of their conscription.

Desertion was a crime of abstention that was nevertheless reversable if a deserter settled their status after one of several state amnesties. The Syrian Amnesty Law (No. 18), passed in October 2018, formalized a pattern of presidential amnesties that had been issued once or twice a year since the beginning of the conflict. The law criminalized desertion while simultaneously providing a mechanism for deserters to fulfill their conscription without penalty. Deserters were required to turn themselves in, pay a fee, and commit to completing their military conscription by reporting to their units within six months (in some cases this time frame was reduced to three months). Anyone who deserted but took up arms against the state was not eligible for amnesty. The Amnesty Law created new subjects around military conscription principally by tying desertion to property forfeiture.

Absenteeism was applied to military deserters by Law No. 35 (2017), which explicitly labeled deserters as disloyal "terrorists" whose assets could be confiscated by the state. Along with Law No. 63 allowing for the appropriation of deserters' assets these measures framed desertion as an act of disloyalty that necessitated punishment. Desertion was the equivalent to a crime of terrorism and prosecuted accordingly. Conscript-aged men inside and outside of Syria experienced anxiety, worry, and fear about the possibility of forced conscription into the army (and in some cases, local militias). Compounding these concerns were legal mechanisms aimed at punishing evaders. A 2019 amendment (Law No. 39) to the Military Service Law (2007) authorized the seizure of the assets of any conscript evader over the age of forty-two, regardless of whether they are inside or outside of Syria, if they had evaded conscription or failed to pay the estimated US$8,000–US$10,000 "exemption fee" (*badal al-nakdi*) for getting out of service. In practice, this fee could become much higher as people were forced to pay bribes up the chain of command before even paying the official fee. Those who had served at least five years in the army were exempt, meaning that people already conscripted once could be conscripted again, as were people with disabilities, or anyone from a family that had lost two sons while serving in the army. Otherwise, all Syrians inside and outside of the country were expected to abide by conscription orders.

Although the amendment was clearly aimed at evaders themselves, statements from regime officials raised fears that seizures would be extended to the families of evaders. Brigadier General Elias Bitar, head of the army's Allowance and Exemption Branch, publicly stated that the amendment to the law would also apply to the families and relatives of evaders despite there being no provision for the seizure of funds or property of anyone other than the evader. The Syrian Public Funds Collection Law, however, did provide measures for the "precautionary seizure" (this was also used in antiterrorism cases) of the monetary assets of evaders' relatives in certain cases. The ensuing confusion and fear this sowed was aggravated by the Central Bank of Syria's official policy toward allowances, which set an exchange rate for the Syrian pound for the payment for exemption fees that was double the official exchange rate (SYP2,550/US$1 rather than SYP1,256/US$1). Fears that the punishment of evaders would be extended to kin reflected societal anxiety about how crimes of disloyalty could be extended to people who were otherwise innocent of any crime.

KIN PUNISHMENT

The kin of wanted or absent subjects were subject to punishment despite their presence in Syria, a nominal prerequisite for the demonstration of loyalty to the state. These present subjects were targeted for punishment through a variety of measures that either severed their relationship to the absent subject (i.e., they were unable to claim property) or rendered them disloyal through association (i.e., kinship was a proxy for disloyalty). For example, the state's attribution of violence in causes of death allows for the extension of punishment to the deceased's kin. Residents of "reconciled" areas that were formally under rebel control were targeted for kinship punishment despite having settled their status with the state. These forms of punishment were simultaneously formally codified in law and enforced by state ministries and informal because they were enacted by militias, profiteers, or squatters. Families of deserters and known opposition fighters who remained in Syria had been subject to social pressure, ostracization, and in many cases violence for their affiliations and presumed affinities with antigovernment people. As Khalifa's book so eloquently shows, one's ancestral village or familial connections were sufficient to cast suspicion on their loyalty to the state. Despite their status as reconciled, many areas that were formally under opposition control remained suspicious in the eyes of state authorities. Such suspicions manifested in extralegal punishments or exclusions against the families of the deceased.

Kin were regularly the objects of suspicion by state authorities, neighbors, and friends. The state enacted punishment against kin through the disruption of property transfers and direct cuts to social services.[19] The withdrawal of subsidy access became a mechanism for the state to punish hundreds of thousands of Syrians for their familial associations. In 2014, the government introduced a long-planned digital subsidy system called the "smart card," literally a physical card resembling a bank card, that allowed all Syrians to purchase fuel-related products such as gas and heating oil at a subsidized rate. The rollout of the system was gradual, and it slowly expanded to include both public and private sector organizations before being extended in 2019 to include key commodities. At that time, Syrians with the card could purchase goods from distribution centers operated by the Syrian Trading Establishment, a government body under the Ministry of Internal Trade and Consumer Protection.[20] A Syrian company named Takamol partnered with the Ministry of Petroleum and Mineral Resources in a public-private partnership using the open-source Humansis web platform to manage the subsidy system.[21]

The smart card system provided the government with a digitized subsidy management system that could regulate prices and access through Takamol's platform. Each Syrian who wanted to obtain a smart card was required to register with Takamol and provide their family information, including their family's registration book and their spouse's and children's national identification numbers. The head of the household was also required to show proof of an identity card and residence if they were outside of their registered governorate. The process of family digital registration allowed the state to repeal subsidies from the kin of those charged with terrorism or other crimes. Digitization also created the kinds of documentation and registration gaps that disproportionately affected Syrian women and compounded problems of property transfer and inheritance, even in cases where people had not been charged with a crime.

Punishing Absence Through Property Appropriation

The state's criminalization of absenteeism, compounded by gaps in people's documentation, created the conditions for the large-scale appropriation of assets. The de-tethering of settlement from restitution was an aggravating factor as one's formal status as settled did not automatically result in the return of all rights and assets. The housing, land, and property (HLP) regime that was constructed during the conflict was specifically aimed at the punishment of disloyal citizens through property appropriation. At the same time, the HLP regime allowed the state to reward local notables and elites for their loyalty by funneling expropriated assets to them. Provisions within the new terrorism law allowed citizens to initiate legal proceedings against other citizens simply by denouncing them to the CTC. Once someone was denounced, they became *matloob* by the security apparatus. The fear that this generated among potential returnees prevented them from trying to reclaim their properties.[22] Because settlement and restitution were de-linked, many returnees whose status was settled also feared reclaiming their lost properties. Damaged homes were often categorized as such, and a bureaucratic process headed by state-affiliated "spatial technical committees" determined whether people could even return to such homes.[23] In many cases these committees rejected applications from residents to return and thus left their ownership and residency status in legal limbo for years. Meanwhile, committees also had the power to identify and oversee lands targeted for auction. In these cases, committees worked to classify appropriated lands and decide on their distribution to certain ministries (such as in the case of agricultural land) or their auctioning off to private investors.

Syria's HLP regime meted out punishment to disloyal citizens while rewarding loyalist elites by allowing them to acquire appropriated assets. Unruh argues that the HLP regime was weaponized through seven methods that the government deployed to deny restitution: destroying HLP records; targeting anti-regime people and places; identifying housing, land, and other property for destruction; confiscating and reselling through false documentation; confiscating legal documents; using of state laws; and creating ungovernable HLP tenure.[24] The main targets for HLP confiscation were absentee subjects. Indeed, dozens of HLP laws were passed after 2011 targeting the absentee subject for state punishment through appropriation. These laws reconstituted the state's HLP regime around the punishment of disloyal subjects by reclassifying property and property rights based either on one's absence or one's status inside state territory.

The HLP regime explicitly targeted absent subjects and those accused of terrorism. Laws No. 19, 22, and 63 (2012) created new legal categories linking the crime of terrorism to property confiscation.[25] Law No. 22 creating the CTC officially enforced Law No. 19's provisions on the appropriation of the property of anyone charged with terrorism. Similarly, military deserters were explicitly targeted for property appropriation in Law No. 35 (2017), which provided an addendum to Law No. 63, to confiscate and sell through auction the assets of military deserters. Collectively, the targeting of these subjects situated terrorism and desertion as acts of disloyalty that necessitated casting citizens out of the body politic through asset appropriation. Absence here was immediately linked to forfeiture and appropriation.

The state also prohibited property transfers or sales by subjecting the power-of-attorney system to security approval. The Ministry of Justice passed Resolution No. 689 formalizing an existing practice requiring those seeking power-of-attorney applications to secure security approval, which in turn subjected the *matloobeen* to further scrutiny. In September 2021, Circular No. 30 required all power-of-attorney applications to receive security approval. Prior to this measure, some people could bypass the security apparatus and acquire power of attorney through sharia courts. The circular was justified by the Ministry of Finance as a response to the overwhelming requests for power of attorney, but was a way for the state to subject budgetary decisions, such as the dispensing of salary and pensions or transfer of assets to kin, to security approval.

In addition to these national laws that constitute the HLP regime, HLP laws at the governorate level legitimized the seizure of assets and property. There were several overlapping national laws that constituted the regime.[26] Law No. 66 (2012) reclassified informal settlements and targeted them for planning while giving owners only thirty days to claim their properties or compensation. This law permitted technical committees to assess and categorize land based on its status. This law potentially affected more than a third of all Syrian land, including major areas of settlement on the outskirts of cities such as Damascus, Aleppo, and Homs. Law No. 23 (2012) similarly targeted lands for redevelopment while again only giving owners thirty days to claim their properties or compensation. All property transactions in areas outside of state control were nullified by Law No. 11 (2016), which was retroactive to March 15, 2011. This law effectively created ambiguities around ownership that facilitated state appropriation of land once ownership could not be established. Owners whose property was restored to them had a narrow time frame (from one year to as little as one month) to reclaim their lands. If they were not able to do so the lands could be appropriated. Law No. 33 (2017) regulated the issuance of property documentation and created new criteria for absentee subjects to secure title to prove ownership. Finally, Law No. 10 (2018) legalized the state's appropriation of lands targeted for redevelopment. The categorization of land for redevelopment was outside of appeal. Together, these laws legalized property appropriation.

The collective (and intended) effects of Syria's HLP regime were to actively discourage property reclamation. De-linking settlement from restitution forced returnees to undergo an altogether different process to prove both loyalty and property ownership. People were forced to do so while the state was transforming existing tenure laws to impose new ownership requirements that were virtually impossible for many people to satisfy. These new ownership requirements, especially around documentation, were enacted under the guise of rationalizing and modernizing the current system. However, these provisions almost always contained gaps that made it difficult for people to establish ownership, particularly in cases of collectively held land. Returnees also faced several other problems when trying to reclaim property. Many found that their homes were totally or partially destroyed and that state bodies had deemed them uninhabitable. Others returned to homes that were taken over by armed groups or civilians with close attachments to them. Returnees had little legal recourse to deal with squatters who were protected from eviction through their connections to the security apparatus. In some cases, these squatters were simply able to acquire documentation for the properties they stole.

The state's return to "reconciled areas" paralleled practices that concretized people's displacement from those territories. Return to reconciled areas required residents to submit applications to a "public safety committee" that included proof of ownership, family identification, and other relevant legal documentation demonstrating residency in an area.[27] The role of the committees was to determine whether it was safe for people to return. However, because these committees worked with municipal authorities and the security apparatus, their decisions were not based on any comprehensive engineering or building assessments but rather amounted to political decisions about who gets to return. In one case, 1,350 applications to return to the village of al-Hajr al-Aswad were submitted to a public safety committee, of which only 300 were approved. Of these 300 applicants, only 40 were able to return.[28] Decisions about who can and cannot return were based not on technical assessments of property but on political decisions about which citizens were considered loyalist and worthy of return. Public safety committees were also tasked with making decisions about how to reclassify land in reconciled areas, and some even legalized the destruction of damaged buildings without the consent of property owners.

Until late November 2023, when Law No. 26 was passed, almost all the appropriation decisions contained some mechanism for appeal. In that month, parliament passed a draconian law called "Managing and Investing Transferrable and Non-Transferrable Assets That Were Seized Pursuant to an Unappealable Judicial Ruling."[29] The law said explicitly that any state confiscation of assets or properties was final and would not be subject to appeal. Removing the possibility to appeal state confiscation rendered all forfeitures complete and final. The law also contained a retroactive provision that allowed the state to remove appeals on existing confiscated assets and property. This meant that any confiscated assets or property from 2011 onward seized in fulfillment of an order against "terrorists" or absent subjects could not be appealed, and that the relevant state authorities could confiscate and distribute those assets or property. The law also contained several provisions for the seizure of assets and property. There were two ministries most affected by this law. All assets inside agriculture zones were to be seized and managed by the Ministry of Agriculture and Agrarian Reform. All other assets were controlled by the Ministry of Finance, which maintained authority over property, company assets, private assets, and anything else seized by state authorities in fulfillment of a confiscation order.

These two ministries were entrusted with executive authority to order asset seizures, manage assets, and prevent their transfer to kin. The basis of this new law was Decree No. 63 (2012), which empowered the Ministry of Finance to order asset seizures against people suspected of crimes against the state. Slowly, the power of the ministry to manage assets grew as the categories of subjects who were targets of asset expropriation grew. The ministry thus sat at the pinnacle of an institutional structure oriented toward the seizure of assets and property. It has been estimated that sixty-eight separate executive and judicial bodies in Syria issued decisions ordering the Ministry of Finance to seize someone's assets and property between March 2011 and November 2023, including the Ministries of Justice, Endowments, Agriculture and Agrarian Reform, and Defense, the CTC, the Central Bank of Syria, the National Defense Bureau, and the Directorate General of Real Estate.[30] These bodies requested that the minister of finance issue a seizure order against individuals and their families.

The legal basis of state appropriation of citizen assets was the categorization of the criminal or absent subject whose betrayal of the homeland targeted them for punishment. Categorizing absence required a commonsense narration of the conflict that could absolve some citizens of their absence while condemning others for the same. Various public safety and spatial technical committees represented the institutionalization of the politics of appropriation by giving a veneer of bureaucratic rationalization to the state's appropriation of the assets of criminalized and absent subject assets. These committees functioned to categorize land in ways that facilitated appropriation. These dual processes of categorizing both land and people intertwined to restrict HLP rights and provide state-connected networks opportunities to acquire appropriated assets.

Cementing Absence Through Erasure

Syria's territorial fragmentation created several large pockets of territory outside of state control. After 2015, much of this territory started to fall back under state authority. This was a complicated, gradual process whereby state presence was reestablished after reconciliation agreements and the withdrawal of former oppositionists. State presence was often minimal in reconciled areas. These territories tended to be depopulated and the most in need of reconstruction due to severe material damage. State reconstruction policies varied by locale. In some areas civil committees deemed the reconstruction and engineering demands to be so substantive that returnees were not allowed back into their villages. In other areas residents were allowed to apply for reconstruction permits and received state allowances to rebuild their homes. There was nothing resembling a national policy toward reconstruction. Instead, the areas that fell back under state control were reinscribed with state power through exclusionary strategies intended to prevent the return of disloyal subjects.

The problem of how to reestablish state authority in these areas was superseded by the problem of how to erase the vestiges of opposition rule in those same territories. The ebb and flow of territorial control on the Syrian battlefield produced several competing governance projects to administer life outside of regime control. The most ambitious of these projects was the "state" proclaimed by the ISIS, which attempted to establish a caliphate across the territories the organization controlled in Syria and Iraq. The Rojava, later the Autonomous Administration of North and East Syria (AANES), similarly sought to codify legal practices and administrative authority across areas controlled by the Kurdish YPG-dominated SDF, although the northeastern administration never formally committed to building state institutions as ISIS did. In these areas different governance projects emerged with differing levels of institutionalization and reach.

The question of how to incorporate wartime non-sate and informal governance structures into post-conflict states is an important one for understanding the distribution of power. Some have argued that stitching together state, non-state, and informal structures in post-conflict state building can enhance reconciliation and administrative integration.[31] These arguments rest on the assumption that the mainstreaming of wartime non-state governance structures will enhance the legitimacy of post-conflict state building.[32] These concerns with how non-state governance structures are or are not integrated into post-conflict state building tend to deflect from the question of how everyday life happens and is governed in conflict zones. Students need schooling, people need vaccinations, people sell homes and assets, and births and deaths all occur. One of the several governance bodies in Syria registered life events for people. Various governance bodies, especially those associated with the Syrian Interim Government, sought to administratively document everyday life events precisely so that Syrians would have access to documentation. Even in cases where no existing authority could document life events, social networks and citizen organizing sought to ensure the delivery of key services, such as education.[33]

The state's response to life outside of its territorial control was to render all life events in such places effectively null and void through a process of erasure that rejected any documentation for life events not issued by the Syrian state. Most importantly, the state rejected documentation for births, deaths, and property transfers, and used the ensuing ambiguities to appropriate property or inflict kin punishment on people whose life events had been rendered invisible by new state laws. The nonrecognition of documents had a cascading effect on families who are unable to register life events. These effects include problems in claiming inheritance or transferring property. Ultimately, they create a void in the documented life of a citizen that was upheld by Syrian laws. Decree No. 11 (2016) formalized the state's nonrecognition of property transactions registered by nongovernment authorities. All property transactions in areas outside of government control were effectively nullified and ownership, in bureaucratic terms, was restored to the original property owners through reversion to the authority of civil registry documentation. Decree No. 11 also created the category of the absentee owner who did not reclaim their property. All absentee properties would then be placed under the authority of the relevant ministry.

Subjecting real estate transactions to security approval tethered the state's legal categorization of absenteeism to kin punishment. In August 2015, the Council of Ministers passed Decree No. 4554 requiring the Ministry of Local Administration and Environment to secure security approval for the sale of all residential and commercial properties. The requirement for security approval was henceforth expanded to include almost all facets of the transaction process, from power of attorney to sale. The process for obtaining security approval was essentially the same throughout Syria. An application for property transfer was submitted to the political security branch in the area where the transfer was supposed to occur. Once received, the security branch distributed the application to other intelligence agencies and awaited approval or rejection. During this time, each agency would check the names of the applicants against their blacklists of wanted people. If approved, the Ministry of Interior would officially issue a document sanctioning the transaction. This process of security approval was effectively the same in all cases where Syrians were required to obtain it. Denials were common and could occur because a person was located "outside of state territory" (i.e., living in opposition areas), undergoing trial, facing a travel ban, was in financial arrears, or was believed to have pro-opposition sympathies.[34]

The Absent and Wanted as Disloyal Subjects

The categories created out of Syrians' absence from areas under state control indexed disloyal and loyal citizens while creating legal categories that facilitated widespread appropriation. Absence was a problem to be governed through new HLP regimes that would punish subjects for leaving the country, failing to serve in the military, or committing crimes. The corresponding categories of the *matloob*, absent, and absent from state territory became the organizing basis for punishment. Spatial technical and public safety committees supported the work of civil committees in producing knowledge about the population that enhanced the state's capacity to manage absence. The politics of absence was only possible through a knowledge-generating process that linked local elites and notables with the security apparatus to determine who was absent, the nature of their absence, and who their kin were to target for punishment.

The effect of the state's management of absence was to render substantial portions of Syrian territory targetable for appropriation. Categorizing absence and attendant appropriation laws dovetailed perfectly with new laws about documentation and zoning and categorizing land. This made appropriation much easier while disincentivizing restitution claims. As the brief interlude at the beginning of this chapter demonstrated, even when someone was not *matloob*, they did not necessarily feel confident in returning and reclaiming their lands. Besides creating a legal environment hostile to restitution, the state's politics of absence also created an affective climate that invoked fear in Syrians wishing to return. Categorizing land and housing through various committees made appeals difficult until they were forbidden altogether. The mechanisms of appropriating the assets of the absent had thus become embedded in the machinations of state power and the devolved power centers in various governorates.

6

The Regime Falls

Managing Syria's Transition

Those who think that the time of hardship has passed, and that comfort has come, are wrong. Syria's needs are greater than ever. Just as we were determined previously to liberate it, we must be determined to build and develop it.

—SYRIAN PRESIDENT AHMED AL-SHARAA

Introduction

On November 11–12, 2024, the Astana powers of Russia, Turkey, and Iran met for the twenty-second time to discuss the state of the Syrian conflict. The statement they released at the end of the meeting sounded like many previous declarations in its eschewing of any commitment to political change in Syria in favor of a vague commitment to a "comprehensive political solution." Within a month of this meeting the trajectory of contemporary Syria was forever altered. Ten days after the Astana meeting ended, Hayat Tahrir al-Sham (HTS) began an unexpected military campaign against pro-regime forces in the areas bordering HTS-controlled territories. The campaign ended on December 8, 2024—less than two weeks after it started—when Bashar al-Assad fled Syria and his regime collapsed. After more than fifty-four years of one-party rule Syria was, shockingly, no longer governed by the regime that al-Assad family (father Hafez followed by son Bashar) had controlled for more than forty years.

The regime has collapsed, but the effects of Ba'athist authoritarian rule and more than a decade of violent conflict will persist for years to come. Conflict leaves irreparable imprints on individuals and societies. The Syrian conflict's many legacies will persist in the hearts of Syrians, in the institutions that govern them, in the language that people use and how they speak to each other, and in the memories that future generations will retain from thirteen years of brutal conflict and fifty-four years of Ba'athist rule. Syria's transitional authorities, as well as those who will govern in the future, will inevitably grapple with how to embrace, reject, appropriate, or erase these many vestiges while families and cultural producers navigate shifting terrains of memory making and political contestation. The conflict's many legacies will continue to be reflected in how Syria's post-Assad political system, constitution, legal structure, and state institutions are oriented around the management of transition and post-conflict stabilization. *Betrayal of the Homeland* has traced the institutional, legal, political, and discursive legacies of conflict as they materialized in the state apparatus. The arguments advanced in the previous chapters raise important questions about both how the regime was able to sustain its rule during the conflict and the residual effects of the regime's conflict management strategies and the challenges these for the authorities to initiate a political transition: How much of the "old" state will remain? What laws, decrees, and bureaucratic practices will persist through the transition period and beyond? How will transitional authorities attempt to erase the vestiges of regime rule? What will reconciliation look like?

With these questions in mind, this chapter asks how we can understand the possible trajectories for Syria's political transition vis-à-vis the legacies of decades of authoritarian rule and the state's conflict management strategies. I begin by detailing the dramatic events that transformed the conflict over twelve days and concluded with the regime's collapse. I then turn my attention to the first major transition period between December 8, 2024 (when Assad left the country) and March 1, 2025 (when the SSG-led new government claimed it would dissolve into a new transitional authority). I use this period to highlight the challenges transitional authorities face in constructing a post-conflict political system. Finally, the latter part of the chapter identifies several key issues that will define Syria's political transition going forward. This section raises several questions that Syria's future political authorities must struggle with as they seek a new political order amid the many catastrophes wrought by the conflict.

The Battlefield Shifts

For years, the frontlines between regime-held areas and the large enclaves stretching across most of Idlib and part of Aleppo Governorates that were controlled by the Turkish-backed Syrian National Army (SNA) and the HTS-dominated Syrian Salvation Government (SSG) stayed relatively stable. Skirmishes along these de facto borderlands were common, as were aerial bombardments from the regime and Russian air forces, but the frontlines rarely shifted. That changed dramatically on the evening of November 27, when an HTS-led offensive culminated in the collapse of the regime in less than two weeks. By December 8, 2024, Bashar al-Assad had fled the country and his regime had collapsed. A military offensive from Idlib was able to overrun and assume control over Syria's major cities before congealing in the capital, Damascus. Prior to these dramatic and shocking two weeks, the frontlines separating regime-held areas from the northwestern areas of HTS control in Idlib and northern Aleppo Governorates had stayed the same since 2018. Skirmishes within the areas under rebel control were common, but the frontlines separating pro- and anti-regime forces rarely shifted. The Astana powers ensured that this status quo stuck for almost seven years by preventing any major incursions into either territory along the de facto borders. During this time, the SSG emerged as a governance structure for almost four million citizens who lived in areas under their control. In other words, something akin to military and political stasis defined the borderlands and relations between the SSG, the SNA, the Astana powers, and the regime forces.

This all changed two weeks after the last Astana meeting when, on November 27, 2024, rebel groups attacked several villages in western Aleppo Governorate that were under regime control. The attack was the first major fighting between forces on either side of the border in several years. In the aftermath of the attack thirteen villages in the governorate fell under rebel control. Three days later rebel forces entered Aleppo city, Syria's second-largest city and an urban center that had come under full regime control in 2016. The Syrian army had retreated and barely fought back. Most importantly, it was clear that the Russian and Iranian forces inside of Syria were not reinforcing the Syrian army in its attempt to repel the rebel offensive. The fall of Aleppo was, in several ways, the most significant moment in the offensive as it revealed the Iranian and Russian withdrawal, demoralized the (already demoralized) Syrian military, exposed the collapse of the command structure, and demonstrated that the rebels could militarily control a major city. Several days later, on December 5, 2024, the rebels took control of the next major city, Hama, which provided them a direct geographic link to Damascus along the important M5 highway axis. Daraa, a city in southern Syria far removed from the northwestern battlefield, fell the next day, December 6, 2024, after a coalition of existing rebel factions overran what remained of regime forces. Homs fell to rebel forces on December 7, 2024, marking the fourth major city in just one day to fall (Daraa, Quneitra, and Suwayda in the South also fell).

At this point, the entire Syrian command structure had collapsed and there was very little resistance to the rebel advancements. Measured by the duration and brutality of the conflict, the rebels' advance and the regime's collapse were relatively quick and peaceful. The speed at which the regime collapsed caught everyone, including al-Assad's closest confidants, by surprise.[1] By the time the president had fled the country and rebels and citizens occupied the presidential palace, army barracks, and state institutions, the future of Syria had been forever altered. Jubilant scenes of rebels liberating prisoners from the regime's torture chambers in Saydnaya, Tadmoor, and elsewhere filled Syrians with a renewed sense of hope for the post-Assad future of their country. For the first time since the uprising began, many Syrians began to collectively wonder and dream about a radically new future.

These visions of Syria's future quickly ran up against the reality of the political transition and the challenges the country's new authorities would face. The vacuum created by the collapse of the regime was immediately filled by the SSG, which assumed responsibility as a caretaker government until a transitional road map could be agreed upon by March 1. Syrians were greeted to hitherto unthinkable scenes of the existing prime minister, Mohammed Ghazi al-Jalali, being escorted peacefully out of his offices by armed HTS soldiers to formally hand power to SSG Prime Minister

Mohammed al-Bashir. In the days, weeks, and months that followed, the SSG government was transplanted to Damascus, its ministers assumed responsibility for national portfolios, and the peaceful transition of authority from the former regime's ministers and ministries occurred. An Idlib-based governance model was transplanted wholesale to Damascus and henceforth assumed responsibility for governing areas nominally under state control.

Syria in Transition

The SSG essentially served as a caretaker, substitute transitional government until a new government could be formed. This has the stabilizing effect of maintaining continuity in governance and state institutions, but it also creates a complicated situation where power is vested in one of the many groups party to the conflict. In previous years, the SSG proved ineffective in negotiating political and military agreements with the SDF-controlled AANES. The SSG had also responded to opposition and dissent inside of Idlib through repression. Whether or not the SSG-dominated transitional authorities can adopt a more deliberative model of politics remains to be seen. On the one hand, these authorities are not strong enough to govern the entire country and will inevitably need to consider models for incorporating opposing social and political forces into the ruling coalition. On the other hand, opening the political space for new kinds of encounters between different actors inside of Syria creates new terrains of conflict and contestation that may hamper transition. In the absence of a negotiated end to the conflict these tensions are even more acute.

One of the principal arguments advanced in this book is that the Syrian regime sought to manage, rather than resolve, the conflict through the punishment of citizens deemed disloyal. A resolution to the conflict would have involved a negotiated settlement likely ending in a power-sharing agreement in which the regime would have engaged in reforms and ceded some political control to various opposition groups. However, the Syrian regime pursued a zero-sum approach to the conflict and refused concessions to the opposition. As the arguments in this book demonstrate, the erasure of any vestiges of opposition control was central to the regime's conflict management strategies. The regime's refusal to negotiate with opposition forces contributed to its collapse and the short-term challenges facing the transitional authorities. As a unique moment in Syria's postcolonial state formation the conflict created new social and political forces that will contend over a weakened state apparatus, fragmented country, and competing military and governance projects. In other words, Syria's transitional authorities are facing several of the same problems faced by the regime. In the remainder of this section, I identify two broad but important questions that can help us frame an understanding of Syria's transition in the key period between December and March 1: What are the breaks and continuities with the previous regime? And what is Syria transitioning to?

The starting point for our understanding of Syria's political transition is in the political reality of the regime's collapse and the assumption of power by a new coalition of political and military forces. This inflection point in the Syrian conflict raises the important question of what breaks and continuities from the ancien régime will shape the future. There are two divergent bodies of literature that give us insight into this question: that pertaining to civil war settlement, on the one hand, and the anthropology of war and state violence, on the other. Literature on civil war settlement differs from that of authoritarian conflict management in that it takes a specific moment, event, or period as the starting point for thinking about political transition. Whereas conflict management literature asks how regimes sustain conflict both on and away from the battlefield, civil war settlement scholarship asks how civil wars end and what these "end" points mean for the trajectory of a post-conflict state. Civil war settlement literature identifies several different ways that conflicts end through negotiated settlements, military victories (by either incumbent regimes or rebel groups), stalemates, or permanent ceasefires, and the role that different actors (domestic or foreign), institutions, constitutional processes, elections, and reconstruction projects play in shaping contingent post-conflict trajectories.[2] One of the central questions that this literature is interested in relates to the inclusion or exclusion of former belligerents in post-conflict political processes. At stake here is the extent to which the post-conflict political system is accessible to warring parties, opposition groups, and different political factions, and how a national political process signals the inclusion/exclusion of different political forces.[3]

While literature on civil war settlement takes key inflection points and processes as evidence of a political transition's trajectory, scholarship on the anthropology of war and state violence reminds us that wars persist long after the formal settlement of conflict, peace agreements, or the fall of a regime.[4] The regime's collapse creates the opportunity for a new political order to emerge. That political order, however, will be imbued with the legacy of conflict, state violence, and authoritarian rule. There are existing laws, institutions, ministries, bureaucracies, and, indeed, people, who are holdovers from the previous regime that had oriented the state apparatus around the punishment of disloyal subjects. What will the new authorities do with the edifice of the state? What will happen to the bureaucrats, workers, and security officials who were part of the state? Memories and narratives about the conflict shape institutions and state practices in ways that correspond to specific legacies of conflict. How the conflict gets narrated today and what this means for the creation of state enemies tomorrow will have a profound impact on how the state materializes a post-conflict political order. The question of how the conflict will persist (or not) in Syria's state institutions is an extremely important one that will determine much of Syria's trajectory.

The question of what Syria will be transitioning to is a similarly important one. Transitions literature takes for granted that the collapse of authoritarianism will inevitably produce momentum toward democratization. However, as much of the experience and literature on the trajectory of the Arab uprisings demonstrates there are several divergent trajectories that do not produce democratic orders.[5] The transfer of the SSG model of governance from Idlib to Damascus, while it may be a necessary stabilizing measure for Syria's short-term political transition, nonetheless risks perpetuating the exclusion of anti-regime forces over the long term should this substitute for a comprehensive national political process. Herein lies the political stakes in Syria's transition. If the transition authorities can expand the political space for the inclusion of various political forces, then the chances for stabilization increase. The regime's collapse will then be understood as having occasioned a more inclusive political transition. However, if the transition remains dominated by the SSG authorities then Syria's transition trajectory may be toward a more Damascus- and Idlib-centered exclusionary authority.

The larger issue around the question of what Syria is transitioning to relates to which actors will bring their pressure and power to bear on the transition so as to shift the country's trajectory. This includes domestic actors as well as regional ones who may be less incentivized to support a "democratic" transition in Syria. For Syrians, visions of a post-Assad future will inevitably clash as the trauma and memories produced by the conflict inform political visions of the future. The transition has created the political terrain for clashes, which I conceptualize here as a series of political encounters between different forces in Syria that will shape the transition.

Syria's Transition Challenges as Political Encounters

The core argument in this book is that the state was oriented around the punishment of disloyal subjects through various measures that extended the enmity of the battlefield to "terrorists," the displaced, and otherwise "disloyal" subjects. My arguments in the previous chapter were motivated by the question of how the state was oriented around the extension of the battlefield to the social and political lives of Syrians as a related form of punishment. Similarly, the fall of the regime raises the question of how the state will be oriented around the punishment of specific populations and/or the reconciliation of formerly belligerent actors. How will Syria's transitional and future authorities frame victim/perpetrator binaries? Who will be held responsible for Syria's catastrophe, and how? How will competing memory projects be reconciled? How will narratives about the conflict materialize into state institutions and practices? The regime's fall has raised a set of challenges occasioned by the inevitable political encounters that will emerge in the wake of its collapse. These political encounters between different power centers will determine the trajectory of Syria's transition. For example, the encounters between the SSG and SDF have been radically reshaped as the former attempts to exercise sovereign control over Syria from the seat of state power in Damascus. How will the Sunni religious establishment and Damascene business elites who have endured decades of Ba'athist rule react to an SSG-dominated transition? What political concessions will powerful commanders such as

Ahmad al-Awda in the South demand for demilitarization and allegiance to the state? How will ordinary citizens react to encountering their former jailers, torturers, or tormentors? The political transition occasioned by the fall of the regime has created the context for a series of political encounters between entrenched and newly created social and political forces inside of Syria. These encounters had largely been mediated by the presence of the regime prior to its collapse.

DEALING WITH THE FORMER REGIME

One of the most important encounters will be between the current and future authorities, on the one hand, and the remnants of the former regime, on the other. The early transition period witnessed a restrictive identification of former regime officials as Syria's new enemies. One of the first measures taken by the new authorities was the declaration of a blanket amnesty for conscripts. Public sector workers and even the prime minister were guaranteed safety and not targeted for retribution. The authorities publicly and regularly spoke about the need to bring the regime's upper echelons to justice. This meant targeting jailers, torturers, military commanders, and the *shabiha* infrastructure, not the judges, lawyers, bureaucrats, and other civil service workers associated with the regime. Transitional authorities thus adopted a narrow definition of who was to be targeted for transitional justice. This does not mean, however, that the political space for who constitutes an enemy of the state will not be expanded in the future.

One of the most alarming continuities with the previous regime was the new authorities' creation of a settlement process to identify, document, and demilitarize soldiers and intelligence officials from the previous regime. Settlement centers were established throughout the country and anyone associated with the regime's security apparatus was invited to surrender themselves and their weapons and to receive official documentation exonerating them—temporarily—for crimes committed. The process discursively and politically reproduced that of the settlement process enacted by the regime in parsing out potential enemies were and forcing them to adopt a narrative of loyalty to ensure their integration into the "new" Syria. This was a remarkable early development in Syria's transition as it borrowed wholly from one of the regime's most brutal bureaucratic methods of separating the loyal from the disloyal, redirecting the practice against former regime officials. Much of the media coverage of the new settlement process did not, however, point out the irony that this practice had been continued. Instead, news reports tended to replicate the same structure of previous reporting from settlement centers, showing images of people walking into settlement centers (in some cases across a makeshift carpet of abandoned posters of Bashar al-Assad),[6] followed by images of long lines of people holding their weapons and turning them in before being interviewed by balaclava-clad armed men who would then write down their answers to questions about what units they belonged to, where they were stationed, the identities of their commanding officers, and so on. One of the criteria for these soldiers' settlement was proof that their hands "were not stained in Syrian blood."[7] This was a direct appropriation of the regime's language for determining who was a loyal citizen. Once the interviews were completed several of the newly "settled" subjects would be interviewed by reporters, at which time they would express regret for their actions and confirm their desire to work "hand in hand" with the transition authorities.

The transitional authorities' deployment of a settlement process was similarly intended to bifurcate former regime loyalists who could be integrated into the "new" Syria and those who refused to settle and thus would be targeted for prosecution. The initial period for people to settle their status was one month but was eventually extended to three months. Those who were settled and not accused of major crimes were given documentation allowing them to travel throughout the country and a temporary reprieve from prosecution. This is precisely how the regime dealt with those disloyal subjects who were forced to perform loyalty to be able to return and live in the country. Encounters between elements of the former regime, on the one hand, and the transitional authorities and people who were victimized by the regime, on the other, are important determinants of Syria's post-conflict trajectory.

TRANSITIONAL JUSTICE

One of the declared priorities of the Syrian transitional authorities was their intent to create a transitional justice process to prosecute officials within the former regime. In any post-conflict context, the pursuit of transitional justice requires the delineation of victims and perpetrators and the pursuit of justice for the former.[8] The victim/perpetrator binaries that shape transitional justice processes reflect a dominant narrative of why the conflict happened and who is responsible. Inevitably, such dominant narratives clash with others that hold equally powerful affective and political resonance among those who experienced the war. Transitional justice is thus a highly contested process. The relitigation of the conflict in the pursuit of justice and reconciliation can have counterbalancing effects that aggravate certain actors' historic wounds, and that create obstacles in a country's political transition. Transitional justice is a deeply political process and will become a new terrain for memory contestation among different actors in Syria. In Lebanon, for example, the approach of "official amnesia" about the civil war has effectively erased any state-led memory projects or transitional justice to absolve the civil war's militia leaders—many of whom, thirty years later, remain in power in the 2020s—for their crimes during the war. This suppression of an official narrative created the space for leaders to advance confessional and sectarian memories of the war that informed encounters between different sectarian communities decades after the civil war ended.[9] "Official amnesia" suppresses transitional justice and prevents a dominant memory politics of the Lebanese Civil War from emerging. In Syria, transitional authorities have rejected this approach and committed to some form of transitional justice. Public declarations about the intent to turn the regime's prisons into museums and to provide other ways of memorializing Syrian victims also suggest that these authorities will support public discussion of the conflict.

Any transitional justice process will create altogether new forms of political encounters between different actors in Syria in which the memory politics of the war are litigated in the name of reconciliation, accountability, and justice. Selim has argued that in the case of Nepal, transitional justice has become a mechanism for certain actors to advance their specific political interests by appropriating the language, processes, and institutions of transitional justice. Politics was thus reoriented around the transitional justice process, providing a new terrain for political encounters between different actors. In this new terrain, different social and political actors related to each other via transitional justice on a continuum running from co-option, to resistance, to contestation, to compliance.[10] As the above Lebanese example shows, the war memories of different communities continue to inform their collective politics in the present. The absence of a collective process to pursue justice and create an "official" narrative of the conflict can thus have long-lasting effects on the political encounters between different actors. Inevitably, however, any transitional justice process will contain exclusions that aggravate the war memories and experiences of certain communities and actors.

As a new terrain for political encounters between different actors in Syria, the transitional justice process raises several questions concerning future relations between Syrian communities and different actors and the conflict memories that shape their politics. How will the state construct an official narrative about the conflict? Will this official narrative be compatible with the individual and localized experiences of conflict that shape people's memories? Who will be defined as a victim and who as a perpetrator? What will the pursuit of justice look like? What role will outside actors such as human rights groups and the United Nations play in transitional justice? Will armed groups beyond regime forces be prosecuted? These questions have no clear answers in the Syrian case, and inevitably an answer for one of them complicates an answer for another. One of the principal questions about transitional justice in Syria is how to approach the issue, prevalent since the fall of the regime, of vendettas or vigilante justice. State or local authorities' decisions about whether to prevent these sorts of attacks will reflect the political will and ability of authorities to protect people (even those associated with the regime) and influence the legitimacy that communities afford the transitional authorities. If state power cannot be projected into the localities in which these vendettas are being pursued then any transitional justice process risks being politically hollow, delegitimized, and a backwards step toward societal reconciliation.

Any form of transitional justice—whether state-led or of the vigilante type—will inevitably lay the foundation for the litigation of the conflict and the clashing of memory politics between different actors. Transitional justice is never an objective process; rather, it is deeply imbued with the politics of conflict and the post-conflict visions of state authorities. In Syria today it is unlikely that any of the armed groups will be prosecuted under any transitional justice scheme. Singling out regime officials will no doubt provide a degree of healing for many people, but solely targeting the upper echelons of the regime risks alienating those for whom the horrors of war were inflicted by the regime's lower-level personalities and other armed groups.

RECONSTRUCTION AND REFUGEE REPATRIATION

Quantifying Syria's economic destruction is virtually impossible given the duration of the conflict, the decimation of key infrastructures, and the failure of the previous regime to engage in any substantial physical reconstruction inside of the country. The figures put forth by the United Nations Development Programme to quantify the destruction wrought by the Syrian conflict are truly staggering, with estimates of around USD$800 billion lost during the war, more than 600,000 deaths, half the population displaced, a 90 percent poverty rate, limited energy production, and almost one-third of all housing stock damaged or destroyed.[11] At the current rate of growth, it would take Syria fifty-five years simply to return to pre-conflict GDP levels. The scale of destruction and the challenges ahead are exacerbated by the lack of any substantive financial base from which to initiate large-scale reconstruction. Relations with the Arab Gulf states and Turkey will certainly help provide funds for physical reconstruction. The authorities, however, have not advanced a vision for the country's reconstruction beyond some vague commitments to the free market as the basis of Syria's future economic system and reducing "waste" by eliminating one-third of all public sector jobs and privatizing many public sector enterprises.[12]

Syria's transitional president, Ahmed al-Sharaa, has regularly declared his desire for Syrian refugees to be repatriated, but this will be extremely difficult if there is not immediate progress in improving physical infrastructure, housing, and services. Throughout this book, I have detailed how the internally and externally displaced were narrated as disloyal subjects who could only prove their loyalty by either reconciling or settling with the state. Displacement was indexed as an act of disloyalty that the state punished through legal appropriation and enacting other forms of social erasure that prevented Syrians from transferring property or even working in the country. While the collapse of the regime has created an opportunity for many of the displaced to return, the transitional authorities will face important questions about, first, how to facilitate large-scale repatriation and, second, how to pursue a project of restitution for returnees. Thousands of properties were confiscated under Syria's antiterrorism laws. Absentee laws and other, more localized property decisions taken by various state committees led to the appropriation of even more properties and lands that were taken over by the state and auctioned to loyalists. Compounding these appropriations are the legal property transactions between buyer and seller that were conducted using forged documents. Throughout the country tens of thousands of properties were illegally transferred to people using fake documentation who then sold those same properties to unknowing buyers. Severe destruction of physical homes and ongoing state-led engineering assessments of their habitability have also created categories of homes and properties that cannot be reclaimed by their original owners. What approach will transitional and future state authorities take toward property and asset restitution?

The politics of repatriation and restitution will create new types of political encounters between returnees and those who stayed and returnees and both local and federal authorities. The complicated and delicate politics of restitution that transitional and future authorities will face hinge significantly on how returnees are incorporated into the new Syria. Refugee return has become an important political and symbolic aim of the transitional government. However, repatriation will inevitably create overlapping legal disputes that reveal both local and national legal gaps in the system for addressing property restitution. The resolution of property disputes—both as individual disputes between landowners and as collective problems posed by legal classifications—will likely emerge as a space for the relitigation of the conflict around questions of loyalty and disloyalty. Should those who profited from the conflict be allowed to retain their properties? What conflict-era laws will remain? Complicating these questions is the ongoing analog-to-digital transition that Syria's property documentary regime is undergoing.[13] In this transition, analog (i.e., paper) forms of documentation were slowly being digitized into a large state database. This transition became an opportunity for the regime to further appropriate properties from those who could not provide proof of ownership. There are thus several bureaucratic as well as political questions facing the transitional authorities about how to classify property and ownership and whether (and how) to link property transfers to the conflict. In other words, should anyone who profited through property acquisition during the conflict be subject to appropriation?

The particular approach that state authorities adopt to the question of property restitution will have long-standing effects on how returnees and those who remained relate to each other. Property restitution can contribute to or impede reconciliation.[14] In Syria's complicated case, the path toward restitution of properties appropriated under the state's antiterrorism laws will require a new legal regime, changes to the constitution, and the creation of a large-scale national project for restitution akin to the Dayton Accords.[15] In the meantime, state authorities declared a total suspension of property transfers in January 2025 to prevent the fraudulent transfer of illegally obtained properties. Property restitution in post-conflict Syria will be a new terrain for encounters between those who left and lost their properties and those who stayed, some of whom benefited from property appropriations. The encounter between returnees and those who stayed will thus have a profound impact on Syria's transition and reconciliation. There are very deep wounds in Syria today that will not be easily healed. As Schwartz has argued, the encounters between returnee and nonmigrant groups can be destabilizing if state institutions favor one at the expense of the other.[16] Moreover, different forms of land competition can create the conditions for further violence in the country. Schwartz's research raises two relevant questions: How will the state create the conditions for repatriation and restitution? And will these state-led projects produce divisions between returnee and nonmigrant groups?

REGIONAL RELATIONS

The Astana process has collapsed, bringing with it the tripartite guarantor structure that linked Iran, Russia, and Turkey in a collaborative structure to manage Syria's conflict. Syria's regional and geopolitical alignments radically changed when the regime fell. President Ahmed al-Sharaa immediately signaled Syria's new regional orientation by traveling to Saudi Arabia on his first official visit to meet Crown Prince Mohammed Bin Salman, before continuing on to Turkey to meet Turkish President Recep Tayyip Erdoğan. He also received the emir of Qatar, Tamim bin Hamad al-Thani, in late January on an official state visit. These diplomatic measures to move Syria closer to the Turkey-Gulf political orbit coincided with al-Sharaa's repeated declarations that Iran was no longer a welcome Syrian ally. This set off a series of diplomatic tussles between the two countries, with Iranian officials demanding repayment of the debts accrued by the former regime. Amid this dramatic reorientation of Syria's regional relations al-Sharaa declared that Syria would remain close with Russia, noting the "deep strategic interests between Russia and Syria" and making clear he did not want Russia to depart Syria "in a way that undermines its relationship with our country."[17]

Syria faces other serious regional problems in the wake of the regime's collapse. The most destabilizing of these is Israel's expansion of its occupation zone beyond the Golan Heights. Within hours of the regime's collapse Israeli Prime Minister and accused war criminal Benjamin Netanyahu declared the 1974 border agreement with Syria "null and void" and ordered the Israeli military to extend the occupation zone into a "buffer zone." The Israeli military subsequently extended the occupation zone and destroyed Syria's naval and aerial forces while also targeting dozens of state institutions. The Israeli military struck nearly five hundred major targets within seventy-two hours of the regime's collapse.[18] The long-term consequences of these attacks are profoundly destabilizing by decimating the state's capacity to defend its territory (not only from Israel but from other potential aggressors as well) and the physical infrastructure of the state bureaucracy. For example, the Israeli military destroyed several buildings housing property and identification records. This creates a bureaucratic nightmare for the authorities. In addition to this wanton destruction, Israel has also adopted a new justification for its southern occupation of Syria under the guise of protecting Syria's Druze community. Except for a few opportunistic warlords, residents in southern Syria have overwhelmingly rejected Israel's occupation and continue to demand the withdrawal of the country's forces. However, Israel's declared intention to also "protect" Syria's Kurdish population has been met with some warmth by Syrian Kurdish leaders, who have publicly supported Israeli intervention into Syria's affairs. SDF General Mazloum Abdi even went so far as to say, "If [Israel] can prevent attacks against us and stop the killing of our people ... we welcome that and appreciate it."[19] Syrian Kurds' open collaboration with Israel will only hamper Syria's successful political transition.

Western powers have been much more cautious in their approach to the new Syrian reality. European leaders have visited the country and committed to supporting the transition. In late February 2025 the European Union took the important step of lifting its sanctions against Syrian. The United States has thus far not signaled an interest in terminating sanctions, but it has quietly lifted a $10 million reward for the arrest of Ahmed al-Sharaa (formerly Abu Mohammed al-Jolani) after a US delegation led by the assistant secretary of state for Near Eastern affairs visited Damascus in mid-December 2024. There appears to be little interest in the Trump administration in supporting Syrian reconstruction. The United Nations remains present in Syria, but it is largely peripheral to ongoing public discussions about the constitution or political transition. It appears, then, that Western powers and the United Nations are in a weaker position to exert influence over Syria's political transition than the country's neighbors.

GOVERNANCE AND DEMILITARIZATION

Syria's transitional authorities have repeatedly declared their intention to create a new constitutional structure to govern the country, one that would inevitably restructure many facets of Syrian political life, including state institutions, the judiciary, state-governorate relations, and the nature of Syrian citizenship. The euphoria caused by al-Assad's collapse will inevitably give way to the realities of governing a war-torn country that remains territorially fragmented with several armed groups exercising control in various territories. Hinnebusch's claim in the wake of the Arab uprisings that "it is . . . one thing to remove a leader and quite another to create stable and inclusive 'democratic' institutions" reminds us of both the immense challenges facing Syria and the divergent trajectories that the country may take in the wake of the regime's collapse.[20] In the interim transition period, al-Sharaa and his ministers have regularly signaled their intention to create a constitutional process that would bring different visions of Syria together in shared dialogue.

These constitutional encounters will certainly test the political power of the transitional authorities as well as the organizational capacity of various Syrian political and social forces that, at the time of writing, do not have institutional expression in the form of political parties. How will the power and interests of the religious establishment, business elites, warlords, returnees, and fragmented opposition be reflected in the dialogue over Syria's new constitution? What will the encounters between these forces mean for the new political structure in Syria? There is no clear path toward a new constitution and governance structure in Syria. New arenas for dialogue and encounters between different groups will have to emerge—even cosmetically—to give meaning to the process of constitutional and political change. The Syrian National Dialogue Conference held in February 2025 was a first attempt at this process, despite most observers deeming the conference an utter failure.[21] The National Dialogue Conference was the first major attempt to bring people together to discuss Syria's future. Its failure should only be understood as one moment in a long political trajectory that will be granular, frustrating, and certainly not linear.

A more immediate issue facing the authorities is how to initiate the demilitarization and demobilization of armed groups. The first major step in this direction occurred when transitional authorities announced the absorption of all armed groups, including HTS, into the national army. Deploying the language of sovereignty, the authorities have entered into agreements with several armed groups to disband their militia structures and remobilize their members into the national army. The settlement process described above targeting former regime soldiers and intelligence agents similarly seeks to separate those individuals and groups who are loyal to the transition authorities from those who are potential threats. The most obvious case is that of the SDF, which has insisted on retaining autonomy from the national army as a bargaining chip in its political negotiations with the transitional authorities over its future autonomous status. Warlords and militias in the country's South and North continue to exercise substantial influence in the locales under their control, and they are, similarly, refusing to abide by government decrees to disband, either as a bargaining tactic or simply out of a genuine sense of refusal. Finally, there remain remnants of the former regime and its loyalists who have organized into militias and have begun targeting people and symbols associated with the transitional authorities.

The continued presence of armed groups and militias will pose serious challenges to the transitional authorities. The encounters among these groups and between them and the state will both reflect and determine the state's capacity to project sovereignty throughout the country. The continued fragmentation of Syria and the control of pockets of territory by different groups would resemble the country's situation throughout most of the conflict. At risk here is not only the state's capacity to project sovereign power but the very real possibility that the state authorities are not able to project sovereign control outside the two major urban centers of Idlib and Damascus.

Managing Syria's Transition

This book has asked how the Syrian regime managed the conflict. This chapter similarly asked how the new authorities that emerged after the collapse of the regime will manage the political transition. From outside of the country, the HTS-led forces and SSG government became the symbol of the anti-regime forces when they declared themselves the new transitional authorities. The reality of the Syrian political landscape is much more complex. In addition to the several other armed groups and warlords unaligned with HTS that led the military campaign against the regime, there are hundreds of thousands, if not millions, of Syrians whose vision for the future of their country may be incompatible with the direction that the transitional authorities pursue. The issue here is not whether there are various options for how Syria's post-conflict politics will unfold, but how the current transition authorities will respond to, exclude, appropriate, or incorporate into the political structures of the country moving forward.

I have focused in this chapter on the brief transition period from December 8 to March 1 in order to identify some of the challenges facing Syria's authorities through the new political encounters occasioned by the regime's collapse. Questions of Syria's transition and its political future will be determined by the outcomes of these encounters between Syria's different social and political forces. From the vantage point of early 2025 it appears that the two major political forces remaining are the HTS-led federal government and the SDF-led Autonomous Administration of Northeastern Syria. If we consider the political transition to be determined solely by the negotiations between these two power centers then we ignore the very real, granular, and sometimes even bureaucratic ways that the conflict will continue to be litigated between different actors vying over property rights, reconstruction funds, transitional justice, and so on. The central government is today weaker than it has ever been, and this means that decentralized authorities in the governorates have a degree of latitude to enact new laws and practices that materialize transition in ways that may be incompatible with central state directives.

Syria's transition may thus follow several possible trajectories, most of which are impossible to fully understand barely a year into the transition. What we do know, however, is that the state will play a major role in shaping this trajectory and establishing the legal and political basis for the management of transition. The arguments in this book demonstrate how a specific form of conflict management can materialize an illiberal state oriented toward the suppression of conflict through punishment and the abandonment of negotiations and reconciliation with opposing groups. Similarly, the forms of transition management adopted by the Syrian authorities will materialize a state structure that acts on the lives of citizens in specific ways. Syria is in transition; how, to what, and where it is impossible to know without the benefit of hindsight. The questions informing this chapter, however, give us insight into what this transition will look like and the ways that different encounters around the challenges of dealing with the former regime, transitional justice, reconstruction and refugee repatriation, regional relations, and governance structures and demilitarization, will determine the transition's inevitably fraught trajectory.

Conclusion
Authoritarian Conflict Management and Its Legacies

> *In light of what history has taught us, it is too early to think of the Arab revolutions of 2011 as over or failed.*
>
> —LISA WEDEEN

Introduction

What are the political and affective legacies of the Syrian regime's conflict management strategies? How will Syria's future political authorities erase the vestiges of regime rule? What conflict management practices will persist into Syria's future? The state's management of conflict did not have absolute, universal effects on the citizenry, but instead constructed a terrain for state-citizen relations to unfold during wartime. This terrain was described by Ismail as a civil war regime in which the state was constantly at war with its citizens as it sought to produce the affect and subjectivity necessary for authoritarian rule. In this understanding of war, the state seeks to construct affect and subjectivity through violence. I have argued that the bureaucratization of war alongside its violent unfolding is also consequential in terms of how wartime Syrian subjectivity was constructed and governed. The regime's conflict management practices ensured that loyalty became the politically relevant cleavage that ran through Syrian society, separating Syrians into loyal and disloyal subjects.

Betrayal of the Homeland argues that the state sought to create a political order in the aftermath of violent conflict through the institutionalization of enmity and the targeting of disloyal subjects for various forms of punishment. While most literature on state punishment in Syria rightly focuses on the exercise of battlefield and carceral violence, I have argued that a parallel infrastructure of punishment existed through laws, institutions, and state practices that sought to exclude citizens categorized as disloyal. These categorizations exist in relation to a series of absences (from work, from home, from school), acts (social media posts, taking up arms), feelings (emotional betrayal of the homeland), and non-acts (failing to protect the homeland) that indexed a subject as disloyal. Over the course of the conflict, the categorizations that state officials used to narrate the conflict to the Syrian public were eventually given legal subjectivity and institutionalized through courts and laws oriented toward their punishment. To be categorized in a way that indexed disloyalty was to be subject to measures that effectively cast someone out from the body politic.

The arguments in this book bring together the regional and international dynamics of the conflict's trajectory alongside granular domestic transformations that oriented the state around the punishment of disloyal subjects. The Astana process made Syria's conflict management strategies possible by insulating the country from outside liberal intervention. The absence of a peace process or political solution allowed the state to envision an alternative that reflected its ideas about victory, reconciliation, and peace. These visions wholly excluded parts of the population deemed terrorist or disloyal. The spectral terrorist was constructed as the supreme state enemy at which enmity was directed. By expanding the definition of terrorism to include both violent and nonviolent acts as well as non-acts the state was able to cast a wide net in articulating who its enemies were and how they should be punished. I have shown how through the reconciliation and settlement processes a vision of Syria's future was enacted. This future was characterized by exclusion, violence, and appropriation. By extending enmity to absent Syrians, not just those willing to return or stay in Syria's national territory, the state was able to provide broad categorizations that could apply to all citizens. Once absence was codified as disloyalty the process of appropriation and casting out could be enacted.

Creating Political Order Through Conflict Management

Betrayal of the Homeland sheds light on the problem of how states manage conflict and seek to create durable political orders in the wake of violence. The arguments in this book demonstrate how a parallel narrative and legal war emerges alongside the violence of the battlefield and how states institutionalize the political hatred generated during conflict. In this way, this book orients our understanding of wartime Syria away from a focus on mass violence to understanding how states attempt to create political order out of conflict. In doing so, I hope that this book will provide context for scholars interested in the many institutional, political, and affective legacies of Syria's conflict and how the regime was able to persist amid rapidly deteriorating political conditions. I also hope that this book will compel scholars to inquire into the bureaucratic machinations of the Syrian regime and how the conflict reshaped the roles of party, state, and regime. The prospect of access to the vast state, party, and security archives occasioned by the regime's collapse will certainly expand how scholars can understand the figures and inner workings of the regime.

I have taken up several themes that are of interest to conflict scholars. The theme of conflict management shifts attention away from the battlefield to the effects on and machinations of state power during civil violence. How states create dense, continuous narratives about conflict that create a commonsense narration sheds insight into how conflict legacies materialize as institutions, laws, and practices toward certain populations. By thinking about conflict as existing along a continuum rather than having a beginning and an end we can also see how Syria's pre-2011 governance structures informed post-2011 conflict management practices and how these, in turn, contributed to different forms of power. The regional and international contexts in which all of this occurred have also been a major theme of the book and are reflective of new global power dynamics that influence conflict trajectories. Finally, I have highlighted the relational power dynamics between state institutions, localized power centers (such as civil committees), and security interests in enacting bureaucratic state power in wartime.

I have made several claims about how we think about authoritarian conflict management (ACM), specifically about how a conflict logic is absorbed by the state and materialized through practices and institutions that punish disloyal subjects. Advocates of liberal peace are often criticized for divorcing conflict resolution strategies from the ontologies of conflict. Universal approaches to peace and conflict resolution risk reproducing the power dynamics that created the conditions for conflict in the first place, producing illiberal or hybrid forms of peace, or creating altogether new terrains for conflict. Liberal peace strategies in the policy world have shaped how knowledge about conflict is produced in academia. Knowledge production about conflict ontologies and trajectories is often tethered to liberal visions of what conflicts should look like, rather than how they look in reality. One of the main motivations behind the ACM literature was to expand our understanding of war and peace by pointing to conflicts whose trajectories do not have easy liberal explanations. My arguments contribute to broadening our understanding of modern conflict by showing, first, the regional and international conditions of possibility for the creation of a non-liberal transition, and second, how a commonsense narrative of conflict materializes a bifurcation of society into loyal and disloyal subjects who are acted upon through various reward and punishment regimes. The story presented here is neither a liberal one about how conflicts begin and end nor a sectarian one explaining Syria's conflict trajectory, but rather a story about how an authoritarian regime managed conflict and punished its enemies away from the battlefield.

The regime's management of conflict encourages us to think anew about conflict in several ways. First, Syria's conflict demonstrates the existence of credible alternatives to the liberal management of peace and conflict. These alternatives offer incumbent regimes a set of norms, strategies, and alliances to ensure their survival at the expense of creating inclusive political orders in the wake of conflict. These alternatives have cohered not into global institutions, but as a set of disparate conflict management practices around the world that undermine liberalism's hegemony. Similarly, the Astana process provided a model for the regional management of conflict that has successfully peripheralized disinterested Western states and a frustrated United Nations conflict resolution apparatus. Turkey and Russia's cooperation in Libya, for example, has provided a credible competitor to liberal approaches to conflict resolution there.

The political strategy of managing rather than resolving conflict offers authoritarian states alternative methods of maintaining power amid civil conflict. Conflict management seeks to reduce violence to a containable simmer while maintaining incumbent regime power. Regional conflict management structures such as Astana provide political cover to forestall or prevent entirely forms of international intervention that, at best, could overthrow an incumbent regime or, at worst, dramatically reduce their share of power. In doing so, regional conflict management structures facilitate the continued targeting of state enemies and the denial of opposition political demands by incumbent regimes. In Syria's case, the collapsing of all anti-regime opposition into the category of "terrorists" allowed the regime to frame its conflict management strategies through its own "war on terror." These domestic conflict management strategies cohered with the Astana powers' specific political design for Syria, which maintained the country's territorial fragmentation and subjected all major battlefield decisions to tripartite consensus. Astana thus provided both the political and battlefield context for the regime to pursue a project of punishing disloyal subjects and demonstrated how regional states could cooperate to manage conflict through new deliberative structures and the proffering of new norms.

The second contribution this book makes is in locating conflict management practices along a historical continuum. The state's bifurcation of Syrians into disloyal and loyal and the enactment of punishment against the former has its antecedents in the Syrian civil war regime dating back to the 1960s. This trajectory should encourage us to think about conflict along a continuum and to reject teleological explanations for Syria's conflict and its periodization. In rejecting teleological views of conflict, we should also ask what contributes to the creation of violent, exclusionary political orders. I have tried to encourage scholars to consider what discourses, norms, laws, and institutions create the conditions for a political order grounded in enmity and political hatred of state enemies. The threat of or actual exercise of violence certainly helps us understand these questions, but durability extends beyond the battlefield and prison to the state bureaucracy, decentralized power constellations, and legal infrastructures that also sustain state rule. Here, a more banal form of politics is apparent when we read the *Official Gazette*, for example, which blandly details the hundreds and thousands of property expropriations each week. It is in the banal state declaration of asset appropriation and related acts of punishment that I believe we can locate the contours of the kind of political order the state sought to create.

Similarly, this book demonstrates how neo-patrimonial rule adapted to civil war and how decades of authoritarian learning about how to bifurcate and govern society helped the regime develop conflict management practices. The regime faced serious political and economic losses in the first years of conflict as territory fell to armed groups and business elites fled the country in droves. The entire structure of elite Syrian politics was reoriented around the effects of conflict, including the deaths, defections, and displacement of key figures in the networks that bound the state, party, economic elite, and security apparatus together. This, however, did not lead to the regime's collapse in the early years of the conflict. Instead, new centers of social and economic power were cultivated in a context of sanctions and metastasizing conflict. Economic elites who fled were quickly replaced on the boards of holding companies and chambers of commerce and industry by a new conflict elite that willingly seized the economic opportunities posed by Syria's war economies. Local elites in rural and peripheral areas were incorporated into the state project of conflict management through various civil committees that positioned them as state intermediaries. This not only enhanced their power vis-à-vis the state and local populations but also gave them direct access to the spoils of war that asset appropriation afforded. While many of these local elites had social standing within their communities prior to the war, it was their incorporation into the state project of punishing disloyal subjects that brought them into proximity with the security apparatus and state power.

The state project of punishing disloyal subjects through asset appropriation and forced divesture produced new forms of state power that linked local elites to the economic opportunities of conflict. The members of the civil committees responsible for categorizing absentees and initiating appropriation measures through the Ministry of Finance were often the first people to gain access to auctioned assets. Property auctions of appropriated assets became one mechanism for the regime to garner loyalty and support among new networks of power that emerged during the conflict. These networks benefiting from state appropriation varied widely, from the new conflict elite that took over the levers of Syria's economy, to the local elites represented in the civil committees, to members of the security apparatus, or simply enterprising and opportunistic businesspeople whose continued presence in the country indexed loyalty and provided access to the state's distribution of appropriated assets. The settlement process and its attendant bifurcation of the loyal and disloyal contributed to shaping the political economy of wartime Syria by providing the state with resources in the form of appropriated assets to distribute to loyalist networks.

A third contribution that this book makes to the study of conflict is in showing how a commonsense narrative of conflict materializes as a set of categorizations and attendant punishments that are institutionalized through new laws, government bodies, and courts. The study of Syrian state power has rightly focused on the exercise of violence (or the threat of it) and what this means for the citizenry. In this book, I have tried to take state discourse, laws, and institutional innovations seriously as indicators of how the conflict was narrated and rendered into a governance problem. If the bifurcating line between "us" and "them" has always shifted in Syria based on differing state enemies, then the conflict created altogether new conflict subjectivities from which the state could bifurcate and act upon enemies. Framing the conflict as a "war on terror" allowed the regime to situate the terrorist subject as a state enemy who had to be punished. From here flowed a series of other categorizations, such as the absent, the unreconciled, or the unsettled, that similarly indexed disloyalty. An expanding array of categories throughout the conflict allowed the state to collapse all disloyal subjects into the same punishment regime aimed at inflicting forms of social death on the citizenry by appropriating property, forbidding return, or preventing people from working, opening bank accounts, or receiving subsidies.

The creation of subjectivities tied to the commonsense narration of conflict meant that new legal categories emerged that corresponded to how state officials and everyday people spoke of the conflict. These legal categories included everything from those who were "deceived" to the "terrorist" to the "mentally unstable." These categories created the discursive and political conditions for either the condemnation of the disloyal subject or their repentance. On the one hand, the disloyal subject had to be carved out of the body politic as a punishment for their disloyalty. Some acts of disloyalty, such as terrorism, could never be forgiven and the terrorist subject had to be punished through imprisonment, murder, displacement, or appropriation. Their disloyalty was unforgiveable. On the other hand, a citizen could repent for their disloyalty by embracing state narratives about their deception and mental state when submitting themselves to the settlement process. The political function of punishing some while allowing others to repent was to aggravate the loyal-disloyal cleavage within society and to render people fearful of how to narrate their supposed disloyalty in ways that were consistent with the commonsense narrative of the conflict. The disloyal subject in Syria demonstrates how authoritarian states construct subjectivity and create societal cleavages in wartime. These cleavages not only create "us" and "them" categories but are also mobilized through the law and state institutions to subjectivize the population and govern them accordingly.

The strategies for population management, information gathering, and legal categorizations of different segments of the population form a fourth contribution this book makes. One of the central problems that any state has during wartime is how to generate knowledge about its population: Who are the loyalists? Who is fighting against the state? What are people's political beliefs? In Syria's case, the politically relevant cleavage running through society was loyalty/disloyalty. The state sought to generate information along a continuum that indexed people's actions as either loyal or disloyal. For the latter category, some acts and feelings could be forgiven, while others could not. Armed fighters, for example, were refused settlement for having "hands stained in Syrian blood." Conversely, a deserter could narrate his desertion as resulting from his "weak mental state" or "deception," thus inviting state forgiveness through repentance. The Syrian state's strategy to develop information about its population relied on two complementary approaches linking subjectivization to categorization. The first was by indexing physical presence in areas under state control as a form of loyalty and to categorize Syrians in areas outside of state control or outside of the country as disloyal. Here, absence was a proxy for disloyalty, presence a proxy for loyalty. Those not in areas under state control were thus acted upon as absentees and deserters whose absence was narrated and categorized as a betrayal of the homeland. The second strategy was to marshal denunciations gleaned through torture, imprisonment, the settlement process, or simply citizen reporting toward an ever-growing list of *matloobeen* (wanted) that allowed the state to identify people engaged in broad political activities against the homeland.

The state's population management strategies relied heavily on the violent extraction of information from the incarcerated but also the information generated by civil and settlement committees. Bifurcating society into loyal and disloyal created the specific conditions for governing loyal populations while punishing disloyal subjects. To do so, however, required the state to solve the supreme wartime problem of gathering information about its population. The state's strategy was primarily to index absence as disloyalty and to punish accordingly. It is important to emphasize again here that the bifurcation of Syrian society did not rely entirely on state violence and punishment away from the battlefield; it also depended on the continued acceptance of state rule by both loyalist populations and the "uncommitted centrists" whose ambivalence toward the regime contributed to its durability in the early years of conflict.[1] Loyalist and ambivalent subjects were politically "safe" because their presence inside of Syria was taken as a proxy for loyalty. Population management strategies that bifurcate and categorize different segments of the population provide insight into both how commonsense narratives materialize during wartime and how states construct enemy subjectivities.

Finally, the book contributes to the growing ACM literature by introducing Syria as a case study and expanding our understanding of spatial, discursive, and economic strategies of conflict management to include legal infrastructures. Debates about whether liberalism is dead, dying, or waning are inconsequential on the reality that liberal interveners are increasingly peripheralized in how states manage conflict and how their allies create forums to buttress these strategies. In this context, the literature on ACM is appealing because it encourages us to ask about the presence of something—authoritarian conflict management—rather than the absence of something—that of liberal intervention. By introducing the Syrian case to the literature on ACM this book should contribute to how scholars understand the repertoire of conflict management strategies deployed by authoritarian states, particularly how the discursive strategies to narrate conflict materialize in a set of punishment regimes targeting specific segments of the population. My emphasis on the importance of law, courts, and legal structures of appropriation is intended to complement how scholars think of conflict management strategies beyond the battlefield or carceral violence. The state's spatial division of society, for example, is buttressed by categorizations and appropriations that peripheralize disloyal populations and prevent their presence in areas under state control.

While this book offers insights into the expanding array of conflict management strategies deployed by authoritarian states it also gestures toward some of the major challenges facing countries after regime collapse. The literature on ACM is largely framed around the question of how conflict management strategies create the conditions for durable political order. Indeed, as I began this book, I was similarly interested in how the state was oriented around stability and durability in the wake of violent conflict. Questions about why regimes such as Syria's collapsed while others in Eurasia remain relatively stable will inform the work of scholars of Syria for decades to come. Of course, the answer to why the regime collapsed is an overdetermined one, as was the question of why the uprising began. Nevertheless, answers can certainly be found in the regime's inability to sufficiently manage simmering conflict over the long term. The strategies deployed against opposition armed groups and disloyal subjects was aimed at their total marginalization if not outright elimination from the body politic. In some cases, this bifurcation of society between loyal and disloyal has contributed to regime stability, while in Syria's case, over the long term at least, the state was unable to withstand continued pressures.

I have tried to encourage scholars to ask different questions about the Syrian conflict. How did people experience categorization as disloyal? How did Syrians choose between a hostile external environment and the fear of returning to the country? How do we understand paradoxes of state power alongside state weakness or failure?[2] How did informal networks of power, such as the civil committees, enact state power? What role did state institutions play in materializing the punishment of disloyal populations? How did a commonsense narrative of conflict materialize? And now that the regime has collapsed, what are the legacies of more than five decades of regime rule oriented around the punishment of state enemies and disloyal subjects?

The Future of Syria

Syria's future will largely be determined by how the political authorities address the legacies of regime rule and the fragmentations and traumas of the conflict. I have argued that the state created disloyal subjects who were punished away from the battlefield through forms of social death that prevented them from returning and living in Syria. These practices were aimed at preserving regime power throughout the conflict. While they ultimately failed, the regime's durability after 2011 was remarkable given the immense pressures arrayed against it. The political and legal afterlives of the punishment regimes that the state enacted to preserve regime power will persist into the future alongside the emotional scars that all Syrians carry. At the same time, Syria's territorial fragmentation will remain a major challenge when it comes to moving the country toward reconciliation. Initial agreements between the central government and the SDF in the Northeast and armed commanders in the Southwest are positive steps toward reconstituting Syria's territorial integrity. These agreements, however, are premised on a much more decentralized model of political power in the country. Decentralization will create localized power centers that are likely to control decisions over repatriation and restitution. It is at the level of the locality, then, where the continued contestation over the effects of the punishment of disloyal subjects may continue to take place.

Questions about where political power lies in Syria will also determine the forms of memory politics that emerge in the coming decades and how these victim/perpetrator binaries materialize. If a narrative of conflict shaped how the state functioned toward certain segments of the population rendered as enemies, then memories of the conflict are likely to similarly produce categorizations that inform Syria's future political system, especially around questions of justice and restitution. Revenge killings in the aftermath of the regime's collapse portend a scary future in which vengeance and vigilantism serve as substitutes for collective healing and justice. Similarly, forms of amnesia around state violence could serve to suppress memories and create the conditions for future tension among citizens. The work of creating collective memories of the conflict will be difficult. As in most post-conflict cases, the dominant memory narratives will coexist alongside complementary or contradictory individual and local memories. How these memories materialize into a political project of healing, justice, or revenge will largely shape Syria's future.

The transitional authorities' wholesale adoption of the state's settlement process to distinguish between "good" and "bad" elements of the regime signals a future in which the state's conflict management practices may be repurposed and deployed by Syria's new authorities. There is an apparent political utility in drawing on the regime's own tools of population management. If this is the case, and new state enemies emerge in the wake of the regime's collapse, then the vestiges of regime rule may take no longer to banish than some would hope.

Notes

Introduction

Epigraph: Achille Mbembe, *Necropolitics* (Duke University Press, 2019), 7.

1. "President Al-Assad: The War Was Between Us Syrians and Terrorism, We Triumph Together Not Against Each Other," Syrian Arab News Agency, February 17, 2019, https://www.sana.sy/en/?p=158819.
2. Samer Abboud, "'The Decision to Return to Syria Is Not in My Hands': Syria's Repatriation Regime as Illiberal Statebuilding," *Journal of Refugee Studies* 37, no. 1 (2023): 181–200, https://doi.org/10.1093/jrs/fead065.
3. John Heathershaw and Catherine Owen, "Authoritarian Conflict Management in Post-Colonial Eurasia," *Conflict, Security & Development* 19, no. 3 (May 4, 2019): 269–273, https://doi.org/10.1080/14678802.2019.1608022; David Lewis et al., "Illiberal Peace? Authoritarian Modes of Conflict Management," *Cooperation and Conflict* 53, no. 4 (2018): 486–506, https://doi.org/10.1177/0010836718765902; Philipp Lottholz et al., "Governance and Order-Making in Central Asia: From Illiberalism to Post-Liberalism?," *Central Asian Survey* 39, no. 3 (2020): 420–437, https://doi.org/10.1080/02634937.2020.1803794; David G. Lewis, "Sri Lanka's Schmittian Peace: Sovereignty, Enmity and Illiberal Order," *Conflict, Security & Development* 20, no. 1 (2020): 15–37, https://doi.org/10.1080/14678802.2019.1705067.
4. Catherine Owen et al., eds., *Interrogating Illiberal Peace in Eurasia: Critical Perspectives on Peace and Conflict* (Rowman and Littlefield, 2018).
5. Salwa Ismail, *The Rule of Violence: Subjectivity, Memory and Government in Syria* (Cambridge University Press, 2018); Lisa Blaydes, *State of Repression: Iraq Under Saddam Hussein* (Princeton University Press, 2018); Dina Rizk Khoury, *Iraq in Wartime: Soldiering, Martyrdom, and Remembrance* (Cambridge University Press, 2013).

6. David Lewis, "The Myopic Foucauldian Gaze: Discourse, Knowledge, and the Authoritarian Peace," *Journal of Intervention and Statebuilding* 11, no. 1 (2017): 35, https://doi.org/10.1080/17502977.2016.1276677.
7. Claire Q. Smith et al., "Illiberal Peace-Building in Asia: A Comparative Overview," *Conflict, Security & Development* 20, no. 1 (2020): 1–14, https://doi.org/10.1080/14678802.2019.1705066.
8. Ismail, *The Rule of Violence*.
9. Ismail.
10. "Country Profile: Syrian Arab Republic," Internal Displacement Monitoring Center, accessed July 18, 2025, https://www.internal-displacement.org/countries/syria/.
11. "Syrian Regional Refugee Response," United Nations High Commissioner for Refugees Operational Data Portal, accessed July 18, 2025, https://data.unhcr.org/en/situations/syria.
12. "Behind the Data: Recording Civilian Casualties in Syria," United Nations Office of the High Commissioner for Human Rights, May 11, 2023, https://www.ohchr.org/en/stories/2023/05/behind-data-recording-civilian-casualties-syria.
13. "Total Death Toll: Over 606,000 People Killed Across Syria Since the Beginning of the 'Syrian Revolution,' Including 495,000 Documented by SOHR," Syrian Organization for Human Rights, June 1, 2021, https://www.syriahr.com/en/217360/.
14. Jaber Baker and Ugur Ümit Üngör, *Syrian Gulag: Inside Assad's Prison System* (I. B. Tauris, 2023).
15. Maja Janmyr, "UNHCR and the Syrian Refugee Response: Negotiating Status and Registration in Lebanon," *International Journal of Human Rights* 22, no. 3 (2018): 393–419, https://doi.org/10.1080/13642987.2017.1371140.
16. Feyzi Baban et al., "Syrian Refugees in Turkey: Pathways to Precarity, Differential Inclusion, and Negotiated Citizenship Rights," *Journal of Ethnic and Migration Studies* 43, no. 1 (2017): 41–57, https://doi.org/10.1080/1369183X.2016.1192996.
17. Lamis Abdelaaty, "Refugees and Guesthood in Turkey," *Journal of Refugee Studies* 34, no. 3 (2021): 2827–2848, https://doi.org/10.1093/jrs/fez097.
18. See "Missing Migrants Project," International Organization for Migration, accessed July 18, 2025, https://missingmigrants.iom.int/region/mediterranean.
19. Samer Abboud, *Syria*, 1st ed. (Polity, 2015).
20. Samer Abboud, *Syria*, 2nd ed. (Polity, 2018).
21. Robin Yassin-Kassab and Leila Shami, *Burning Country: Syrians in Revolution and War* (Pluto Press, 2016); Yasser Munif, *The Syrian Revolution: Between the Politics of Life and the Geopolitics of Death* (Pluto Press, 2020).
22. Emile Hokayem, *Syria's Uprising and the Fracturing of the Levant* (Routledge, 2017); Christopher Phillips, *The Battle for Syria: International Rivalry in the New Middle East* (Yale University Press, 2020).
23. Josepha Ivanka Wessels, *Documenting Syria: Film-Making, Video Activism and Revolution* (I. B. Tauris, 2019); Donatella Della Ratta, *Shooting a Revolution: Visual Media and Warfare in Syria* (Pluto Press, 2018).

24. Wendy Pearlman, *We Crossed a Bridge and It Trembled: Voices from Syria* (Custom House, 2017); Rania Abouzeid, *No Turning Back: Life, Loss, and Hope in Wartime Syria* (W. W. Norton, 2018).
25. Sam Dagher, *Assad or We Burn the Country: How One Family's Lust for Power Destroyed Syria* (Little, Brown and Company, 2019); Samar Yazbeck, *A Woman in the Crossfire: Diaries of the Syrian Revolution*, trans. Max Weiss (Haus Publishing, 2012); Charles Glass, *Syria in Ashes* (Or Publishing, 2024).
26. Maja Janmyr, "Ethnographic Approaches and International Refugee Law," *Journal of Refugee Studies* 37, no. 4 (2024): 871–885, https://doi.org/10.1093/jrs/feac042; Arif Akgul et al., "Exploring the Victimization of Syrian Refugees Through the Human Security Model: An Ethnographic Approach," *Studies in Ethnicity and Nationalism* 21, no. 1 (2021): 46–66, https://doi.org/10.1111/sena.12338; Areej Al-Hamad et al., "Listening to the Voices of Syrian Refugee Women in Canada: An Ethnographic Insight Into the Journey from Trauma to Adaptation," *Journal of International Migration and Integration* 24, no. 3 (2023): 1017–1037, https://doi.org/10.1007/s12134-022-00991-w; An Van Raemdonck, "Syrian Refugee Men in 'Double Waithood': Ethnographic Perspectives on Labour and Marriage in Jordan's Border Towns," *Gender, Place & Culture* 30, no. 5 (2023): 692–713, https://doi.org/10.1080/0966369X.2023.2178390.
27. Şule Can, *Refugee Encounters at the Turkish-Syrian Border: Antakya at the Crossroads* (Routledge, 2019).
28. Phillips, *The Battle for Syria*.
29. Linda Matar and Ali Kadri, eds., *Syria: From National Independence to Proxy War* (Palgrave, 2019); Raymond Hinnebusch and Adham Saouli, *The War for Syria: Regional and International Dimensions of the Syrian Uprising* (Routledge, 2019); Christopher Phillips and Morten Valbjørn, "'What Is in a Name?': The Role of (Different) Identities in the Multiple Proxy Wars in Syria," *Small Wars & Insurgencies* 29, no. 3 (2018): 414–433, https://doi.org/10.1080/09592318.2018.1455328; Geraint Alun Hughes, "Syria and the Perils of Proxy Warfare," *Small Wars & Insurgencies* 25, no. 3 (2014): 522–538, https://doi.org/10.1080/09592318.2014.913542.
30. Asli Bâli and Aziz Rana, "The Wrong Kind of Intervention in Syria," in *The Land of Blue Helmets: The United Nations and the Arab World*, ed. Karim Makdisi and Vijay Prashad (University of California Press, 2017).
31. Alex J. Bellamy, *Syria Betrayed: Atrocities, War, and the Failure of International Diplomacy* (Columbia University Press, 2022); Fadi Nicholas Nassar, *UN Mediators in Syria: The Challenges and Responsibilities of Conflict Resolution* (Cambridge University Press, 2024).
32. Mona Yacoubian, "What Is Russia's Endgame in Syria? Lacking Better Options, Russia Appears to Be Pursuing a 'Spheres Of Influence' Model," United States Institute of Peace, February 16, 2021, https://www.usip.org/publications/2021/02/what-russias-endgame-syria; Julie Wilhelmsen, "Putin's Power Revisited: How Identity Positions and Great Power Interaction Condition Strategic Cooperation on Syria," *Europe-Asia Studies* 71, no. 7 (2019): 1091–1121, https://doi.org/10.1080

/09668136.2019.1602594; Anna Borshchevskaya, *Putin's War in Syria: Russian Foreign Policy and the Price of America's Absence* (I. B. Tauris, 2021).
33. Vera Mironova, *From Freedom Fighters to Jihadists: Human Resources of Non-State Armed Groups* (Oxford University Press, 2019).
34. Adam Baczko et al., *Civil War in Syria: Mobilization and Competing Social Orders* (Cambridge University Press, 2018).
35. Robin Yassin-Kassab and Leila al-Shami, *Burning Country: Syrians in Revolution and War*, 2nd ed. (Pluto Press, 2018).
36. Munif, *The Syrian Revolution*.
37. Dipali Mukhopadhyay and Kimberly Howe, *Good Rebel Governance* (Cambridge University Press, 2023).
38. Marwa Daoudy, *The Origins of the Syrian Conflict: Climate Change and Human Security* (Cambridge University Press, 2020).
39. Roschanack Shaery-Yazdi and Uğur Ümit Üngör, "Mass Violence in Syria: Continuity and Change," *British Journal of Middle Eastern Studies* 49, no. 3 (2022): 399, https://doi.org/10.1080/13530194.2021.1916146.
40. Uğur Ümit Üngör, "Forum: Mass Violence in Syria," *Journal of Genocide Research* 25, no. 1 (2023): 84–88, https://doi.org/10.1080/14623528.2021.1979907.
41. James Worrall and Victoria Penziner Hightower, "Methods in the Madness? Exploring the Logics of Torture in Syrian Counterinsurgency Practices," *British Journal of Middle Eastern Studies* 49, no. 3 (2022): 418–432, https://doi.org/10.1080/13530194.2021.1916154.
42. Baker and Üngör, *Syrian Gulag*.
43. Üngör, "Forum," 84.
44. Ora Szekely, *Syria Divided: Patterns of Violence in a Complex Civil War* (New York: Columbia University Press, 2023), 2.
45. Szekely, 12.
46. Szekely, 17.
47. Josepha Wessels, "Killing the Dispensables: Massacres Perpetrated in the Villages of Eastern Aleppo Province in 2013," *British Journal of Middle Eastern Studies* 49, no. 3 (2022): 463–485, https://doi.org/10.1080/13530194.2021.1920267.
48. Uğur Ümit Üngör, "Shabbiha: Paramilitary Groups, Mass Violence and Social Polarization in Homs," *Violence: An International Journal* 1, no. 1 (2020): 59–79, https://doi.org/10.1177/2633002420907771; Samer Jabbour and Nasser Fardousi, "Violence Against Health Care in Syria: Patterns, Meanings, Implications," *British Journal of Middle Eastern Studies* 49, no. 3 (2022): 403–417, https://doi.org/10.1080/13530194.2021.1916153; Haian Dukhan, "The ISIS Massacre of the Sheitat Tribe in Der Ez-Zor, August 2014," *Journal of Genocide Research* 25, no. 1 (2023): 113–121, https://doi.org/10.1080/14623528.2021.1979912; Ali Aljasem, "Queiq: The River That Streamed Bodies in Aleppo," *Journal of Genocide Research* 25, no. 1 (2023): 104–112, https://doi.org/10.1080/14623528.2021.1979911; Wessels, "Killing the Dispensables."

49. Ismail, *The Rule of Violence*.
50. Ismail, 1.
51. Sabrina Melenotte, "Perpetrating Violence Viewed from the Perspective of the Social Sciences: Debates and Perspectives," *Violence: An International Journal* 1, no. 1 (2020): 40–58, https://doi.org/10.1177/2633002420924963.
52. Gary Uzonyi, "Bureaucratic Quality and the Severity of Genocide and Politicide," *Dynamics of Asymmetric Conflict* 13, no. 2 (2020): 125–142, https://doi.org/10.1080/17467586.2019.1650387.
53. Ismail, *The Rule of Violence*, 2.
54. Jon D. Unruh, "Weaponization of the Land and Property Rights System in the Syrian Civil War: Facilitating Restitution?," *Journal of Intervention and Statebuilding* 10, no. 4 (2016): 453–471, https://doi.org/10.1080/17502977.2016.1158527.
55. Christopher Phillips, "Sectarianism and Conflict in Syria," *Third World Quarterly* 36, no. 2 (2015): 357–376, https://doi.org/10.1080/01436597.2015.1015788.
56. Samer Bakkour, "Beyond Genocide: Towards an Improved Analysis and Understanding of the Syrian Regime's Mass Atrocity Crimes in the Syrian Civil War," *Digest of Middle East Studies* 32, no. 4 (2023): 300–320, https://doi.org/10.1111/dome.12304.
57. Leon Goldsmith, *Cycle of Fear: Syria's Alawites in War and Peace* (Hurst, 2015).
58. Lewis et al., "Illiberal Peace?," 491.
59. Lewis et al., 491. My emphasis.
60. Lewis et al.
61. Lewis et al.
62. Lewis et al.
63. Lewis et al., 494.
64. Lewis et al.
65. Lewis et al., 498.
66. Rungrawee Chalermsripinyorat, "Dialogue Without Negotiation: Illiberal Peace-Building in Southern Thailand," *Conflict, Security & Development* 20, no. 1 (2020): 71–95, https://doi.org/10.1080/14678802.2019.1705069.
67. Mbembe, *Necropolitics*.
68. Carl Schmitt, *The Concept of the Political* (University of Chicago Press, 2007), 26.
69. Lewis, "Sri Lanka's Schmittian Peace."
70. Achille Mbembe, "The Society of Enmity," *Radical Philosophy*, no. 200 (November–December 2016): 24, https://www.radicalphilosophy.com/article/the-society-of-enmity.
71. Mbembe, 26. My emphasis.
72. Mbembe, 27.
73. Mbembe, *Necropolitics*.
74. Khoury, *Iraq in Wartime*, 1.
75. Khoury, 2.
76. Khoury.

77. Samer Abboud, "Conflict Absorption and the Paradox of State Power in Syria," *Syria Studies* 16, no. 1 (2025), https://ojs.st-andrews.ac.uk/index.php/syria/article/view/2868/2161.
78. Joseph Daher, "Expelled from the Support System: Austerity Deepens in Syria," *Middle East Directions Programme Blog*, February 15, 2022, https://blogs.eui.eu/medirections/expelled-from-the-support-system-austerity-deepens-in-syria/.
79. Ismail, *The Rule of Violence*.
80. Samer Abboud, "Syria's Repressive Peace," in *Struggles for Political Change in the Arab World*, ed. Hesham Sallam et al. (University of Michigan Press, 2022), 124–147.
81. Smith et al., "Illiberal Peace-Building in Asia," 4.
82. Smith et al., 4.
83. Samuel Helfont, *Iraq Against the World: Saddam, America, and the Post-Cold War Order* (Oxford University Press, 2023); Samuel Helfont, *Compulsion in Religion: Saddam Hussein, Islam, and the Roots of Insurgencies in Iraq* (Oxford University Press, 2018); Blaydes, *State of Repression*.
84. Moyukh Chatterjee, *Composing Violence: The Limits of Exposure and the Making of Minorities* (Duke University Press, 2023).
85. Chatterjee.
86. Chatterjee, 4.
87. Chatterjee.

1. The Astana Process and the Regional Context of Conflict Management

Epigraph: "Astana Process Most Effective Move for Political Solution in Syria: Erdogan," Islamic Republic News Agency, July 20, 2022, https://en.irna.ir/news/84827431/Astana-process-most-effective-move-for-political-solution-in.

1. Emel Parlar Dal, "Rising Powers in International Conflict Management: An Introduction," *Third World Quarterly* 39, no. 12 (2018): 2207–2221, https://doi.org/10.1080/01436597.2018.1503048.
2. Xinyu Yuan, "The Chinese Approach to Peacebuilding: Contesting Liberal Peace?," *Third World Quarterly* 43, no. 7 (2022): 1798–1816, https://doi.org/10.1080/01436597.2022.2074389.
3. Kwok Chung Wong, "The Rise of China's Developmental Peace: Can an Economic Approach to Peacebuilding Create Sustainable Peace?," *Global Society* 35, no. 4 (2021): 522–540, https://doi.org/10.1080/13600826.2021.1942802.
4. Özker Kocadal, "Emerging Power Liminality in Peacebuilding: Turkey's Mimicry of the Liberal Peace," *International Peacekeeping* 26, no. 4 (2019): 431–456, https://doi.org/10.1080/13533312.2019.1615575.
5. Kristian Stokke, "Crafting Liberal Peace? International Peace Promotion and the Contextual Politics of Peace in Sri Lanka," *Annals of the Association of American Geographers* 99, no. 5 (2009): 932–939, https://doi.org/10.1080/00045600903245920.

6. Bayram Balci and Nicolas Monceau, eds., *Turkey, Russia and Iran in the Middle East* (Springer International Publishing, 2021), https://doi.org/10.1007/978-3-030-80291-2.
7. Stephen Lubkemann, *Culture in Chaos: An Anthropology of the Social Condition in War* (University of Chicago Press, 2007).
8. For the former, see Mary Kaldor et al., "Local Agreements—an Introduction to the Special Issue," *Peacebuilding* 10, no. 2 (2022): 107–121, https://doi.org/10.1080/21647259.2022.2042111; for the latter, Santiago Sosa, "The Micro-Dynamics of Conflict and Peace: Evidence from Colombia," *International Interactions* 49, no. 2 (2023): 163–170, https://doi.org/10.1080/03050629.2023.2189705.
9. Milena Dieckhoff, "Reconsidering the Humanitarian Space: Complex Interdependence Between Humanitarian and Peace Negotiations in Syria," *Contemporary Security Policy* 41, no. 4 (2020): 564–586, https://doi.org/10.1080/13523260.2020.1773025.
10. Nazih Richani, "The Political Economy and Complex Interdependency of the War System in Syria," *Civil Wars* 18, no. 1 (2016): 45–68, https://doi.org/10.1080/13698249.2016.1144495.
11. Line Khatib, "Syria, Saudi Arabia, the U.A.E. and Qatar: The 'Sectarianization' of the Syrian Conflict and Undermining of Democratization in the Region," *British Journal of Middle Eastern Studies* 46, no. 3 (2019): 385–403, https://doi.org/10.1080/13530194.2017.1408456.
12. "Syria Conflict Update," Carter Center, October 30, 2015, https://www.cartercenter.org/resources/pdfs/peace/conflict_resolution/syria-conflict/syria-conflict-update-103015.pdf.
13. Samer Abboud, "Conflict, Governance, and Decentralized Authority in Syria," in *The Levant in Turmoil: Syria, Palestine, and the Transformation of Middle Eastern Politics*, ed. Martin Beck et al. (Palgrave, 2016), 57–77.
14. Christopher Phillips, *The Battle for Syria: International Rivalry in the New Middle East*, 2nd ed. (Yale University Press, 2020).
15. Samer Abboud, "Social Change, Network Formation and Syria's War Economies," *Middle East Policy* 24, no. 1 (2017): 92–107, https://doi.org/10.1111/mepo.12254.
16. Richani, "The Political Economy and Complex Interdependency of the War System in Syria."
17. Ohannes Geukjian, *The Russian Military Intervention in Syria* (McGill-Queen's University Press, 2022); Babak Rezvani, "Russian Foreign Policy and Geopolitics in the Post-Soviet Space and the Middle East: Tajikistan, Georgia, Ukraine and Syria," *Middle Eastern Studies* 56, no. 6 (2020): 878–899, https://doi.org/10.1080/00263206.2020.1775590.
18. "Analyzing Shifts in Territorial Control Within Syria Offers Glimpse of Future Challenges," Carter Center, May 13, 2020, https://www.cartercenter.org/news/features/p/conflict_resolution/syria-mapping-shifts-in-territorial-control.html.
19. "Russian Airstrikes Update," Carter Center, January 29, 2016, https://www.cartercenter.org/resources/pdfs/peace/conflict_resolution/syria-conflict/Russian-Airstrikes-Update-Jan-29-2016.pdf.

20. Raymond Hinnebusch and I. William Zartman, *UN Mediation in the Syrian Crisis: From Kofi Annan to Lakhdar Brahimi* (International Peace Institute, March 2016), https://www.ipinst.org/wp-content/uploads/2016/03/IPI-Rpt-Syrian-Crisis2.pdf.
21. Aslı Bâli and Aziz Rana, "The Wrong Kind of Intervention in Syria," in *Land of Blue Helmets: The United Nations and the Arab World*, ed. Karim Makdisi and Vijay Prashad (University of California Press, 2017), 115.
22. Alexander Kentikelenis and Erik Voeten, "Legitimacy Challenges to the Liberal World Order: Evidence from United Nations Speeches, 1970–2018," *Review of International Organizations* 16, no. 4 (2021): 721–754, https://doi.org/10.1007/s11558-020-09404-y.
23. Outi Keranen, "Building States and Identities in Post-Conflict States: Symbolic Practices in Post-Dayton Bosnia," *Civil Wars* 16, no. 2 (2014): 127–146, https://doi.org/10.1080/13698249.2014.904984.
24. Megan Bradley, *Refugee Repatriation: Justice, Responsibility and Redress* (Cambridge University Press, 2013).
25. Karim Makdisi and Coralie Pison Hindawi, "The Syrian Chemical Weapons Disarmament Process in Context: Narratives of Coercion, Consent, and Everything in Between," *Third World Quarterly* 38, no. 8 (2017): 1691–1709, https://doi.org/10.1080/01436597.2017.1322462.
26. Pınar Akpınar, "The Limits of Mediation in the Arab Spring: The Case of Syria," *Third World Quarterly* 37, no. 12 (2016): 2288–2303, https://doi.org/10.1080/01436597.2016.1218273.
27. Akpınar.
28. "Press Remarks by UN Special Envoy for Syria, Mr. Staffan de Mistura, in Astana, Kazakhstan, 24 January 2017," United Nations Office for the Special Envoy for Syria, January 24, 2017, https://reliefweb.int/report/syrian-arab-republic/press-remarks-un-special-envoy-syria-mr-staffan-de-mistura-astana.
29. Fadi Nicholas Nassar, *UN Mediators in Syria: The Challenges and Responsibilities of Conflict Resolution* (Cambridge University Press, 2024).
30. Nassar.
31. Bâli and Rana, "The Wrong Kind of Intervention in Syria."
32. Samer Abboud, "Making Peace to Sustain War: The Astana Process and Syria's Illiberal Peace," *Peacebuilding* 9, no. 3 (2021): 326–343, https://doi.org/10.1080/21647259.2021.1895609.
33. Irene Costantini and Ruth Hanau Santini, "Power Mediators and the 'Illiberal Peace' Momentum: Ending Wars in Libya and Syria," *Third World Quarterly* 43, no. 1 (2022): 131–147, https://doi.org/10.1080/01436597.2021.1995711.
34. Seçkin Köstem, "Russian-Turkish Cooperation in Syria: Geopolitical Alignment with Limits," *Cambridge Review of International Affairs* 34, no. 6 (2021): 795–817, https://doi.org/10.1080/09557571.2020.1719040.
35. Kocadal, "Emerging Power Liminality in Peacebuilding."
36. Kocadal.

37. Abboud, "Making Peace to Sustain War."
38. Samer Abboud, "Imagining Localism in Post-Conflict Syria: Prefigurative Reconstruction Plans and the Clash Between Liberal Epistemology and Illiberal Conflict," *Journal of Intervention and Statebuilding* 15, no. 4 (2021): 543–561, https://doi.org/10.1080/17502977.2020.1829360.
39. David Rieff, "A New Age of Liberal Imperialism?," *World Policy Journal* 16, no. 2 (1999): 1–10, https://www.jstor.org/stable/40209622.
40. "Can the Astana Agreement End the Syrian War?" [in Arabic], *Annabaa*, May 7, 2017, https://annabaa.org/arabic/reports/10894.
41. Abboud, "Making Peace to Sustain War."
42. Ilsur Nafikov and Rinat Nabiev, "The Astana Process as an International Platform for Middle Eastern Regional Security: The Russian Mission," in *Contemporary Turkish-Russian Relations from Past to Future*, ed. İlyas Topsakal and Ali Askerov (Istanbul University Press, 2021), 197–212, https://doi.org/10.26650/B/SS52.2021.011.10.
43. Nafikov and Nabiev.
44. Abboud, "Making Peace to Sustain War."
45. Zenonas Tziarras, *Ethical Issues and Controversies in the Astana Process: Questioning Representation and Ownership*, FAIR Case Brief 4 (Peace Research Institute Oslo, 2022), 6, https://www.prio.org/publications/13046.
46. Andrey Kortunov, "The Astana Model: Methods and Ambitions of Russian Political Action," in *The MENA Region: A Great Power Competition*, ed. Karim Mezran and Arturo Varvelli (ISPI and Atlantic Council, 2019), 53–63.
47. Lars Hauch, *Mixing Politics and Force Syria's Constitutional Committee in Review*, CRU Report (Netherlands Institute of International Relations Clingendael, 2020), https://www.clingendael.org/pub/2020/the-politics-of-syrias-constitutional-committee/.
48. Karam Shaar and Ayman Dasouki, "Syria's Constitutional Committee: The Devil in the Detail," Middle East Institute, January 6, 2021, https://www.mei.edu/publications/syrias-constitutional-committee-devil-detail.
49. Shaar and Dasouki.

2. The Spectral Terrorist as State Enemy

Epigraphs: Achille Mbembe, *Necropolitics* (Duke University Press, 2019), 49; James T. Siegel, *A New Criminal Type in Jakarta: Counter-Revolution Today* (Duke University Press, 1998), 1.

1. "Walid Moallem at Press Conference: Combatting Terrorism Is a Duty of Every Syrian to Protect Their Land and Homeland" [in Arabic], *Dam Press*, February 14, 2014, https://www.dampress.net/mobile/?page=show_det&category_id=5&id=39328&_x_tr_sl=en&_x_tr_tl=ar&_x_tr_hl=en&_x_tr_pto=wapp.

2. Lisa Blaydes, *State of Repression: Iraq Under Saddam Hussein* (Princeton University Press, 2018); Dina Rizk Khoury, *Iraq in Wartime: Soldiering, Martyrdom, and Remembrance* (Cambridge University Press, 2013).
3. Lisa Wedeen, *Ambiguities of Domination: Politics, Rhetoric, and Symbols in Contemporary Syria* (University of Chicago Press, 2015).
4. Salwa Ismail, *Political Life in Cairo's New Quarters: Encountering the Everyday State* (University of Minnesota Press, 2006).
5. Interview with author, July 8, 2022. In order to preserve speakers' anonymity, names and identifying details have been withheld from all interviews cited in the notes.
6. Blaydes, *State of Repression*.
7. Blaydes.
8. Charles Glass, *Syria Burning: A Short History of a Catastrophe* (Verso, 2016); Kevin Mazur, *Revolution in Syria: Identity, Networks, and Repression* (Cambridge University Press, 2021); Leon Goldsmight, *Cycle of Fear: Syria's Alawites in War and Peace* (Hurst, 2015).
9. Salwa Ismail, *The Rule of Violence: Subjectivity, Memory and Government in Syria* (Cambridge University Press, 2018).
10. Ismail, 9.
11. Ismail, 18.
12. Ismail, 31–32.
13. Haian Dukhan, *State and Tribes in Syria: Informal Alliances and Conflict Patterns* (Routledge, 2018).
14. Ismail, *The Rule of Violence*.
15. Ismail, 160.
16. Ismail.
17. Ismail.
18. Blaydes, *State of Repression*.
19. Blaydes; Khoury, *Iraq in Wartime*.
20. Samer Abboud, "Reconciling Fighters, Settling Civilians: The Making of Post-Conflict Citizenship in Syria," *Citizenship Studies* 24, no. 6 (2020): 751–768, https://doi.org/10.1080/13621025.2020.1720608.
21. Abboud.
22. Catherine Owen et al., eds., *Interrogating Illiberal Peace in Eurasia: Critical Perspectives on Peace and Conflict* (Rowman and Littlefield, 2018).
23. Sean Lee, "How Bashar Al-Asad Learned to Stop Worrying and Love the 'War on Terror,'" *International Studies Quarterly* 68, no. 2 (2024): sqae066, https://doi.org/10.1093/isq/sqae066.
24. David Lewis et al., "Illiberal Peace? Authoritarian Modes of Conflict Management," *Cooperation and Conflict* 53, no. 4 (2018): 486–506, https://doi.org/10.1177/0010836718765902.
25. Lewis et al.
26. Lewis et al.

27. Samer Abboud, "Narrating Crisis Through the Loyalist Witness," *Middle East Journal of Culture and Communication* 16, no. 1 (2023): 1–19, https://doi.org/10.1163/18739865-tat00003.
28. Lee, "How Bashar Al-Asad Learned to Stop Worrying and Love the 'War on Terror'"; Alice Martini, "The Syrian Wars of Words: International and Local Instrumentalisations of the War on Terror," *Third World Quarterly* 41, no. 4 (2020): 725–743, https://doi.org/10.1080/01436597.2019.1699784.
29. "A Unified Stance Rejects Attacking Iraq" [in Arabic], *Al Jazeera*, February 18, 2002, https://www.aljazeera.net/news/presstour/2002/2/18/العراق-ضرب-يرفض-موحد-موقف.
30. "Guarantor States of the Cessation of Hostilities Agreement: Supporting the Sovereignty and Unity of Syria" [in Arabic], Syrian Arab News Agency, April 5, 2018, https://archive.sana.sy/?p=734747.
31. Nasir Qandil, "Putin and Assad . . . and Roosevelt and Stalin—al-Thawra Newspaper" [in Arabic], Syrian Arab News Agency, October 23, 2015, https://archive.sana.sy/?p=287488.
32. Lee, "How Bashar Al-Asad Learned to Stop Worrying and Love the 'War on Terror.'"
33. Toufiq al-Madani, *The Nationalist Syrian State and the War on Terror* [in Arabic] (Syrian National Book Authority, 2018).
34. Al-Madani.
35. "'The War on Syria Has Failed,' Foreign Minister Says in UN Speech, Denouncing the West's Hegemonic Ambitions," *UN News*, September 22, 2022, https://news.un.org/en/story/2022/09/1128011.
36. "Kremlin: The Syrian Arab Army Is the Only Force Capable of Combatting Terrorism on the Ground" [in Arabic], Syrian Arab News Agency, November 27, 2015, https://archive.sana.sy/?p=303771.
37. Ismail, *The Rule of Violence*.
38. Violations Documentation Center, *Counter-Terrorism Court: A Tool for War Crimes: Special Report on Counter-Terrorism Law No. 19 and the Counter-Terrorism Court in Syria* (Violations Documentation Center, April 2015), https://icct.nl/sites/default/files/import/publication/1430186775-English.pdf.
39. Syrian Arab Republic Parliament, "Law No. 19 of 2012, the Anti-Terrorism Law" [in Arabic] (2012), http://www.parliament.gov.sy/arabic/index.php?node=55151&nid=4306&First=0&Last=23&CurrentPage=0&mid=&refBack=.
40. Syrian Arab Republic Parliament, "Law No. 20 of 2012 Dismisses from State Service Anyone Convicted by Court Decision of Committing Any Terrorist Act" [in Arabic] (2012), http://www.parliament.gov.sy/arabic/index.php?node=201&nid=4307&ref=tree&.
41. Syrian Arab Republic Parliament, "Legislative Decree No. 20 of 2013 Criminalizing and Punishing the Kidnapping of Persons" [in Arabic] (2012), http://www.parliament.gov.sy/arabic/index.php?node=55151&cat=4278; Syrian Arab Republic Parliament, "Law No. 21 of 2012 Amending the Penal Code 556 Issued by Decree No. 148 of 1949" [in Arabic] (2012), http://www.parliament.gov.sy/arabic/index.php?node=57151&.

42. Syrian Arab Republic Parliament, "Establishing a Court to Prosecute Terrorism Cases Law No. 22 of 2012 Based in Damascus" [in Arabic] (2012), http://parliament.gov.sy/arabic/index.php?node=201&nid=4304&ref=tree&.
43. Haid Haid, "The Syrian Regime Is Pursuing Its Opponents Through the Use of a Loophole—Private Prosecution," *Syndication Bureau*, July 1, 2019.
44. Abdel Rahman al-Khader, "Human Rights Report: About 1000 Syrians Tried in Counter-Terrorism Court" [in Arabic], *Al-Araby*, October 15, 2020, https://www.alaraby.co.uk/politics/تقرير-حقوقي-نحو-11-ألف-سوري-يخضعون-لمحكمة-قضايا-الإرهاب.
45. Abir Haider, "In Syria, a 'Terrorism Court'" [in Arabic], *As-Safir al-Araby*, January 22, 2014, https://assafirarabi.com/ar/2839/2014/01/22/محكمة-الإرهاب-في-سوريا/.
46. Violations Documentation Center, *Counter-Terrorism Court*, 12.
47. Violations Documentation Center.
48. "Decree to Reconstitute Counter-Terrorism Court" [in Arabic], *Shaam Times*, March 2019, https://www.shaamtimes.net/300675/مرسوم-بإعادة-تشكيل-محكمة-قضايا-الإرهاب/.
49. Dourayd Salloum, "Decree to Reconstitute the Counter Terrorism Court and Appoint Investigative Judges and Prosecutors" [in Arabic], *Syrian Days*, February 25, 2020, https://www.syriandays.com/index.php?page=show_det&select_page=50&id=61312.
50. Haider, "In Syria, a 'Terrorism Court.'"
51. Kamal Sheikho, "Interview with Lawyer and Human Rights Activist Michel Shamas" [in Arabic], *Suwar Magazine*, November 2, 2015, https://www.suwar-magazine.org/articles/1138/مجلة-34صو-ر-34تحاور-المحامي-والحقوقي-ميشيل-شماس.
52. Violations Documentation Center, *Counter-Terrorism Court*.
53. Violations Documentation Center, *Counter-Terrorism Court*; Nael Georges, "The Syrian Regime Legal 'Reforms' (III) Security vs. Counterterrorism Courts: Different Names, Same Function," Legal Agenda, January 10, 2014, https://english.legal-agenda.com/the-syrian-regime-legal-reforms-iii-security-vs-counterterrorism-courts-different-names-same-function/; "Syria: Counterterrorism Court Used to Stifle Dissent," Human Rights Watch, June 25, 2013, https://www.hrw.org/news/2013/06/25/syria-counterterrorism-court-used-stifle-dissent.
54. Manal Munjid, "Criminal Prosecution of Terrorism Crimes in Syrian Law (an Analytical Study)" [in Arabic], *Damascus University Journal for Economic and Legal Studies*, no. 2 (2014), https://www.damascusuniversity.edu.sy/mag/law/images/stories/2-2014/ar/103-148.pdf.
55. Munjid.
56. Munjid.
57. Jad al-Karim al-Jabaae, "Parallel Society: A Background to Understanding What Is Happening in Syria" [in Arabic], *Omran* 3, no. 7 (2014), https://omran.dohainstitute.org/ar/issue007/Pages/jadkharimjabay.pdf.
58. Al-Jabaae, 104.
59. Al-Jabaae, 108.
60. Khaled Khalifa, *Death Is Hard Work*, trans. Leri Price (Farrar, Straus and Giroux, 2019).

61. Blaydes, *State of Repression*.
62. Lewis et al., "Illiberal Peace? Authoritarian Modes of Conflict Management," 25.
63. Lewis et al.
64. Siegel, *A New Criminal Type in Jakarta*.
65. Interview with author, April 20, 2022.
66. Interview with author, April 20, 2022.
67. Hazem Mustafa, "/تجارة-معتقلي-الإرهاب-كيف-تصبح-إرهابيا/," *Syria Untold*, December 4, 2017, https://syriauntold.com/2017/12/04.

3. The Reconciliation Process

Epigraph: "Assad Pledges to Regain Control of Northern Syria by Force If Needed," Reuters, June 24, 2018. https://www.reuters.com/article/world/assad-pledges-to-regain-control-of-northern-syria-by-force-if-needed-idUSKBN1JK0JV/.

1. Personal communication, January 25, 2018.
2. Samer Abboud, "Imagining Localism in Post-Conflict Syria: Prefigurative Reconstruction Plans and the Clash Between Liberal Epistemology and Illiberal Conflict," *Journal of Intervention and Statebuilding* 15, no. 4 (2021): 543–561, https://doi.org/10.1080/17502977.2020.1829360.
3. Kristian Stokke, "Crafting Liberal Peace? International Peace Promotion and the Contextual Politics of Peace in Sri Lanka," *Annals of the Association of American Geographers* 99, no. 5 (2009): 932–939, https://doi.org/10.1080/00045600903245920.
4. Samer Abboud, "Making Peace to Sustain War: The Astana Process and Syria's Illiberal Peace," *Peacebuilding* 9, no. 3 (2021): 326–343, https://doi.org/10.1080/21647259.2021.1895609.
5. Anika Oettler and Angelika Rettberg, "Varieties of Reconciliation in Violent Contexts: Lessons from Colombia," *Peacebuilding* 7, no. 3 (2019): 329–352, https://doi.org/10.1080/21647259.2019.1617029.
6. Giulia Piccolino, review of *Winning Wars, Building (Illiberal) Peace? The Rise (and Possible Fall) of a Victor's Peace in Rwanda and Sri Lanka*, ed. Scott Straus et al., *Third World Quarterly* 36, no. 9 (2015): 1770–1785, http://www.jstor.org/stable/24523149.
7. George Joffé, "National Reconciliation and General Amnesty in Algeria," *Mediterranean Politics* 13, no. 2 (2008): 213–228, https://doi.org/10.1080/13629390802127539.
8. Burcu Özçelik, "What Can a Political Form of Reconciliation Look Like in Divided Societies?," *Democratic Theory* 9, no. 1 (2022): 52–72, https://doi.org/10.3167/dt.2022.090104.
9. Darrel Moellendorf, "Reconciliation as a Political Value," *Journal of Social Philosophy* 38, no. 2 (2007): 205–221, https://doi.org/10.1111/j.1467-9833.2007.00375.x.
10. Janine Natalya Clark, "National Unity and Reconciliation in Rwanda: A Flawed Approach?," *Journal of Contemporary African Studies* 28, no. 2 (2010): 137–154, https://doi.org/10.1080/02589001003736793.

11. Clark.
12. May Hamidouche, "From the Pen of May Hamidouche . . ." [in Arabic], *Dam Press*, May 15, 2014, https://www.dampress.net/mobile/?page=show_det&category_id=28&id=43955&lang=ar.
13. "Syrian Government Ends Reconciliation System," North Press Agency, October 23, 2020. https://npasyria.com/en/48653/.
14. "The Regime's Parliament Has Decided to Suspend National Reconciliation" [in Arabic], *Syria TV*, October 22, 2020.
15. "Haidar: Words Are the Most Effective Means of Achieving True National Reconciliation" [in Arabic], Syrian Arab News Agency, April 5, 2017, https://archive.sana.sy/?p=533776.
16. "People's Assembly Discusses the Performance of the Ministry of National Reconciliation and the Expansion of Local Reconciliations" [in Arabic], Syrian Arab News Agency, March 6, 2016, https://archive.sana.sy/?p=347987.
17. Rim Turkmani, "Local Agreements as a Process: The Example of Local Talks in Homs in Syria," *Peacebuilding* 10, no. 2 (2022): 156–171, https://doi.org/10.1080/21647259.2022.2032941.
18. "On the Ministry of Oil's Investment Budget and the Work of the Ministry of National Reconciliation" [in Arabic], Syrian Arab News Agency, November 12, 2018, https://pministry.gov.sy/contents/13904/contents/14243/م-في-الحسابات-و الموازنة-لجنة جلس-الشعب-تناقش-مشروع-قانون-الموازنة-العامة-للدولة-لعام-2019 مع-وزارات-الصناعة،الزراعة،الموارد- المائية،النفط،النقل،السياحة،الأوقاف،الصحة.
19. Jeffrey T. Checkel, "Socialization and Violence," *Journal of Peace Research* 54, no. 5 (2017): 592–605, https://doi.org/10.1177/0022343317721813.
20. "Video: Launching the Civi Initiative for Local Reconciliation" [in Arabic], Syrian Arab News Agency, September 5, 2023, https://sana.sy/?p=379699.
21. Jenniffer Vargas Reina, "Coalitions for Land Grabbing in Wartime: State, Paramilitaries and Elites in Colombia," *Journal of Peasant Studies* 49, no. 2 (2022): 288–308, https://doi.org/10.1080/03066150.2020.1835870.
22. Benedetta Berti and Marika Sosnowski, "Neither Peace nor Democracy: The Role of Siege and Population Control in the Syrian Regime's Coercive Counterinsurgency Campaign," *Small Wars & Insurgencies* 33, no. 6 (2022): 954–972, https://doi.org/10.1080/09592318.2022.2056392.
23. See "Peace Agreements Database," University of Edinburgh, accessed February 21, 2024, https://www.peaceagreements.org.
24. Jan Pospisil, "Dissolving Conflict. Local Peace Agreements and Armed Conflict Transitions," *Peacebuilding* 10, no. 2 (2022): 122–137, https://doi.org/10.1080/21647259.2022.2032945.
25. Christine Bell and Laura Wise, "The Spaces of Local Agreements: Towards a New Imaginary of the Peace Process," *Journal of Intervention and Statebuilding* 16, no. 5 (2022): 563–583, https://doi.org/10.1080/17502977.2022.2156111.
26. Bell and Wise.

27. Marika Sosnowski, "Reconciliation Agreements as Strangle Contracts: Ramifications for Property and Citizenship Rights in the Syrian Civil War," *Peacebuilding* 8, no. 4 (2020): 460–475, https://doi.org/10.1080/21647259.2019.1646693; Samer Abboud, "Social Change, Network Formation and Syria's War Economies," *Middle East Policy* 24, no. 1 (2017): 92–107, https://doi.org/10.1111/mepo.12254.
28. Sosnowski.
29. Sosnowski.
30. Fadi Adleh and Agnes Favier, *"Local Reconciliation Agreements" in Syria: A Non-Starter for Peacebuilding* (European University Institute, 2017).
31. Samer Abboud, "Reconciling Fighters, Settling Civilians: The Making of Post-Conflict Citizenship in Syria," *Citizenship Studies* 24, no. 6 (2020): 751–768, https://doi.org/10.1080/13621025.2020.1720608.
32. Samer Abboud, "Conflict, Governance, and Decentralized Authority in Syria," in *The Levant in Turmoil: Syria, Palestine, and the Transformation of Middle Eastern Politics*, ed. Martin Beck et al. (Palgrave, 2016), 57–77.
33. Mazen Ezzi, "How the Syrian Regime Is Using the Mask of 'Reconciliation' to Destroy Opposition Institutions," Chatham House, June 26, 2017, https://kalam.chathamhouse.org/articles/how-the-syrian-regime-is-using-the-mask-of-reconciliation-to-destroy-opposition-institutions/.
34. Abboud, "Reconciling Fighters, Settling Civilians."
35. Abboud.
36. Manar Abdel Razzak, "Syrian Regime Agrees with Kurds and ISIS Over Property Confiscation" [in Arabic], *Al-Quds al-Arabi*, October 1, 2015, https://www.alquds.co.uk/%EF%BB%BFالنظام-السوري-يتفق-مع-الأكراد-وتنظيم/.
37. Adleh and Favier, *"Local Reconciliation Agreements."*
38. Kalam Admin, "How Russia and the Regime Manipulate the Reconciliation Process in Dear Ez-Zor Governorate," Chatham House, February 13, 2019, https://kalam.chathamhouse.org/articles/how-russia-and-the-regime-manipulate-the-reconciliation-process-in-deir-ez-zor-governorate/.
39. Abboud, "Reconciling Fighters, Settling Civilians."
40. Gregory Waters, "The Growing Role of Reconciled Rebels in Syria," *International Review*, April 21, 2018, https://international-review.org/the-growing-role-of-reconciled-rebels-in-syria/https://international-review.org/the-growing-role-of-reconciled-rebels-in-syria/
41. Waters.
42. Waters.
43. Ashraf Suleiman, "The Regime Continues to Pursue Reconciliation Factions in Barzeh" [in Arabic], *Baladi News*, January 8, 2019, https://www.baladi-news.com/ar/news/details/39919/النظام-يواصل-ملاحقة-قادة-وعناصر-فصائل-المصالحات-في-برزة.
44. Zaman al-Wasl, "Military Security Arrests Former Rebel Commanders Who Agreed Reconciliation Deal," *Syrian Observer*, July 25, 2019, https://syrianobserver.com/foreign-actors/military-security-arrests-former-rebel-commanders-who

-agreed-reconciliation-deal.html; "Life After Reconciliation Marred by Arrests, Broken Promises as Syria's Southwest Returns to Government Control," *Syria Direct*, October 16, 2018 https://syriadirect.org/life-after-reconciliation-marred-by-arrests-broken-promises-as-syrias-southwest-returns-to-government-control/; AFP, "After 'Reconciliation': Syria Regime's Silent Crackdown," *Deccan Herald*, July 3, 2020, https://www.deccanherald.com/world/after-reconciliation-syria-regimes-silent-crackdown-856099.html.
45. Sosnowski, "Reconciliation Agreements as Strangle Contracts."
46. Raymond Hinnebusch and Omar Imady, "Syria's Reconciliation Agreements," *Syria Studies* 9, no. 2 (2017), https://ojs.st-andrews.ac.uk/index.php/syria/article/view/1558/1193.

4. Settling Friends, Unsettling Enemies

Epigraph: "Settling the Status of Hundreds of Wanted Persons in Hama Governorate" [in Arabic], Syrian Arab News Agency, October 19, 2022, https://sana.sy/?p=1766132
1. "Authorities Continue to Settle the Status of Wanted Persons in the Workers' Hall in Deri ez-Zor" [in Arabic], Syrian Arab News Agency, April 17, 2022, https://www.sana.sy/?p=1629926.
2. Samer Abboud, "'The Decision to Return to Syria Is Not in My Hands': Syria's Repatriation Regime as Illiberal Statebuilding," *Journal of Refugee Studies* 37, no. 1 (2024): 181–200, https://doi.org/10.1093/jrs/fead065.
3. Abboud.
4. May Hamidouche, "From the Pen of May Hamidouche . . ." [in Arabic], *Dam Press*, May 15, 2014, https://www.dampress.net/mobile/?page=show_det&category_id=28&id=43955&lang=ar.
5. "Ambassador Ala: The Issue of Syrian Refugees Displaced by Terrorism Must Not Be Politicized, and the Syrian Government's Efforts to Facilitate Their Return Must Be Encouraged," *Al-Thawra*, July 10, 2020, https://thawra.sy/?p=236140.
6. Lisa Blaydes, *State of Repression: Iraq Under Saddam Hussein* (Princeton University Press, 2018).
7. Interview with author, April 20, 2022.
8. Burcu Özçelik, "What Can a Political Form of Reconciliation Look Like in Divided Societies?," *Democratic Theory* 9, no. 1 (2022): 52–72, https://doi.org/10.3167/dt.2022.090104.
9. "Popular Support for Settlements in Deir ez-Zor, Raqqa, and Aleppo" [in Arabic], *Al-Wahda*, April 10, 2022, http://wehda.alwehda.gov.sy/?p=49965.
10. Kristin Conner Doughty, *Remediation in Rwanda: Grassroots Legal Forums* (University of Pennsylvania Press, 2016).

11. Doughty.
12. Abboud, "'The Decision to Return to Syria Is Not in My Hands.'"
13. Interview with author, March 2, 2023.
14. Susanne Buckley-Zistel, "We Are Pretending Peace: Local Memory and the Absence of Social Transformation and Reconciliation in Rwanda," in *After Genocide: Transitional Justice, Post-Conflict Reconstruction, and Reconciliation in Rwanda and Beyond*, ed. Phillip Clark and Zachary D. Kaufman (Columbia University Press, 2009), 153–171.
15. Ahmed Hamadeh, "Tolerance Is Our Character" [in Arabic], Syrian Arab News Agency, May 22, 2022, https://sana.sy/?p=1641114.
16. "Dozens Join Settlement Process in Hama and the Damascus Countryside" [in Arabic], Syrian Arab News Agency, October 30, 2022, https://sana.sy/?p=1773626.
17. Asma Khaira, "Culture and Art: The Amnesty Decree Opened the Door to Shaking Hands and Forgiveness in Addition to Dialogue and Reconciliation," *Al Jamahir*, May 4, 2022.
18. Stephanie Schwartz, "Home, Again: Refugee Return and Post-Conflict Violence in Burundi," *International Security* 44, no. 2 (2019): 110–145, https://doi.org/10.1162/isec_a_00362.
19. miriam cooke, *Dissident Syria: Making Oppositional Arts Official* (Duke University Press, 2007); Lisa Wedeen, *Ambiguities of Domination: Politics, Rhetoric, and Symbols in Contemporary Syria* (University of Chicago Press, 2015).
20. Moyukh Chatterjee, *Composing Violence: The Limits of Exposure and the Making of Minorities* (Duke University Press, 2023).
21. Abboud, "'The Decision to Return to Syria Is Not in My Hands.'"
22. Abboud.
23. Abboud.
24. "Increase in the Wanted Joining Numbers of Settlement Process in Deir Ezzor and Raqqa," Syrian Arab News Agency, February 20, 2022, https://sana.sy/en/?p=264140.
25. Interview with author, May 7, 2022.
26. Abboud, "'The Decision to Return to Syria Is Not in My Hands.'"
27. Eldar Sarajlić, "Conceptualising Citizenship Regime(s) in Post-Dayton Bosnia and Herzegovina," *Citizenship Studies* 16, nos. 3–4 (2012): 367–381, https://doi.org/10.1080/13621025.2012.683247.
28. Biljana Đorđević, "Whose Rights, Whose Return? The Boundary Problem and Unequal Restoration of Citizenship in the Post-Yugoslav Space," *Ethnopolitics* 14, no. 2 (2015): 121–139, https://doi.org/10.1080/17449057.2014.991150.
29. Abboud, "'The Decision to Return to Syria Is Not in My Hands.'"
30. Interview with author, July 8, 2022.
31. Interview with author, April 20, 2022.
32. Interview with author, March 8, 2023.

5. Absence as Disloyalty

Epigraphs: Mai el-Sadany, "When Assad Asks Syrians to Come Home, Here's What He Really Means," *Hill*, October 16, 2018, https://thehill.com/opinion/international/401638-when-assad-asks-syrians-to-come-home-heres-what-he-really-means/.

1. Interview with author, July 12, 2022.
2. Mollie Gerver, "Refugee Repatriation and Voluntariness," *International Journal of Human Rights* 19, no. 1 (2015): 32–52, https://doi.org/10.1080/13642987.2014.981535.
3. Jeffrey A. Sluka, "Introduction: State Terror and Anthropology," in *Death Squad: The Anthropology of State Terror*, ed. Jeffrey A. Sluka (University of Pennsylvania Press, 2000), 1–45.
4. Haid Haid, "The Syrian Regime Is Pursuing Its Opponents Through the Use of a Loophole—Private Prosecution," *Syndication Bureau*, July 1, 2019, https://syndicationbureau.com/en/النظام-السوري-يعاقب-معارضيه-باستغلال/.
5. Ninna Nyberg Sørensen and Laura Huttunen, "Missing Migrants and the Politics of Disappearance in Armed Conflicts and Migratory Contexts," *Ethnos* 87, no. 2 (2022): 321–337, https://doi.org/10.1080/00141844.2019.1697333.
6. Sørensen and Huttunen.
7. Steffen Jensen and Henrik Ronsbo, eds., *Histories of Victimhood* (University of Pennsylvania Press, 2014).
8. Jensen and Ronsbo.
9. Martin Clutterbuck et al., "Legal Preparedness for Return to Syria," *Forced Migration Review*, no. 62 (2019): 48–51, https://www.fmreview.org/wp-content/uploads/2024/08/FMR62-EN.pdf.
10. Norwegian Refugee Council, "Syrian Refugees' Right to Legal Identity: Implications for Return," Briefing Note, January 2017, https://www.nrc.no/resources/briefing-notes/syrian-refugees-right-to-legal-identity-implications-for-return.
11. Emily Stubblefield and Sandra Joireman, "Law, Violence, and Property Expropriation in Syria: Impediments to Restitution and Return," *Land* 8, no. 11 (2019): 173, https://doi.org/10.3390/land8110173.
12. Independent International Commission of Inquiry on the Syrian Arab Republic, *Gendered Impact of the Conflict in the Syrian Arab Republic on Women and Girls* (United Nations Office of the High Commissioner for Human Rights, 2023), https://www.ohchr.org/sites/default/files/documents/hrbodies/hrcouncil/coisyria/policypapersieges29aywar/2023-06-12-Gendered-impact-women-girls-Syria.pdf.
13. Stubblefield and Joireman, "Law, Violence, and Property Expropriation in Syria."
14. "How Non-Recognition of Official Documents Impacts HLP Rights," *Syria Report*, October 17, 2023, https://hlp.syria-report.com/hlp/how-non-recognition-of-official-documents-impacts-hlp-rights/.

15. Abir Hamdar, "The Syrian Corpse: The Politics of Dignity in Visual and Media Representations of the Syrian Revolution," *Journal for Cultural Research* 22, no. 1 (2018): 73–89, https://doi.org/10.1080/14797585.2018.1429083.
16. Hamdar.
17. Samer Abboud, "Narrating Crisis Through the Loyalist Witness," *Middle East Journal of Culture and Communication* 16, no. 1 (2023): 1–19, https://doi.org/10.1163/18739865-tat00003.
18. Dina Rizk Khoury, *Iraq in Wartime: Soldiering, Martyrdom, and Remembrance* (Cambridge University Press, 2013).
19. Joseph Daher, "Expelled from the Support System: Austerity Deepens in Syria," *Middle East Directions Programme Blog*, February 15, 2022, https://blogs.eui.eu/medirections/expelled-from-the-support-system-austerity-deepens-in-syria/.
20. Rohan Advani, "Smart Cards for Rationing: How the Syrian Government Is Outsmarting Accountability," *Syria Direct*, February 17, 2020, https://syriadirect.org/smart-cards-for-rationing-how-the-syrian-government-is-outsmarting-accountability/.
21. Advani.
22. Samer Abboud, "'The Decision to Return to Syria Is Not in My Hands': Syria's Repatriation Regime as Illiberal Statebuilding," *Journal of Refugee Studies* 37, no. 1 (2024): 181–200, https://doi.org/10.1093/jrs/fead065.
23. "Regime Tallies IDP Properties in Idlib and Hama for Auction," *Syria Report*, June 22, 2021, https://hlp.syria-report.com/hlp/regime-tallies-idp-properties-in-idlib-and-hama-for-auction/.
24. Jon D. Unruh, "Weaponization of the Land and Property Rights System in the Syrian Civil War: Facilitating Restitution?," *Journal of Intervention and Statebuilding* 10, no. 4 (2016): 453–471, https://doi.org/10.1080/17502977.2016.1158527.
25. Violations Documentation Center, *Counter-Terrorism Court: A Tool for War Crimes: Special Report on Counter-Terrorism Law No. 19 and the Counter-Terrorism Court in Syria* (Violations Documentation Center, April 2015), https://icct.nl/sites/default/files/import/publication/1430186775-English.pdf.
26. "Legislative Decrees and Laws of Property Rights in Syria," *Enab Baladi*, July 20, 2022, https://english.enabbaladi.net/archives/2020/06/legislative-decrees-and-laws-of-property-rights-in-syria/.
27. "Explained: Public Safety Committees," *Syria Report*, May 31, 2022, https://hlp.syria-report.com/hlp/explained-public-safety-committees/#:~:text=Recently%20in%20Syria%20there%20has,by%20fighting%20during%20the%20conflict.
28. "Returnee Numbers Remain Very Low in Al-Hajar Al-Aswad as Looting Continues," *Syria Report*, March 8, 2022, https://hlp.syria-report.com/hlp/returnee-numbers-remain-very-low-in-al-hajar-al-aswad-as-looting-continues/.
29. Syrian Arab Republic Parliament, "The People's Assembly Approves the Draft Law on the Management and Investment of Movable and Immovable Assets" [in

Arabic], November 30, 2023, http://parliament.gov.sy/arabic/index.php?node=554&nid=23767&First=2&Last=3172&CurrentPage=3&mid=&refBack=.
30. Syrian Network for Human Rights, "Preliminary Analysis of the Law on Managing and Investing Transferrable and Non-Transferrable Assets That Were Seized Pursuant to an Unappealable Judicial Ruling, as Promulgated by the People's Assembly of Syria," December 9, 2023.
31. Daniel G. Ogbaharya, "(Re-)Building Governance in Post-Conflict Africa: The Role of the State and Informal Institutions," *Development in Practice* 18, no. 3 (2008): 395–402, https://doi.org/10.1080/09614520802030482.
32. Sukanya Podder, "Mainstreaming the Non-State in Bottom-Up State-Building: Linkages Between Rebel Governance and Post-Conflict Legitimacy," *Conflict, Security & Development* 14, no. 2 (2014): 213–243, https://doi.org/10.1080/14678802.2014.889878.
33. Kjetil Selvik and Tamar Groves, "'The Generation That Will Inherit Syria': Education as Citizen Aid and Political Opportunity," *Third World Quarterly* 44, no. 5 (2023): 930–945, https://doi.org/10.1080/01436597.2023.2167705.
34. "Explained: Security Approval for Real Estate Actions," *Syria Report*, October 18, 2022, https://hlp.syria-report.com/hlp/explained-security-approval-for-real-estate-actions/#:~:text=Security%20approval%20is%20required%20for,%2C%20inheritances%2C%20and%20public%20auctions.

6. The Regime Falls

Epigraph: "Video: Syria's al-Sharaa Sets Out Priorities as Transitional President," *Al Jazeera*, January 30, 2025, https://www.aljazeera.com/video/newsfeed/2025/1/30/video-syrias-al-sharaa-sets-out-priorities-as-transitional-president.

1. "A Palace in Shock: Bashar al-Assad's Final Moments in Syria," *France 24*, December 14, 2024, https://www.france24.com/en/live-news/20241214-a-palace-in-shock-bashar-al-assad-s-final-moments-in-syria.
2. Barbara F. Walter, *Committing to Peace: The Successful Settlement of Civil Wars* (Princeton University Press, 2002).
3. Katia Papagianni, "Political Transitions After Peace Agreements: The Importance of Consultative and Inclusive Political Processes," *Journal of Intervention and Statebuilding* 3, no. 1 (2009): 47–63, https://doi.org/10.1080/17502970802608175.
4. Sami Hermez, *War Is Coming: Between Past and Future Violence in Lebanon* (University of Pennsylvania Press, 2017); Munira Khayyat, *A Landscape of War: Ecologies of Resistance and Survival in South Lebanon* (University of California Press, 2022).
5. Raymond Hinnebusch, "Introduction: Understanding the Consequences of the Arab Uprisings—Starting Points and Divergent Trajectories," *Democratization* 22, no. 2 (2015): 205–217, https://doi.org/10.1080/13510347.2015.1010807.
6. "Scenes from Settling the Status of Military and Police Personnel in Damascus After Bashar al-Assad Fled" [in Arabic], *Step News*, December 24, 2024, https://www.youtube.com/watch?v=E2NSD659Gjc.

7. "Receiving Applications for the Settlement of Status of Former Regime Security Personnel in Damascus" [in Arabic], *Al Arabiyya Syria*, December 21, 2024, https://youtu.be/95vX7mzkdMI?si=Sy8KxoPf_uyY9_AB.
8. Kevin Hearty, "'Victims of' Human Rights Abuses in Transitional Justice: Hierarchies, Perpetrators and the Struggle for Peace," *International Journal of Human Rights* 22, no. 7 (2018): 888–909, https://doi.org/10.1080/13642987.2018.1485656.
9. Bassel F. Salloukh, "War Memory, Confessional Imaginaries, and Political Contestation in Postwar Lebanon," *Middle East Critique* 28, no. 3 (2019): 341–359, https://doi.org/10.1080/19436149.2019.1633748.
10. Yvette Selim, "Contestation and Resistance: The Politics of and Around Transitional Justice in Nepal," *Conflict, Security & Development* 18, no. 1 (2018): 39–60, https://doi.org/10.1080/14678802.2017.1420314.
11. "Accelerating Economic Recovery Is Critical to Reversing Syria's Decline and Restoring Stability," United Nations Development Programme, February 20, 2025, https://www.undp.org/syria/press-releases/accelerating-economic-recovery-critical-reversing-syrias-decline-and-restoring-stability.
12. Timour Azhari, "Exclusive: Syria's New Rulers Back Shift to Free-Market Economy, Business Leader Says," Reuters, December 10, 2024, https://www.reuters.com/world/middle-east/syrias-new-rulers-back-shift-free-market-economy-business-leader-says-2024-12-10/; "Syria's Interim Govt Overhauls Economy with Privatizations, Layoffs," Reuters, January 31, 2025, https://www.dailysabah.com/business/economy/syrias-interim-govt-overhauls-economy-with-privatizations-layoffs.
13. "Explained: Similarities and Differences Between Land Registry Digitisation and Restoration of Damaged Records," *Syria Report*, September 11, 2024, https://hlp.syria-report.com/hlp/explained-similarities-and-differences-between-land-registry-digitisation-and-restoration-of-damaged-records/.
14. Megan Bradley, *Refugee Repatriation: Justice, Responsibility and Redress* (Cambridge University Press, 2013).
15. "Explained: Mechanisms for Recovering Properties Confiscated Under the Anti-Terrorism Court," *Syria Report*, January 7, 2025, https://hlp.syria-report.com/hlp/explained-mechanisms-for-recovering-properties-confiscated-under-the-anti-terrorism-court/.
16. Stephanie Schwartz, "Home, Again: Refugee Return and Post-Conflict Violence in Burundi," *International Security* 44, no. 2 (2019): 110–145, https://doi.org/10.1162/isec_a_00362.
17. George Wright, "Sharaa Vows to Pursue Criminals as Syria's Transitional President," *BBC News*, January 31, 2025, https://www.bbc.com/news/articles/czep8kyeeyyo.
18. Mick Krever, "Israel Strikes Syria 480 Times and Seizes Territory as Netanyahu Pledges to Change Face of the Middle East," *CNN*, December 11, 2024, https://www.cnn.com/2024/12/10/middleeast/israel-syria-assad-strikes-intl.
19. "AANES Kurdish Leader Ilham Ahmed Urges Israeli 'Intervention' in Syria," *New Arab*, February 3, 2025, https://www.newarab.com/news/kurdish-pyd-leader-urges-israeli-intervention-syria; Azhari, "Exclusive."

20. Hinnebusch, "Introduction"; Joshua Stacher, "Fragmenting States, New Regimes: Militarized State Violence and Transition in the Middle East," *Democratization* 22, no. 2 (2015): 259–275, https://doi.org/10.1080/13510347.2015.1010810.
21. "The View from Damascus: Failure of Syria's National Dialogue Conference and Its Implications," *Syrian Observer*, March 25, 2025, https://syrianobserver.com/syrian-actors/the-view-from-damascus-failure-of-syrias-national-dialogue-conference-and-its-implications.html.

Conclusion

Epigraph: Lisa Wedeen, "Epilogue," *British Journal of Middle Eastern Studies* 49, no. 3 (May 27, 2022): 505, https://doi.org/10.1080/13530194.2021.1920280.
1. Lisa Wedeen. *Authoritarian Apprehensions: Ideology, Judgment, and Mourning in Syria* (University of Chicago Press, 2019).
2. Raymond Hinnebusch, "State De-Construction in Iraq and Syria," *Politische Vierteljahresschrift* 57, no. 4 (2016): 560–585.

Bibliography

"AANES Kurdish Leader Ilham Ahmed Urges Israeli 'Intervention' in Syria." *New Arab*, February 3, 2025. https://www.newarab.com/news/kurdish-pyd-leader-urges-israeli-intervention-syria.

Abboud, Samer. "Conflict, Governance, and Decentralized Authority in Syria." In *The Levant in Turmoil: Syria, Palestine, and the Transformation of Middle Eastern Politics*, edited by Martin Beck, Dietrich Jung, and Peter Seeberg. Palgrave, 2016.

Abboud, Samer. "'The Decision to Return to Syria Is Not in My Hands': Syria's Repatriation Regime as Illiberal Statebuilding." *Journal of Refugee Studies* 37, no. 1 (2024): 181–200. https://doi.org/10.1093/jrs/fead065.

Abboud, Samer. "Imagining Localism in Post-Conflict Syria: Prefigurative Reconstruction Plans and the Clash Between Liberal Epistemology and Illiberal Conflict." *Journal of Intervention and Statebuilding* 15, no. 4 (2021): 543–561. https://doi.org/10.1080/17502977.2020.1829360.

Abboud, Samer. "Making Peace to Sustain War: The Astana Process and Syria's Illiberal Peace." *Peacebuilding* 9, no. 3 (2021): 326–343. https://doi.org/10.1080/21647259.2021.1895609.

Abboud, Samer. "Narrating Crisis Through the Loyalist Witness." *Middle East Journal of Culture and Communication* 16, no. 1 (2023): 1–19. https://doi.org/10.1163/18739865-tat00003.

Abboud, Samer. "Reconciling Fighters, Settling Civilians: The Making of Post-Conflict Citizenship in Syria." *Citizenship Studies* 24, no. 6 (2020): 751–768. https://doi.org/10.1080/13621025.2020.1720608.

Abboud, Samer. "Social Change, Network Formation and Syria's War Economies." *Middle East Policy* 24, no. 1 (2017): 92–107. https://doi.org/10.1111/mepo.12254.

Abboud, Samer. "Syria's Repressive Peace." In *Struggles for Political Change in the Arab World*, edited by Hesham Sallam, Amr Hamzway, and Lisa Blaydes. University of Michigan Press, 2022. https://doi.org/10.1353/book.103145.

Abboud, Samer. *Syria*. 1st ed. Polity, 2015.

Abboud, Samer. *Syria*. 2nd ed. Polity, 2018.

Abdel Razzak, Manar. "Syrian Regime Agrees with Kurds and ISIS Over Property Confiscation" [in Arabic]. *Al-Quds al-Arabi*, October 1, 2015.

Abdelaaty, Lamis. "Refugees and Guesthood in Turkey." *Journal of Refugee Studies* 34, no. 3 (2021): 2827–2848. https://doi.org/10.1093/jrs/fez097.

Abouzeid, Rania. *No Turning Back: Life, Loss, and Hope in Wartime Syria*. W. W. Norton, 2018.

"Accelerating Economic Recovery Is Critical to Reversing Syria's Decline and Restoring Stability." United Nations Development Programme, February 20, 2025. https://www.undp.org/syria/press-releases/accelerating-economic-recovery-critical-reversing-syrias-decline-and-restoring-stability.

Adleh, Fadi, and Agnes Favier. *"Local Reconciliation Agreements" in Syria: A Non-Starter for Peacebuilding*. European University Institute, 2017.

Admin, Kalam. "How Russia and the Regime Manipulate the Reconciliation Process in Dear Ez-Zor Governorate." Chatham House, February 13, 2019. https://kalam.chathamhouse.org/articles/how-russia-and-the-regime-manipulate-the-reconciliation-process-in-deir-ez-zor-governorate/.

Advani, Rohan. "Smart Cards for Rationing: How the Syrian Government Is Outsmarting Accountability." *Syria Direct*, February 17, 2020. https://syriadirect.org/smart-cards-for-rationing-how-the-syrian-government-is-outsmarting-accountability/.

AFP. "After 'Reconciliation': Syria Regime's Silent Crackdown." *Deccan Herald*, July 3, 2020. https://www.deccanherald.com/world/after-reconciliation-syria-regimes-silent-crackdown-856099.html.

Akgul, Arif, Cuneyt Gurer, and Hasan Aydin. "Exploring the Victimization of Syrian Refugees Through the Human Security Model: An Ethnographic Approach." *Studies in Ethnicity and Nationalism* 21, no. 1 (2021): 46–66. https://doi.org/10.1111/sena.12338.

Akpınar, Pınar. "The Limits of Mediation in the Arab Spring: The Case of Syria." *Third World Quarterly* 37, no. 12 (2016): 2288–2303. https://doi.org/10.1080/01436597.2016.1218273.

Aljasem, Ali. "Queiq: The River That Streamed Bodies in Aleppo." *Journal of Genocide Research* 25, no. 1 (2023): 104–12. https://doi.org/10.1080/14623528.2021.1979911.

"Ambassador Ala: The Issue of Syrian Refugees Displaced by Terrorism Must Not Be Politicized, and the Syrian Government's Efforts to Facilitate Their Return Must Be Encouraged" [in Arabic]. Syrian Arab News Agency, July 10, 2020. https://thawra.sy/?p=236140.

Ashour, Omar. *How ISIS Fights: Military Tactics in Iraq, Syria, Libya and Egypt*. Edinburgh University Press, 2021.

"Assad Pledges to Regain Control of Northern Syria by Force If Needed." Reuters, June 24, 2018. https://www.reuters.com/article/world/assad-pledges-to-regain-control-of-northern-syria-by-force-if-needed-idUSKBN1JK0JV/.

"The Authorities Continue to Settle the Status of the Wanted in the Workers Hall in Deir ez-Zor" [in Arabic]. Syrian Arab News Agency, April 17, 2022. https://www.sana.sy/?p=1627112.

Azhari, Timour. "Exclusive: Syria's New Rulers Back Shift to Free-Market Economy, Business Leader Says." Reuters, December 10, 2024. https://www.reuters.com/world/middle-east/syrias-new-rulers-back-shift-free-market-economy-business-leader-says-2024-12-10/.

Baban, Feyzi, Suzan Ilcan, and Kim Rygiel. "Syrian Refugees in Turkey: Pathways to Precarity, Differential Inclusion, and Negotiated Citizenship Rights." *Journal of Ethnic and Migration Studies* 43, no. 1 (2017): 41–57. https://doi.org/10.1080/1369183X.2016.1192996.

Baczko, Adam, Gilles Dorronsoro, and Arthur Quesnay. *Civil War in Syria: Mobilization and Competing Social Orders*. Cambridge University Press, 2018.

Baker, Jaber, and Ugur Ümit Üngör. *Syrian Gulag: Inside Assad's Prison System*. I. B. Tauris, 2023.

Bakkour, Samer. "Beyond Genocide: Towards an Improved Analysis and Understanding of the Syrian Regime's Mass Atrocity Crimes in the Syrian Civil War." *Digest of Middle East Studies* 32, no. 4 (2023): 300–320. https://doi.org/10.1111/dome.12304.

Balci, Bayram, and Nicolas Monceau, eds. *Turkey, Russia and Iran in the Middle East*. Springer International, 2021. https://doi.org/10.1007/978-3-030-80291-2.

Bâli, Asli, and Aziz Rana. "The Wrong Kind of Intervention in Syria." In *The Land of Blue Helmets: The United Nations and the Arab World*, edited by Karim Makdisi and Vijay Prashad. University of California Press, 2017.

Barbara F. Walter. *Committing to Peace: The Successful Settlement of Civil Wars*. Princeton University Press, 2002.

"Behind the Data: Recording Civilian Casualties in Syria." United Nations Office for the Special Envoy for Syria, May 11, 2023. https://www.ohchr.org/en/stories/2023/05/behind-data-recording-civilian-casualties-syria.

Bell, Christine, and Laura Wise. "The Spaces of Local Agreements: Towards a New Imaginary of the Peace Process." *Journal of Intervention and Statebuilding* 16, no. 5 (2022): 563–583. https://doi.org/10.1080/17502977.2022.2156111.

Bellamy, Alex J. *Syria Betrayed: Atrocities, War, and the Failure of International Diplomacy*. Columbia University Press, 2022.

Berti, Benedetta, and Marika Sosnowski. "Neither Peace nor Democracy: The Role of Siege and Population Control in the Syrian Regime's Coercive Counterinsurgency Campaign." *Small Wars & Insurgencies* 33, no. 6 (2022): 954–972. https://doi.org/10.1080/09592318.2022.2056392.

Blaydes, Lisa. *State of Repression: Iraq Under Saddam Hussein*. Princeton University Press, 2018.

Borshchevskaya, Anna. *Putin's War in Syria: Russian Foreign Policy and the Price of America's Absence*. I. B. Tauris, 2021.

Bradley, Megan. *Refugee Repatriation: Justice, Responsibility and Redress*. Cambridge University Press, 2013.

Buckley-Zistel, Susanne. "We Are Pretending Peace: Local Memory and the Absence of Social Transformation and Reconciliation in Rwanda." In *After Genocide: Transitional Justice, Post-Conflict Reconstruction, and Reconciliation in Rwanda and Beyond*, edited by Phillip Clark and Zachary D. Kaufman. Columbia University Press, 2009.

Can, Şule. *Refugee Encounters at the Turkish-Syrian Border: Antakya at the Crossroads*. Routledge, 2019.

"Can the Astana Agreement End the Syrian War?" [in Arabic]. *Annabaa*, May 7, 2017. https://annabaa.org/arabic/reports/10894.

Chalermsripinyorat, Rungrawee. "Dialogue Without Negotiation: Illiberal Peace-Building in Southern Thailand." *Conflict, Security & Development* 20, no. 1 (2020): 71–95. https://doi.org/10.1080/14678802.2019.1705069.

Chatterjee, Moyukh. *Composing Violence: The Limits of Exposure and the Making of Minorities*. Duke University Press, 2023.

Checkel, Jeffrey T. "Socialization and Violence." *Journal of Peace Research* 54, no. 5 (2017): 592–605. https://doi.org/10.1177/0022343317721813.

Clark, Janine Natalya. "National Unity and Reconciliation in Rwanda: A Flawed Approach?" *Journal of Contemporary African Studies* 28, no. 2 (2010): 137–154. https://doi.org/10.1080/02589001003736793.

Clutterbuck, Martin, Laura Cunial, Paolo Barsanti, and Tina Gewis. "Legal Preparedness for Return to Syria." *Forced Migration Review*, no. 62 (2019): 48–51. https://www.fmreview.org/return/clutterbuck-cunial-barsanti-gewis-2/.

"Conflict Mapping, Research, Analysis, and Documentation." Carter Center. Accessed March 21, 2024. https://www.cartercenter.org/peace/conflict_resolution/syria-conflict-resolution.html#reports.

cooke, miriam. *Dissident Syria: Making Oppositional Arts Official*. Duke University Press, 2007.

Costantini, Irene, and Ruth Hanau Santini. "Power Mediators and the 'Illiberal Peace' Momentum: Ending Wars in Libya and Syria." *Third World Quarterly* 43, no. 1 (2022): 131–147. https://doi.org/10.1080/01436597.2021.1995711.

"Country Profile—Syrian Arab Republic." Internal Displacement Monitoring Center. Accessed July 18, 2025. https://www.internal-displacement.org/countries/syria/.

Dagher, Sam. *Assad or We Burn the Country: How One Family's Lust for Power Destroyed Syria*. Little, Brown and Company, 2019.

Daher, Joseph. "Expelled from the Support System: Austerity Deepens in Syria." *Middle East Directions Programme Blog*, February 15, 2022. https://blogs.eui.eu/medirections/expelled-from-the-support-system-austerity-deepens-in-syria/.

Daoudy, Marwa. *The Origins of the Syrian Conflict: Climate Change and Human Security*. Cambridge University Press, 2020.

"Decree to Reconstitute Counter-Terrorism Court" [in Arabic]. *Shaam Times*, March 2019. https://www.shaamtimes.net/300675/مرسوم-بإعادة-تشكيل-محكمة-قضايا-الإرها/.

Dieckhoff, Milena. "Reconsidering the Humanitarian Space: Complex Interdependence Between Humanitarian and Peace Negotiations in Syria." *Contemporary Security Policy* 41, no. 4 (2020): 564–586. https://doi.org/10.1080/13523260.2020.1773025.

Dinmore, Guy. "US Seeks New Syrian Leader' as Pressure Mounts." *Financial Times*, October 9, 2005. https://www.ft.com/content/42ea38dc-38ea-11da-900a-00000e2511c8.

Đorđević, Biljana. "Whose Rights, Whose Return? The Boundary Problem and Unequal Restoration of Citizenship in the Post-Yugoslav Space." *Ethnopolitics* 14, no. 2 (2015): 121–139. https://doi.org/10.1080/17449057.2014.991150.

Doughty, Kristin Conner. *Remediation in Rwanda: Grassroots Legal Forums*. University of Pennsylvania Press, 2016.

"Dozens Join Settlement Process in Hama and the Damascus Countryside" [in Arabic]. Syrian Arab News Agency, October 30, 2022. https://sana.sy/?p=1773626.

Dukhan, Haian. "The ISIS Massacre of the Sheitat Tribe in Der Ez-Zor, August 2014." *Journal of Genocide Research* 25, no. 1 (2023): 113–121. https://doi.org/10.1080/14623528.2021.1979912.

Dukhan, Haian. *State and Tribes in Syria: Informal Alliances and Conflict Patterns*. Routledge, 2018.

"Erdogan: Astana Process, Most Effective Measure to Push Political Solution for Syria." Islamic Republic News Agency, July 20, 2022. https://en.irna.ir/news/84827431/Astana-process-most-effective-move-for-political-solution-in.

"Explained: Mechanisms for Recovering Properties Confiscated Under the Anti-Terrorism Court." *Syria Report*, January 7, 2025. https://hlp.syria-report.com/hlp/explained-mechanisms-for-recovering-properties-confiscated-under-the-anti-terrorism-court/.

"Explained: Public Safety Committees." *Syria Report*, May 31, 2022. https://hlp.syria-report.com/hlp/explained-public-safety-committees/.

"Explained: Security Approval for Real Estate Actions." *Syria Report*, October 18, 2022. https://hlp.syria-report.com/hlp/explained-security-approval-for-real-estate-actions/.

"Explained: Similarities and Differences Between Land Registry Digitisation and Restoration of Damaged Records." *Syria Report*, September 11, 2024. https://hlp.syria-report.com/hlp/explained-similarities-and-differences-between-land-registry-digitisation-and-restoration-of-damaged-records/.

Ezzi, Mazen. "How the Syrian Regime Is Using the Mask of 'Reconciliation' to Destroy Opposition Institutions." Chatham House, June 26, 2017. https://kalam.chathamhouse.org/articles/how-the-syrian-regime-is-using-the-mask-of-reconciliation-to-destroy-opposition-institutions/.

"Fact Sheet: President Bush Remarks on the War on Terror." White House, October 6, 2005. https://georgewbush-whitehouse.archives.gov/news/releases/2005/10/20051006-2.html.

"Guarantor States of the Cessation of Hostilities Agreement: Supporting the Sovereignty and Unity of Syria" [in Arabic]. Syrian Arab News Agency, April 5, 2018, https://archive.sana.sy/?p=734747.

Georges, Nael. "The Syrian Regime Legal 'Reforms' (III) Security vs. Counterterrorism Courts: Different Names, Same Function." Legal Agenda, January 10, 2014. https://english.legal-agenda.com/the-syrian-regime-legal-reforms-iii-security-vs-counterterrorism-courts-different-names-same-function/.

Gerver, Mollie. "Refugee Repatriation and Voluntariness." *International Journal of Human Rights* 19, no. 1 (2015): 32–52. https://doi.org/10.1080/13642987.2014.981535.

Geukjian, Ohannes. *The Russian Military Intervention in Syria*. McGill-Queen's University Press, 2022.

Glass, Charles. *Syria Burning: A Short History of a Catastrophe*. Verso, 2016.

Glass, Charles. *Syria in Ashes*. Or Publishing, 2024.

Goldsmight, Leon. *Cycle of Fear: Syria's Alawites in War and Peace*. Hurst, 2015.

Goodhand, Jonathan, and Oliver Walton. "The Limits of Liberal Peacebuilding? International Engagement in the Sri Lankan Peace Process." *Journal of Intervention and Statebuilding* 3, no. 3 (2009): 303–323. https://doi.org/10.1080/17502970903086693.

Haid, Haid. "The Syrian Regime Is Pursuing Its Opponents Through the Use of a Loophole—Private Prosecution." *Syndication Bureau*, July 1, 2019.

Haider, Abir. "Terrorism Court in Syria." *As-Safir al-Araby*, January 22, 2014. https://assafirarabi.com/ar/2839/2014/01/22/محكمة-الإرهاب-في-سوريا/.

"Haidar: Words Are the Most Effective Means of Achieving True National Reconciliation" [in Arabic]. Syrian Arab News Agency, April 5, 2017. https://archive.sana.sy/?p=533776.

Hamad, Areej al-, Cheryl Forchuk, Abe Oudshoorn, and Gerald Patrick Mckinley. "Listening to the Voices of Syrian Refugee Women in Canada: An Ethnographic Insight Into the Journey from Trauma to Adaptation." *Journal of International Migration and Integration* 24, no. 3 (2023): 1017–1037. https://doi.org/10.1007/s12134-022-00991-w.

Hamadeh, Ahmed. "Ahmad Hamadeh: Tolerance Is Our Character." Syrian Arab News Agency, May 22, 2022. https://sana.sy/?p=1641114.

Hamdar, Abir. "The Syrian Corpse: The Politics of Dignity in Visual and Media Representations of the Syrian Revolution." *Journal for Cultural Research* 22, no. 1 (2018): 73–89. https://doi.org/10.1080/14797585.2018.1429083.

Hamidouche, May. "From the Pen of May Hamidouche . . ." [in Arabic]. *Dam Press*, May 15, 2014. https://www.dampress.net/mobile/?page=show_det&category_id=28&id=43955&lang=ar.

Hauch, Lars. *Mixing Politics and Force Syria's Constitutional Committee in Review*. CRU Report. Netherlands Institute of International Relations Clingendael, 2020. https://www.clingendael.org/pub/2020/the-politics-of-syrias-constitutional-committee/.

Hearty, Kevin. "'Victims of' Human Rights Abuses in Transitional Justice: Hierarchies, Perpetrators and the Struggle for Peace." *International Journal of Human Rights* 22, no. 7 (2018): 888–909. https://doi.org/10.1080/13642987.2018.1485656.

Heathershaw, John, and Catherine Owen. "Authoritarian Conflict Management in Post-Colonial Eurasia." *Conflict, Security & Development* 19, no. 3 (2019): 269–273. https://doi.org/10.1080/14678802.2019.1608022.

Helfont, Samuel. *Compulsion in Religion: Saddam Hussein, Islam, and the Roots of Insurgencies in Iraq*. Oxford University Press, 2018.

Helfont, Samuel. *Iraq Against the World: Saddam, America, and the Post-Cold War Order*. Oxford University Press, 2023.

Hinnebusch, Raymond. "Introduction: Understanding the Consequences of the Arab Uprisings—Starting Points and Divergent Trajectories." *Democratization* 22, no. 2 (2015): 205–217. https://doi.org/10.1080/13510347.2015.1010807.

Hinnebusch, Raymond. "State De-Construction in Iraq and Syria." *Politische Vierteljahresschrift* 57, no. 4 (2016): 560–585. https://doi.org/10.5771/0032-3470-2016-4-560.

Hinnebusch, Raymond, and Omar Imady. "Syria's Reconciliation Agreements." *Syria Studies* 9, no. 2 (2017). https://ojs.st-andrews.ac.uk/index.php/syria/article/view/1558/1193.

Hinnebusch, Raymond, and Neil Quilliam. "Contrary Siblings: Syria, Jordan and the Iraq War." *Cambridge Review of International Affairs* 19, no. 3 (2006): 513–528. https://doi.org/10.1080/09557570600869564.

Hinnebusch, Raymond, and Adham Saouli. *The War for Syria: Regional and International Dimensions of the Syrian Uprising*. Routledge, 2019.

Hinnebusch, Raymond, and I. William Zartman. *UN Mediation in the Syrian Crisis: From Kofi Annan to Lakhdar Brahimi*. International Peace Institute, March 2016. https://www.ipinst.org/wp-content/uploads/2016/03/IPI-Rpt-Syrian-Crisis2.pdf.

Hof, Frederic C. *Reaching for the Heights: The Inside Story of a Secret Attempt to Reach a Syrian-Israeli Peace*. USIP Press, 2022.

Hokayem, Emile. *Syria's Uprising and the Fracturing of the Levant*. Routledge, 2017.

"How Non-Recognition of Official Documents Impacts HLP Rights." *Syria Report*, October 17, 2023. https://hlp.syria-report.com/hlp/how-non-recognition-of-official-documents-impacts-hlp-rights/.

Hughes, Geraint Alun. "Syria and the Perils of Proxy Warfare." *Small Wars & Insurgencies* 25, no. 3 (2014): 522–538. https://doi.org/10.1080/09592318.2014.913542.

Independent International Commission of Inquiry on the Syrian Arab Republic. *Gendered Impact of the Conflict in the Syrian Arab Republic on Women and Girls*. United Nations Office of the High Commissioner for Human Rights, 2023. https://www.ohchr.org/en/statements-and-speeches/2023/06/gendered-impact-conflict-syrian-arab-republic-women-and-girls.

Iraq Study Group. *The Iraq Study Group Report*. Vintage Books, 2006.

Ismail, Salwa. *Political Life in Cairo's New Quarters: Encountering the Everyday State*. University of Minnesota Press, 2006.

Ismail, Salwa. *The Rule of Violence: Subjectivity, Memory and Government in Syria*. Cambridge University Press, 2018.

Jabaae, Jad al-Karim al-. "Parallel Society: A Background to Understanding What Is Happening in Syria" [in Arabic]. *Omran* 3, no. 7 (2014). https://omran.dohainstitute.org/ar/Documents/issuepdf/Omran07-2014.pdf.

Jabbour, Samer, and Nasser Fardousi. "Violence Against Health Care in Syria: Patterns, Meanings, Implications." *British Journal of Middle Eastern Studies* 49, no. 3 (2022): 403–417. https://doi.org/10.1080/13530194.2021.1916153.

Janmyr, Maja. "Ethnographic Approaches and International Refugee Law." *Journal of Refugee Studies* 37, no. 4 (2024): 871–885. https://doi.org/10.1093/jrs/feac042.

Janmyr, Maja. "UNHCR and the Syrian Refugee Response: Negotiating Status and Registration in Lebanon." *International Journal of Human Rights* 22, no. 3 (2018): 393–419. https://doi.org/10.1080/13642987.2017.1371140.

Jensen, Steffen, and Henrik Ronsbo, eds. *Histories of Victimhood*. University of Pennsylvania Press, 2014.

Joffé, George. "National Reconciliation and General Amnesty in Algeria." *Mediterranean Politics* 13, no. 2 (2008): 213–228. https://doi.org/10.1080/13629390802127539.

Kaldor, Mary, Marika Theros, and Rim Turkmani. "Local Agreements—an Introduction to the Special Issue." *Peacebuilding* 10, no. 2 (2022): 107–121. https://doi.org/10.1080/21647259.2022.2042111.

Kentikelenis, Alexander, and Erik Voeten. "Legitimacy Challenges to the Liberal World Order: Evidence from United Nations Speeches, 1970–2018." *Review of International Organizations* 16, no. 4 (2021): 721–754. https://doi.org/10.1007/s11558-020-09404-y.

Keranen, Outi. "Building States and Identities in Post-Conflict States: Symbolic Practices in Post-Dayton Bosnia." *Civil Wars* 16, no. 2 (2014): 127–146. https://doi.org/10.1080/13698249.2014.904984.

Khader, Abdel Rahman al-. "Human Rights Report: Nearly 1,000 Syrians Have Been Tried in the Terrorism Court" [in Arabic]. *Al-Araby*, October 15, 2020. https://www.alaraby.co.uk/politics/تقرير-حقوقي-نحو--11ألف-سوري-يخضعون-لمحكمة-قضايا-الإرهاب.

Khaira, Asma. "Culture and Art: The Amnesty Decree Opened the Door to Shaking Hands and Forgiveness in Addition to Dialogue and Reconciliation" [in Arabic]. *Al Jamahir*, May 4, 2022. http://jamahir.alwehda.gov.sy/?p=77408.

Khalifa, Khaled. *Death Is Hard Work*. Translated by Leri Price. Farrar, Straus and Giroux, 2019.

Khatib, Line. "Syria, Saudi Arabia, the U.A.E. and Qatar: The 'Sectarianization' of the Syrian Conflict and Undermining of Democratization in the Region." *British Journal of Middle Eastern Studies* 46, no. 3 (2019): 385–403. https://doi.org/10.1080/13530194.2017.1408456.

Khoury, Dina Rizk. *Iraq in Wartime: Soldiering, Martyrdom, and Remembrance*. Cambridge University Press, 2013.

Kocadal, Özker. "Emerging Power Liminality in Peacebuilding: Turkey's Mimicry of the Liberal Peace." *International Peacekeeping* 26, no. 4 (2019): 431–456. https://doi.org/10.1080/13533312.2019.1615375.

Kortunov, Andrey. "The Astana Model: Methods and Ambitions of Russian Political Action." In *The MENA Region: A Great Power Competition*, edited by Karim Mezran and Arturo Varvelli. ISPI; Atlantic Council, 2019.

Köstem, Seçkin. "Russian-Turkish Cooperation in Syria: Geopolitical Alignment with Limits." *Cambridge Review of International Affairs* 34, no. 6 (November 2, 2021): 795–817. https://doi.org/10.1080/09557571.2020.1719040.

"Kremlin: The Syrian Arab Army Is the Only Force Capable of Combatting Terrorism on the Ground" [in Arabic]. Syrian Arab News Agency, November 27, 2015. https://archive.sana.sy/?p=303771.

Labott, Elise. "U.S. Hits Syria with Sanctions." *CNN*, May 12, 2004. https://edition.cnn.com/2004/WORLD/meast/05/11/us.syria/.

"Launching the Civil Initiative for Local Reconciliation ... Haidar: Civil Society Is a State Partner in Achieving Reconciliation" [in Arabic]. Syrian Arab News Agency, September 5, 2023. https://sana.sy/?p=379699.

Lee, Sean. "How Bashar Al-Asad Learned to Stop Worrying and Love the 'War on Terror.'" *International Studies Quarterly* 68, no. 2 (2024): sqae066. https://doi.org/10.1093/isq/sqae066.

"Legislative Decrees and Laws of Property Rights in Syria." *Enab Baladi*, July 20, 2022. https://english.enabbaladi.net/archives/2020/06/legislative-decrees-and-laws-of-property-rights-in-syria/.

Lewis, David G. "Sri Lanka's Schmittian Peace: Sovereignty, Enmity and Illiberal Order." *Conflict, Security & Development* 20, no. 1 (2020): 15–37. https://doi.org/10.1080/14678802.2019.1705067.

Lewis, David, John Heathershaw, and Nick Megoran. "Illiberal Peace? Authoritarian Modes of Conflict Management." *Cooperation and Conflict* 53, no. 4 (2018): 486–506. https://doi.org/10.1177/0010836718765902.

"Life After Reconciliation Marred by Arrests, Broken Promises as Syria's Southwest Returns to Government Control." *Syria Direct*, October 16, 2018. https://syriadirect.org/life-after-reconciliation-marred-by-arrests-broken-promises-as-syrias-southwest-returns-to-government-control/.

Lottholz, Philipp, John Heathershaw, Aksana Ismailbekova, Janyl Moldalieva, Eric McGlinchey, and Catherine Owen. "Governance and Order-Making in Central Asia: From Illiberalism to Post-Liberalism?" *Central Asian Survey* 39, no. 3 (2020): 420–437. https://doi.org/10.1080/02634937.2020.1803794.

Lubkemann, Stephen. *Culture in Chaos: An Anthropology of the Social Condition in War*. University of Chicago Press, 2007.

Madani, Toufiq al-. *The Nationalist Syrian State and the War on Terror* [in Arabic]. Syrian National Book Authority, 2018.

Makdisi, Karim. "Constructing Security Council Resolution 1701 for Lebanon in the Shadow of the 'War on Terror.'" *International Peacekeeping* 18, no. 1 (2011): 4–20. https://doi.org/10.1080/13533312.2011.527502.

Makdisi, Karim, and Coralie Pison Hindawi. "The Syrian Chemical Weapons Disarmament Process in Context: Narratives of Coercion, Consent, and Everything in Between." *Third World Quarterly* 38, no. 8 (2017): 1691–1709. https://doi.org/10.1080/01436597.2017.1322462.

Martini, Alice. "The Syrian Wars of Words: International and Local Instrumentalisations of the War on Terror." *Third World Quarterly* 41, no. 4 (2020): 725–743. https://doi.org/10.1080/01436597.2019.1699784.

Matar, Linda, and Ali Kadri, eds. *Syria: From National Independence to Proxy War*. Palgrave, 2019.

Mazur, Kevin. *Revolution in Syria: Identity, Networks, and Repression*. Cambridge University Press, 2021.

Mbembe, Achille. *Necropolitics*. Duke University Press, 2019.

Mbembe, Achille. "The Society of Enmity." *Radical Philosophy*, no. 200 (November–December 2016): 23–35. https://www.radicalphilosophy.com/article/the-society-of-enmity.

Melenotte, Sabrina. "Perpetrating Violence Viewed from the Perspective of the Social Sciences: Debates and Perspectives." *Violence: An International Journal* 1, no. 1 (2020): 40–58. https://doi.org/10.1177/2633002420924963.

Mick Krever. "Israel Strikes Syria 480 Times and Seizes Territory as Netanyahu Pledges to Change Face of the Middle East." *CNN*, December 11, 2024. https://www.cnn.com/2024/12/10/middleeast/israel-syria-assad-strikes-intl.

Mironova, Vera. *From Freedom Fighters to Jihadists: Human Resources of Non-State Armed Groups*. Oxford University Press, 2019.

"Missing Migrants Project." International Organization for Migration. Accessed July 18, 2025. https://missingmigrants.iom.int/region/mediterranean.

Moellendorf, Darrel. "Reconciliation as a Political Value." *Journal of Social Philosophy* 38, no. 2 (2007): 205–221. https://doi.org/10.1111/j.1467-9833.2007.00375.x.

Mukhopadhyay, Dipali, and Kimberly Howe. *Good Rebel Governance*. Cambridge University Press, 2023. https://doi.org/10.1017/9781108778015.

Munif, Yasser. *The Syrian Revolution: Between the Politics of Life and the Geopolitics of Death*. Pluto Press, 2020.

Munira Khayyat. *A Landscape of War: Ecologies of Resistance and Survival in South Lebanon*. University of California Press, 2022.

Munjid, Manal. "Criminal Prosecution of Terrorism Crimes in Syrian Law (an Analytical Study)" [in Arabic]. *Damascus University Journal for Economic and Legal Studies* 30, no. 2 (2014). https://www.damascusuniversity.edu.sy/mag/law/images/stories/2-2014/ar/103-148.pdf.

Mustafa, Hazem. "The Terrorism Detainees Trade: How to Become a Terrorist" [in Arabic]. *Syria Untold*, December 4, 2017. https://syriauntold.com/2017/12/04.

Nafikov, Ilsur, and Rinat Nabiev. "The Astana Process as an International Platform for Middle Eastern Regional Security: The Russian Mission." In *Contemporary Turkish-Russian Relations from Past to Future*, edited by Ilsur Nafikov and Rinat Nabiev. Istanbul University Press, 2021. https://doi.org/10.26650/B/SS52.2021.011.10.

Nassar, Fadi Nicholas. *UN Mediators in Syria: The Challenges and Responsibilities of Conflict Resolution*. Cambridge University Press, 2024.

Norwegian Refugee Council. "Syrian Refugees' Right to Legal Identity: Implications for Return." Briefing Note, January 2017. https://www.nrc.no/resources/briefing-notes/syrian-refugees-right-to-legal-identity-implications-for-return.

Nyberg Sørensen, Ninna, and Laura Huttunen. "Missing Migrants and the Politics of Disappearance in Armed Conflicts and Migratory Contexts." *Ethnos* 87, no. 2 (2022): 321–337. https://doi.org/10.1080/00141844.2019.1697333.

Oettler, Anika, and Angelika Rettberg. "Varieties of Reconciliation in Violent Contexts: Lessons from Colombia." *Peacebuilding* 7, no. 3 (2019): 329–352. https://doi.org/10.1080/21647259.2019.1617029.

Ogbaharya, Daniel G. "(Re-)Building Governance in Post-Conflict Africa: The Role of the State and Informal Institutions." *Development in Practice* 18, no. 3 (2008): 395–402. https://doi.org/10.1080/09614520802030482.

Öjendal, Joakim, and Sivhuoch Ou. "From Friction to Hybridity in Cambodia: 20 Years of Unfinished Peacebuilding." *Peacebuilding* 1, no. 3 (2013): 365–380. https://doi.org/10.1080/21647259.2013.813178.

Öjendal, Joakim, and Sivhouch Ou. "The 'Local Turn' Saving Liberal Peacebuilding? Unpacking Virtual Peace in Cambodia." *Third World Quarterly* 36, no. 5 (2015): 929–949. https://doi.org/10.1080/01436597.2015.1030387.

"On the Ministry of Oil's Investment Budget and the Work of the Ministry of National Reconciliation" [in Arabic]. Syrian Arab News Agency, November 12, 2018. https://pministry.gov.sy/contents/13904/contents/14243/الش-مجلس-في-والحسابات-الموازنة-لجنة
عب-تناقش-مشروع-قانون-الموازنة-العامة-للدولة-لعام--2019مع-وزارات-الصناعة،الزراعة،الموارد-المائية،النف
ط،النقل،السياحة،الأوقاف،الصحة.

Owen, Catherine, Shairbek Juraev, David Lewis, Nick Megoran, and John Heathershaw, eds. *Interrogating Illiberal Peace in Eurasia: Critical Perspectives on Peace and Conflict.* Rowman and Littlefield, 2018.

Özçelik, Burcu. "What Can a Political Form of Reconciliation Look Like in Divided Societies?" *Democratic Theory* 9, no. 1 (2022): 52–72. https://doi.org/10.3167/dt.2022.090104.

"A Palace in Shock: Bashar al-Assad's Final Moments in Syria." *France 24*, December 14, 2024. https://www.france24.com/en/live-news/20241214-a-palace-in-shock-bashar-al-assad-s-final-moments-in-syria.

Papagianni, Katia. "Political Transitions After Peace Agreements: The Importance of Consultative and Inclusive Political Processes." *Journal of Intervention and Statebuilding* 3, no. 1 (2009): 47–63. https://doi.org/10.1080/17502970802608175.

Parlar Dal, Emel. "Rising Powers in International Conflict Management: An Introduction." *Third World Quarterly* 39, no. 12 (2018): 2207–2221. https://doi.org/10.1080/01436597.2018.1503048.

"Peace Agreements Database." University of Edinburgh. Accessed February 21, 2024. https://www.peaceagreements.org.

Pearlman, Wendy. *We Crossed a Bridge and It Trembled: Voices from Syria.* Custom House, 2017.

"People's Assembly Discusses the Performance of the Ministry of National Reconciliation and the Expansion of Local Reconciliations" [in Arabic]. Syrian Arab News Agency, March 6, 2016. https://archive.sana.sy/?p=347987.

Phillips, Christopher. *The Battle for Syria: International Rivalry in the New Middle East.* Yale University Press, 2016.

Phillips, Christopher. "Sectarianism and Conflict in Syria." *Third World Quarterly* 36, no. 2 (2015): 357–376. https://doi.org/10.1080/01436597.2015.1015788.

Phillips, Christopher, and Morten Valbjørn. "'What Is in a Name?': The Role of (Different) Identities in the Multiple Proxy Wars in Syria." *Small Wars & Insurgencies* 29, no. 3 (2018): 414–433. https://doi.org/10.1080/09592318.2018.1455328.

Piccolino, Giulia. Review of *Winning Wars, Building (Illiberal) Peace? The Rise (and Possible Fall) of a Victor's Peace in Rwanda and Sri Lanka*, by Scott Straus, Lars Waldorf, Maddalena Campioni, Patrick Noack, Filip Reyntjens, Jonathan Goodhand, Benedikt Korf, Jonathan Spencer, Kristian Stokke, and Jayadeva Uyangoda. *Third World Quarterly* 36, no. 9 (2015): 1770–1785. http://www.jstor.org/stable/24523149.

Podder, Sukanya. "Mainstreaming the Non-State in Bottom-Up State-Building: Linkages Between Rebel Governance and Post-Conflict Legitimacy." *Conflict, Security & Development* 14, no. 2 (2014): 213–243. https://doi.org/10.1080/14678802.2014.889878.

"Popular Support for Settlements in Deir ez-Zor, Raqqa, and Aleppo" [in Arabic]. *Al-Wahda*, April 10, 2022. http://wehda.alwehda.gov.sy/?p=49965.

Pospisil, Jan. "Dissolving Conflict. Local Peace Agreements and Armed Conflict Transitions." *Peacebuilding* 10, no. 2 (2022): 122–137. https://doi.org/10.1080/21647259.2022.2032945.

"Preliminary Analysis of the Law on Managing and Investing Transferrable and Non-Transferrable Assets That Were Seized Pursuant to an Unappealable Judicial Ruling, as Promulgated by the People's Assembly of Syria." Syrian Network for Human Rights, December 9, 2023. https://reliefweb.int/report/syrian-arab-republic/preliminary-analysis-law-managing-and-investing-transferable-and-non-transferable-assets-were-seized-pursuant-unappealable-judicial-ruling-promulgated-peoples-assembly-syria-enar.

"President Al-Assad: The War Was Between Us Syrians and Terrorism, We Triumph Together Not Against Each Other." Syrian Arab News Agency, February 19, 2019. https://archive.sana.sy/en/?p=158819.

"Press Remarks by UN Special Envoy for Syria, Mr. Staffan de Mistura, in Astana, Kazakhstan, 24 January 2017." United Nations Office for the Special Envoy for Syria, January 24, 2017. https://www.un.org/sg/en/content/sg/note-correspondents/2017-01-24/note-correspondents-secretary-generals-special-envoy-for-syria-staffan-de-mistura-astana.

Qandil, Nasir. "Putin and Assad . . . and Roosevelt and Stalin—al-Thawra Newspaper." Syrian Arab News Agency, October 23, 2015. https://archive.sana.sy/?p=287488.

Raemdonck, An Van. "Syrian Refugee Men in 'Double Waithood': Ethnographic Perspectives on Labour and Marriage in Jordan's Border Towns." *Gender, Place & Culture* 30, no. 5 (2023): 692–713. https://doi.org/10.1080/0966369X.2023.2178390.

Ratta, Donatella Della. *Shooting a Revolution: Visual Media and Warfare in Syria*. Pluto Press, 2018.

"Receiving Requests to Settle the Status of Former Regime Security Personnel in Damascus" [in Arabic]. *Al Arabiyya Syria*, December 21, 2024. https://youtu.be/95vX7mzkdMI?si=s8iLd1mmtogaTlRK.

"Regime Tallies IDP Properties in Idlib and Hama for Auction." *Syria Report*, June 22, 2022. https://hlp.syria-report.com/hlp/regime-tallies-idp-properties-in-idlib-and-hama-for-auction/.

Reina, Jenniffer Vargas. "Coalitions for Land Grabbing in Wartime: State, Paramilitaries and Elites in Colombia." *Journal of Peasant Studies* 49, no. 2 (2022): 288–308. https://doi.org/10.1080/03066150.2020.1835870.

"Returnee Numbers Remain Very Low in Al-Hajar Al-Aswad as Looting Continues." *Syria Report*, March 8, 2022. https://hlp.syria-report.com/hlp/returnee-numbers-remain-very-low-in-al-hajar-al-aswad-as-looting-continues/.

Reuters. "Syria's Interim Govt Overhauls Economy with Privatizations, Layoffs." *Daily Sabah*, January 31, 2025. https://www.dailysabah.com/business/economy/syrias-interim-govt-overhauls-economy-with-privatizations-layoffs.

Rezvani, Babak. "Russian Foreign Policy and Geopolitics in the Post-Soviet Space and the Middle East: Tajikistan, Georgia, Ukraine and Syria." *Middle Eastern Studies* 56, no. 6 (2020): 878–899. https://doi.org/10.1080/00263206.2020.1775590.

Richani, Nazih. "The Political Economy and Complex Interdependency of the War System in Syria." *Civil Wars* 18, no. 1 (2016): 45–68. https://doi.org/10.1080/13698249.2016.1144495.

Rieff, David. "A New Age of Liberal Imperialism?" *World Policy Journal* 16, no. 2 (1999): 1–10. https://www.jstor.org/stable/40209622.

"Russian Airstrikes Update." Carter Center, January 29, 2016. https://www.cartercenter.org/resources/pdfs/peace/conflict_resolution/syria-conflict/Russian-Airstrikes-Update-Jan-29-2016.pdf.

Sadany, Mai el-. "When Assad Asks Syrians to Come Home, Here's What He Really Means." *Hill*, October 16, 2018. https://thehill.com/opinion/international/401638-when-assad-asks-syrians-to-come-home-heres-what-he-really-means/.

Salloukh, Bassel F. "War Memory, Confessional Imaginaries, and Political Contestation in Postwar Lebanon." *Middle East Critique* 28, no. 3 (2019): 341–359. https://doi.org/10.1080/19436149.2019.1633748.

Salloum, Dourayd. "Decree to Reconstitute the Counter Terrorism Court and Appoint Investigative Judges and Prosecutors" [in Arabic]. *Syrian Days*, February 25, 2020. https://www.syriandays.com/index.php?page=show_det&select_page=50&id=61312.

Sami Hermez. *War Is Coming: Between Past and Future Violence in Lebanon*. University of Pennsylvania Press, 2017.

Sarajlić, Eldar. "Conceptualising Citizenship Regime(s) in Post-Dayton Bosnia and Herzegovina." *Citizenship Studies* 16, nos. 3–4 (2012): 367–381. https://doi.org/10.1080/13621025.2012.683247.

"Scenes from Settling the Status of Military and Police Personnel in Damascus After Bashar al-Assad Fled" [in Arabic]. *Step News*, December 24, 2024. https://www.youtube.com/watch?v=E2NSD659Gjc.

Schmitt, Carl. *The Concept of the Political*. Expanded ed. University of Chicago Press, 2007.

Schwartz, Stephanie. "Home, Again: Refugee Return and Post-Conflict Violence in Burundi." *International Security* 44, no. 2 (2019): 110–145. https://doi.org/10.1162/isec_a_00362.

Selim, Yvette. "Contestation and Resistance: The Politics of and around Transitional Justice in Nepal." *Conflict, Security & Development* 18, no. 1 (2018): 39–60. https://doi.org/10.1080/14678802.2017.1420314.

Selvik, Kjetil, and Tamar Groves. "'The Generation That Will Inherit Syria': Education as Citizen Aid and Political Opportunity." *Third World Quarterly* 44, no. 5 (2023): 930–945. https://doi.org/10.1080/01436597.2023.2167705.

"Settling the Status of Hundreds of Wanted Persons in Hama Governorate" [in Arabic]. Syrian Arab News Agency, October 19, 2022. https://sana.sy/?p=1766132.

Shaar, Karam, and Ayman Dasouki. "Syria's Constitutional Committee: The Devil in the Detail." Middle East Institute, January 6, 2021. https://www.mei.edu/publications/syrias-constitutional-committee-devil-detail.

Shaery-Yazdi, Roschanack, and Uğur Ümit Üngör. "Mass Violence in Syria: Continuity and Change." *British Journal of Middle Eastern Studies* 49, no. 3 (2022): 397–402. https://doi.org/10.1080/13530194.2021.1916146.

Sheikho, Kamal. "Interview with Lawyer and Human Rights Activist Michel Shamas" [in Arabic]. *Suwar Magazine*, November 2, 2015. https://www.suwar-magazine.org/articles/1138_شماس-ميشيل-والحقوقي-المحامي-تحاور34--ر-صو34--مجلة.

Siegel, James T. *A New Criminal Type in Jakarta: Counter-Revolution Today*. Duke University Press, 1998.

Simon, Steven, and Jonathan Stevenson. "The Road to Damascus." *Foreign Affairs* 83, no. 3 (2004): 110–118. https://doi.org/10.2307/20033979.

Sluka, Jeffrey A. "Introduction: State Terror and Anthropology." In *Death Squad: The Anthropology of State Terror*, edited by Jeffrey A. Sluka. University of Pennsylvania Press, 2000.

Smith, Claire Q., Lars Waldorf, Rajesh Venugopal, and Gerard McCarthy. "Illiberal Peace-Building in Asia: A Comparative Overview." *Conflict, Security & Development* 20, no. 1 (2020): 1–14. https://doi.org/10.1080/14678802.2019.1705066.

Sosa, Santiago. "The Micro-Dynamics of Conflict and Peace: Evidence from Colombia." *International Interactions* 49, no. 2 (2023): 163–170. https://doi.org/10.1080/03050629.2023.2189705.

Sosnowski, Marika. "Reconciliation Agreements as Strangle Contracts: Ramifications for Property and Citizenship Rights in the Syrian Civil War." *Peacebuilding* 8, no. 4 (2020): 460–475. https://doi.org/10.1080/21647259.2019.1646693.

Sottimano, Aurora. "Building Authoritarian 'Legitimacy': Domestic Compliance and International Standing of Bashar al-Asad's Syria." *Global Discourse* 6, no. 3 (2016): 450–466. https://doi.org/10.1080/23269995.2016.1152790.

Stacher, Joshua. "Fragmenting States, New Regimes: Militarized State Violence and Transition in the Middle East." *Democratization* 22, no. 2 (2015): 259–275. https://doi.org/10.1080/13510347.2015.1010810.

Stokke, Kristian. "Crafting Liberal Peace? International Peace Promotion and the Contextual Politics of Peace in Sri Lanka." *Annals of the Association of American Geographers* 99, no. 5 (2009): 932–939. https://doi.org/10.1080/00045600903245920.

Stubblefield, Emily, and Sandra Joireman. "Law, Violence, and Property Expropriation in Syria: Impediments to Restitution and Return." *Land* 8, no. 11 (2019): 173. https://doi.org/10.3390/land8110173.

Suleiman, Ashraf. "The Regime Continues to Pursue Reconciliation Factions in Barzeh" [in Arabic]. *Baladi News*, January 8, 2019. https://www.baladi-news.com/ar/news/details/39919/برزة_في_المصالحات_فصائل_وعناصر_قادة_ملاحقة_يواصل_النظام.

"Syria: Counterterrorism Court Used to Stifle Dissent." Human Rights Watch, June 25, 2013. https://www.hrw.org/news/2013/06/25/syria-counterterrorism-court-used-stifle-dissent.

"Syria Conflict Update." Carter Center, October 30, 2015. https://www.cartercenter.org/resources/pdfs/peace/conflict_resolution/syria-conflict/syria-conflict-update-103015.pdf.

Syrian Arab Republic Parliament. "Establishing a Court to Prosecute Terrorism Cases Law No. 22 of 2012 Based in Damascus" [in Arabic]. Accessed February 18, 2024. http://parliament.gov.sy/arabic/index.php?node=201&nid=4304&ref=tree&.

Syrian Arab Republic Parliament. "Law No. 19 of 2012, the Anti-Terrorism Law" [in Arabic]. Accessed February 18, 2024. http://www.parliament.gov.sy/arabic/index.php?node=55151&nid=4306&First=0&Last=23&CurrentPage=0&mid=&refBack=.

Syrian Arab Republic Parliament. "Law No. 20 of 2012 Dismisses from State Service Anyone Convicted by Court Decision of Committing Any Terrorist Act" [in Arabic]. Accessed February 18, 2024. http://www.parliament.gov.sy/arabic/index.php?node=201&nid=4307&ref=tree&.

Syrian Arab Republic Parliament. "Law No. 21 of 2012 Amending the Penal Code 556 Issued by Decree No. 148 of 1949556" [in Arabic]. Accessed February 18, 2024. http://www.parliament.gov.sy/arabic/index.php?node=57151&.

"Syrian Government Ends Reconciliation System." North Press Agency, October 23, 2020. https://npasyria.com/en/48653/.

"Syrian Regional Refugee Response." United Nations High Commissioner for Refugees Operational Data Portal. Accessed July 18, 2025. https://data.unhcr.org/en/situations/syria.

Szekely, Ora. *Syria Divided: Patterns of Violence in a Complex Civil War.* Columbia University Press, 2023.

"Total Death Toll: Over 606,000 People Killed Across Syria Since the Beginning of the 'Syrian Revolution,' Including 495,000 Documented by SOHR." Syrian Observatory for Human Rights, June 1, 2021. https://www.syriahr.com/en/217360/.

Turkmani, Rim. "Local Agreements as a Process: The Example of Local Talks in Homs in Syria." *Peacebuilding* 10, no. 2 (2022): 156–171. https://doi.org/10.1080/21647259.2022.2032941.

Tziarras, Zenonas. *Ethical Issues and Controversies in the Astana Process: Questioning Representation and Ownership.* FAIR Case Brief 4. Peace Research Institute Oslo, 2022. https://cdn.cloud.prio.org/files/9a0008d3-49cd-4070-9a29-32c347621b4a/Tziarras%20-%20Ethical%20Issues%20and%20Controversies%20in%20the%20Astana%20Process%20Questioning%20Representation%20and%20Ownership%20-%20FAIR%20Case%20Brief%204.pdf?inline=true.

Üngör, Uğur Ümit. "Forum: Mass Violence in Syria." *Journal of Genocide Research* 25, no. 1 (2023): 84–88. https://doi.org/10.1080/14623528.2021.1979907.

Üngör, Uğur Ümit. "*Shabbiha*: Paramilitary Groups, Mass Violence and Social Polarization in Homs." *Violence: An International Journal* 1, no. 1 (2020): 59–79. https://doi.org/10.1177/2633002420907771.

"A Unified Stance Rejects Attacking Iraq" [in Arabic]. *Al Jazeera*, February 18, 2002. https://www.aljazeera.net/news/presstour/2002/2/18/العراق-ضرب-يرفض-موحد-موقف.

Unruh, Jon D. "Weaponization of the Land and Property Rights System in the Syrian Civil War: Facilitating Restitution?" *Journal of Intervention and Statebuilding* 10, no. 4 (2016): 453–471. https://doi.org/10.1080/17502977.2016.1158527.

Uzonyi, Gary. "Bureaucratic Quality and the Severity of Genocide and Politicide." *Dynamics of Asymmetric Conflict* 13, no. 2 (2020): 125–142. https://doi.org/10.1080/17467586.2019.1650387.

"The View from Damascus: Failure of Syria's National Dialogue Conference and Its Implications." *Syrian Observer*, March 25, 2025. https://syrianobserver.com/syrian-actors/the-view-from-damascus-failure-of-syrias-national-dialogue-conference-and-its-implications.html.

Violations Documentation Center. *Counter-Terrorism Court: A Tool for War Crimes: Special Report on Counter-Terrorism Law No. 19 and the Counter-Terrorism Court in Syria*. Violations Documentation Center, April 2015. https://icct.nl/sites/default/files/import/publication/1430186775-English.pdf.

"Walid Moallem at Press Conference: Combatting Terrorism Is a Duty of Every Syrian to Protect Their Land and Homeland" [in Arabic]. *Dam Press*, February 14, 2014. https://www.dampress.net/mobile/?page=show_det&category_id=5&id=39328&_x_tr_sl=en&_x_tr_tl=ar&_x_tr_hl=en&_x_tr_pto=wapp.

"'The War on Syria Has Failed,' Foreign Minister Says in UN Speech, Denouncing the West's Hegemonic Ambitions." *UN News*, September 22, 2022. https://news.un.org/en/story/2022/09/1128011.

Wasl, Zaman al-. "Military Security Arrests Former Rebel Commanders Who Agreed Reconciliation Deal." *Syrian Observer*, July 25, 2019. https://syrianobserver.com/foreign-actors/military-security-arrests-former-rebel-commanders-who-agreed-reconciliation-deal.html.

Waters, Gregory. "The Growing Role of Reconciled Rebels in Syria." *International Review*, April 21, 2018. https://international-review.org/the-growing-role-of-reconciled-rebels-in-syria/.

Wedeen, Lisa. *Ambiguities of Domination: Politics, Rhetoric, and Symbols in Contemporary Syria*. University of Chicago Press, 2015.

Wedeen, Lisa. *Authoritarian Apprehensions: Ideology, Judgment, and Mourning in Syria*. University of Chicago Press, 2019.

Wedeen, Lisa. "Epilogue." *British Journal of Middle Eastern Studies* 49, no. 3 (2022): 500–505. https://doi.org/10.1080/13530194.2021.1920280.

Wessels, Josepha. "Killing the Dispensables: Massacres Perpetrated in the Villages of Eastern Aleppo Province in 2013." *British Journal of Middle Eastern Studies* 49, no. 3 (2022): 463–485. https://doi.org/10.1080/13530194.2021.1920267.

Wessels, Josepha Ivanka. *Documenting Syria: Film-Making, Video Activism and Revolution*. I. B. Tauris, 2019.

Wilhelmsen, Julie. "Putin's Power Revisited: How Identity Positions and Great Power Interaction Condition Strategic Cooperation on Syria." *Europe-Asia Studies* 71, no. 7 (2019): 1091–1121. https://doi.org/10.1080/09668136.2019.1602594.

Wolff, Jonas. "Beyond the Liberal Peace: Latin American Inspirations for Post-Liberal Peacebuilding." *Peacebuilding* 3, no. 3 (2015): 279–296. https://doi.org/10.1080/21647259.2015.1040606.

Wong, Kwok Chung. "The Rise of China's Developmental Peace: Can an Economic Approach to Peacebuilding Create Sustainable Peace?" *Global Society* 35, no. 4 (2021): 522–540. https://doi.org/10.1080/13600826.2021.1942802.

Woodward, Susan L. *The Ideology of Failed States: Why Intervention Fails.* Cambridge University Press, 2017.

Worrall, James, and Victoria Penziner Hightower. "Methods in the Madness? Exploring the Logics of Torture in Syrian Counterinsurgency Practices." *British Journal of Middle Eastern Studies* 49, no. 3 (2022): 418–432. https://doi.org/10.1080/13530194.2021.1916154.

Wright, George. "Sharaa Vows to Pursue Criminals as Syria's Transitional President." *BBC News*, January 31, 2025. https://bbc.com/news/articles/czep8kyeeyyo.

Yacoubian, Mona. "What Is Russia's Endgame in Syria? Lacking Better Options, Russia Appears to Be Pursuing a 'Spheres of Influence' Model." United States Institute of Peace, February 16, 2021. https://www.usip.org/publications/2021/02/what-russias-endgame-syria.

Yassin-Kassab, Robin, and Leila al-Shami. *Burning Country: Syrians in Revolution and War.* 2nd ed. Pluto Press, 2018.

Yazbeck, Samar. *A Woman in the Crossfire: Diaries of the Syrian Revolution.* Translated by Max Weiss. Haus Publishing, 2012.

Yuan, Xinyu. "The Chinese Approach to Peacebuilding: Contesting Liberal Peace?" *Third World Quarterly* 43, no. 7 (2022): 1798–1816. https://doi.org/10.1080/01436597.2022.2074389.

Index

AANES. *See* Autonomous Administration of North and East Syria
Abdi, Mazloum, 177
absence, 139; categorization of, 35, 140–147, 160; disloyal subjects and, 160–161; disloyalty contrasted with, 115–116, 137–138, 141–142; erasure and, 158–160; property appropriation and, 153–158
absenteeism, 145, 151
absent subject (*ghayab*), 138
ACM. *See* authoritarian conflict management
Action Group on Syria, 46
Aleppo (Syria), 124, 165
Aleppo Freeze, 50
Allowance and Exemption Branch, of army, 151
alternative approaches, to conflict management, 38–39, 185
Amanah al-Suriah al-Wahidah, al-. *See* Single Syrian Registry
amnesty, 91, 123–124
Amnesty Law No. 18, 150

Annan, Kofi, 46
antiterrorism policies, spectral terrorist undergirding, 141–142
Arab uprisings, 70
armed fighters, 110–111
armed group control, 41
armed groups: demilitarization and demobilization of, 179; reconciliation between, 97–98. *See also specific armed groups*
army, Syrian, 165; Allowance and Exemption Branch of, 151; chemical weapons used by, 47
Assad, Bashar al-, 1–3, 46–47, 68, 70, 86, 137; collapse of regime of, 162–163; on desertion and evasion, 150
asset appropriation, disloyal subjects and, 187
Astana process, 21, 33–34, 38, 49, 60–61, 162; collapse of, 176; designs for, 39–40; Erdoğan on, 37; HTS and SDF excluded from, 57; liberal intervention avoided through, 183; origins and design of, 55–56; as regional conflict

Astana process (*continued*)
    management, 52–60; social death and, 56–57; UN sidelined during, 51–52; violence sanctioned by, 59
authoritarian alchemy, settlement process as, 119–126
authoritarian conflict management (ACM), xiii, 184–185, 190; enmity and, 18–23; hegemonic narrative of conflict created by, 20–21; illiberal peace distinguished from, 5; illiberal state building distinguished from, 19
authoritarian peace, 31
Autonomous Administration of North and East Syria (AANES), 159, 166, 180

Ba'athist authoritarian rule, 163
Ba'athist rule, 66, 169
battlefield, Syrian: conflict management contrasted with, 184; fragmentation of, 41–42, 46; regional conflicts shaping, 41; Russian military intervention shifting, 44–45; shifts in, 164–166
bifurcation, 4–5, 20, 34–35, 63–68, 147, 186, 190; political hatred and, 17; through settlement, 126
bureaucratic capacity, 15–16
bureaucratic governance, war as, 26–27
bureaucratization of conflict, mass violence and, 16–17
bureaucratization of enmity, 15–16, 18

categorization, 20, 61, 74, 107–108, 115–117; of absence, 35, 140–147, 160; commonsense narrative materialized through, 188–189; conflict narration and, 183; of death, 35, 143, 149–150; of the diseased, 147–150; of disloyal subjects, 14; of displacement, 35; the law in relation to, 22–23; of martyrdom, 149–150; through reconciliation agreements, 109; reward and punishment regimes informed by, 25–26; settlement process and, 135; the state absorbing, 4; by state officials, 183, 188; subjectivization linked with, 189; of terrorism, 84
ceasefires (freezes), 49–51, 53–54
Center for Reconciliation of Opposing Sides and Refugee Migration Monitoring in the Syrian Arab Republic (Reconciliation Center), 99–100
Central Real Estate Directorate, 101
Charter for National Reconciliation and Peace, 89
Circular No. 30, 155
citizen assets, state appropriation of, 157
citizen behavior, reward and punishment regimes structuring, 80
citizenship, gradations of, 133
citizenship regimes, as tool of inclusion and exclusion, 134
citizen subjectivity: settlement process and, 121, 131–132; the state constructing, 6–7
civil committees, 96; property and, 28–29; the state backing, 2; outside state oversight, 28
Civil Initiative Committees. *See* National Reconciliation Commission
Civil Initiative for Local Reconciliation (*al Mbadrah al Ahliyah lil Musalahat al Mhliyah*), 95
civil registries, Syrians not registered with, 145–146
Civil Registries Division of the Syrian Ministry of Interior, 144–145
Civil Registry Centers (CRC), xiii, 146
Civil Status, 145–146
Civil Status Code, 100
Civil Status Law No. 13, 146–147
civil war regime, 5, 15, 19, 65, 182, 186
civil war settlement, 167–168
collective victimhood, 130–132

commonsense narrative, 61, 69, 92, 127, 131, 142–143; categorization materializing, 188–189; institutionalization of, 32–33; spectral terrorist and, 88; state officials creating, 20
conflict absorption, 26–31
conflict management, 84–85; alternative approaches to, 38–39, 185; battlefield contrasted with, 184; disloyal subjects and, 6; by illiberal state, 181; outside liberal powers, 60; political order through, 184–191; reconciliation as, 97–103; regime power maintained through, 185–186; regional, 52–60; repatriation as, 135–136; settlement as, 135–136; by Syrian regime, 166–167, 182–183. *See also* authoritarian conflict management
conflict management practices, 95–96
conflict management strategies, 102; reconciliation agreements as, 99; of the state, 3; war on terror and, 2
constitutional reforms, UN and, 57–58
Council of Ministers, 28, 93, 117
counterinsurgency campaign, of the state, 13
counterterrorism: state violence and, 72; war as, 83–84
Counter-Terrorism Court (CTC), xiii, 34, 61, 71, 72–73, 78–79; chambers of, 75–76; Law No. 22 creating, 74, 77
counterterrorism state, Syria as, 72–79
CRC. *See* Civil Registry Centers
CTC. *See* Counter-Terrorism Court

Dayr ez-Zor Governorate, 112
DDR. *See* disarmament, demobilization, and reintegration
death, 139–140; categorization of, 35, 143, 149–150. *See also* social death
deceased, the, categorization of, 147–150
deceived citizens, 116, 119, 128–129

deceived or psychologically unstable citizen, settlement of, 114–115
deceived subjects, 125, 131
decentralization, 192
Decree No. 7, 123, 124
Decree No. 11, 144, 159
Decree No. 14, 99
Decree No. 22, 93
Decree No. 53, 73
Decree No. 63, 74, 157
Decree No. 361, 93
de-escalation zones, 53–54, 57
deliberation, reconciliation eschewing, 124
demilitarization, governance and, 178–180
deserters, 150–152
desertion, 118, 150
digitization, of national registry, 146
Directorate for Managing Seized Funds and Confiscated Property (*Mudeerat al Amwal al Masdrah wu al Mistuli 'Lihah*), 102–103
disappearance, 142–143
disarmament, demobilization, and reintegration (DDR), xiii, 99, 105–106
disloyal citizens, loyal citizens separated from, 4, 133–134
disloyal subjects: absence and, 160–161; asset appropriation and, 187; categorization of, 14; conflict management and, 6; punishment targeting, 183; social death of, 192; the state targeting, 14; wanted category and, 160–161
disloyal Syrians, legal infrastructure and, 94
disloyalty, 79–83; absence contrasted with, 115–116, 137–138, 141–142; as acts, 27; codification of, 26; state officials framing, 69, 80
displaced by terrorism (*al mahajriyn bf'l al irhab*), 116–117, 128
displaced people, 117
displaced Syrians, 7–8

238 INDEX

displacement, 7, 136, 139; categorization of, 35; forced, 87; reconciliation contrasted with, 105; violence and, 140 documentation, 75; of life events, 144–146; of property ownership and life events, 144; property transfers and, 145

Eastern Ghouta, 101
Economic and Social Commission for West Asia (ESCWA), xiii
economic destruction, in Syria, 174
elites, 6, 153, 187
emergency politics, 79
enmity, 23–26; ACM and, 18–23; bureaucratization of, 15–16, 18; politics structured by, 24; society of, 24; the state and, 25, 64; against state enemies, 7. *See also* political hatred
erasure, absence and, 158–160
Erdoğan, Recep Tayyip, 37, 55, 176
ESCWA. *See* Economic and Social Commission for West Asia; United Nations' Economic and Social Commission for West Asia
European Union, 9, 178
evaders, 150–152
exemption fee (*badal al-nakdi*), 151
expropriated assets, the state funneling, 153
expropriation infrastructure, 108

fasaeel al musalahat. *See* reconciliation factions
fear, 79–80, 135
forced displacement, 87
forced expulsion, 100
Fr' al Amn al Dualah. *See* State Security Branch
Fr' al Amn al Siyasi. *See* Political Security Branch
Free Syrian Army (FSA), xiii, 40–41
freezes. *See* ceasefires

friend/enemy binary, 4, 23, 25, 65, 80–81, 119
FSA. *See* Free Syrian Army

genealogy of loyalty, 113–114, 128–129
Geneva III, 48–49
Geneva II talks, 46–47
Geneva I negotiations, 62–63
Geneva Process, 45–52
ghayab. *See* absent subject
global war on terror (GWOT), xiii, 63; Syria embracing, 68–69; Syrian regime instrumentalizing, 70–71
Golan Heights (Israel), 177
governable populations, 64
governance, demilitarization and, 178–180
GWOT. *See* global war on terror

Haidar, Ali, 93, 94, 95
Hajr al-Aswad, al- (Syria), 156
hal ajtma'ee. *See* social solution
Hama (site of massacre), 66–67
Hayat Tahrir al-Sham (HTS), xiii, 53, 57, 59, 162, 180
hegemonic narrative of conflict, ACM creating, 20–21
High Negotiation Committee (HNC), xiii, 49
HLP. *See* housing, land, and property rights
HNC. *See* High Negotiation Committee
housing, land, and property rights (HLP), xiii, 16, 153–154, 155–156. *See also* property
HTS. *See* Hayat Tahrir al-Sham

ideology, 121
Idlib (Syria), 108, 111
illiberal peace, ACM distinguished from, 5
illiberal political order, conflict absorption and, 26–29
illiberal reconciliation, 109–111
illiberal state, conflict management by, 181

illiberal state building, ACM distinguished from, 19
Internal Displacement Monitoring Center, 7
international diplomacy, 11
International Syrian Support Group (ISSG), xiii, 48
Iran, 37, 51–52
Islamic State of Iraq and al-Sham (ISIS), xiii, 12, 41, 158–159
Islamist fighters, FSA in conflict with, 40
Israel, 37, 177
ISSG. *See* International Syrian Support Group

Jabhat an-Nusra (JAN), xiii, 41
Jordan, 8
justice, transitional, 171–174

kin punishment, 152–153, 160
kulna lil watan. *See* "We Are All for the Homeland"
Kurds, 53, 55, 73, 177

LAS. *See* League of Arab States
law, the, categorization in relation to, 22–23
Law No. 4, 100
Law No. 10, 155
Law No. 11, 100, 145, 155
Law No. 19, 68–71, 73, 78, 83, 154
Law No. 20, 74, 77
Law No. 21, 74
Law No. 22, 74, 154
Law No. 23, 100
Law No. 26, 157
Law No. 33, 100, 101, 151, 155
Law No. 35, 151, 154
Law No. 39, Military Service Law amended by, 151
Law No. 63, 151, 154, 155
League of Arab States (LAS), xiii, 40, 45, 46
Lebanon, 8, 172
legal bargaining, 22

legal infrastructure, disloyal Syrians and, 94
legible populations, 23–26, 64
liberal actors, peacebuilding and, 53
liberal intervention, Astana process avoiding, 183
liberalism, 20, 38, 45, 190
liberal peace, 31, 185
liberal powers, conflict management outside, 60
life events, 144–146, 159–160
Llijnah al Ahliyah, al-. *See* National Reconciliation Committees
loyal citizens, disloyal citizens separated from, 4, 133–134
loyal-disloyal cleavage, 189
loyalist subjects, 26
loyalist victim, 131
loyal returnees, 2, 113, 126–132
loyalty, genealogy of, 128–129
loyalty tests, 4, 35

mahajriyn bf'l al irhab, al-. *See* displaced by terrorism
"Managing and Investing Transferable and Non-Transferable Assets That Were Seized Pursuant to an Unappealable Judicial Ruling" (law), 103, 157
markaz al tasaweeah. *See* settlement centers
martyrdom, categorization of, 149–150
Martyrdom Law No. 1, 149
mass violence, 12–13, 63; bureaucratization of conflict and, 16–17; bureaucratization of enmity and, 18; in Syria, 14–15
matloob. *See* wanted category
Mbadrah al Ahliyah lil Musalahat al Mhliyah, al. *See* Civil Initiative for Local Reconciliation
memory politics, 173–174
military intervention, Russian. *See* Russian military intervention

Military Service and Security Personnel Law Decree No. 15, 149
Military Service Law, Law No. 39 amending, 151
Ministry of Agriculture and Agrarian Reform, 157
Ministry of Finance, 74, 96, 102, 103, 157, 187
Ministry of Interior, Civil Registries Division of the Syrian, 144–145
Ministry of Internal Trade and Consumer Protection, 153
Ministry of Justice, 155
Ministry of National Reconciliation (*Wzrat al Dulah Lshun al Musalahat al Wataniyah*), 28, 93–97, 110
Ministry of Petroleum and Mineral Resources, 153
missing, the, 139–140
Mistura, Staffan de, 48–51
mmn lam ttltakh aydiyhm baldma. *See* stained in blood
Moallem, Walid, 62–63
Mudeerat al Amwal al Masdrah wu al Mistuli 'Lihah. *See* Directorate for Managing Seized Funds and Confiscated Property
musalaha. *See* reconciliation
Muslim Brotherhood, 143–144

National Agenda for the Future of Syria project, 86
National Defense Forces (NDF), xiii, 99, 106, 150
National Reconciliation Commission, 93
National Reconciliation Committees (Civil Initiative Committees) (*al Llijnah al Ahliyah*), 93, 94, 96
"National Reconciliation for the Good of the Homeland" (civil initiative), 95
NDF. *See* National Defense Forces
necroviolence, 147–149
neo-patrimonial rule, 6
non-state authority, the state erasing, 100

Norwegian Refugee Council, 144
noufous. *See* registry offices

Obama administration, 47
"official amnesia," in Lebanon, 172
Official Gazette (newspaper), 186
OPCW. *See* Organisation for the Prohibition of Chemical Weapons
Operation Euphrates Shield, 53, 59
opposition presence, erasure of, 21
Organisation for the Prohibition of Chemical Weapons (OPCW), xiii, 47–48
ownership requirements, tenure laws and, 156

parallel societies, 79
peace: authoritarian, 31; illiberal, 5; liberal, 31, 185; Syrian regime crafting, 89
"peace," Russian military intervention followed by, 30–31
peacebuilding: by China, 38–39; liberal actors and, 53
People's Assembly, 93, 103
People's Defense Units (*Yekîneyên Parastina Gel*) (YPG), xiv
political economy: spatial control of territory and, 21–22; violence incentivized by, 42
political encounters, 169–171
political hatred, 6–7, 23; bifurcation and, 17; the state structured, 25
political order, 29–31, 91, 97, 109, 168; through conflict management, 184–191; illiberal, 26–29; moral-, 120; spectral terrorist organizing, 81; Syrian regime creating, 3
political process reconciliation, 88
Political Security Branch (*Fr' al Amn al Siyasi*), 83
political transition, 165–167
population, legible, 23–26, 64

population, of Syria: governable, 64; management of, 189–190; regime distinguished from, 6; the state warring with, 5, 15
post-conflict transitions, universalist liberal ideas and, 45
power dynamics, 184–185
power-of-attorney system, subjected to security approval, 155
power-sharing agreements, 105–106
prison system, Syrian, 13
production of knowledge, by the state, 4
property, 102, 143–144; appropriation of, 103, 153–158; civil committees and, 28–29; disputes over, 175; expropriation of, 186; reclamation of, 156
property confiscation, terrorism tied to, 154–155
property ownership, documentation of, 144
property restitution, 175–176
property rights, 145, 147
property transactions, 102
property transfers, 87; annulment of, 22; documentation and, 145
punishment, 13, 16, 64–65, 81, 137–138, 158; disloyal subjects targeted with, 183; kin, 152–153; of legible populations, 23–26; multidirectionality of, 82; the state enacting, 152. *See also* reward and punishment regimes
Putin, Vladimir, 70

Qatar, 176

real estate transactions, security approval required for, 160
reconciled areas, 88, 100–102, 104, 105, 156
reconciled factions, 88, 106–107
reconciled fighter, 88, 104
reconciled subjects, 88, 104–109
reconciliation (*tusaleeh*) (*musalaha*), 86; between armed groups, 97–98; as conflict management, 97–103; deceived subject and, 125; deliberation eschewed by, 124; displacement contrasted with, 105; illiberal, 109–111; institutionalization of, 93–97; regime-style, 88–93, 104–105; restoration contrasted with, 120; social dimension of, 95
reconciliation agreements (*musalahat*), 44, 53–54, 87–88, 97–98, 103–110, 113, 158; categorization through, 109; as conflict management strategies, 99
Reconciliation Center. *See* Center for Reconciliation of Opposing Sides and Refugee Migration Monitoring in the Syrian Arab Republic
reconciliation factions (*fasaeel al musalahat*), 104
reconciliation process, 4, 34–35, 90, 107–108, 119
reconstruction, refugee repatriation and, 174
refugee repatriation, reconstruction and, 174
regime collapse, 191m 162–163
regime power, conflict management maintaining, 185–186
regime-style reconciliation, 88–93, 104–105
regional alliances, 27
regional conflict management, Astana process as, 52–60
regional conflicts, battlefield shaped by, 41
regional order, 11
regional relations, 176–177
registry offices (*noufous*), 146
regret, 90
remobilization, 106–107
repatriation: as conflict management, 135–136; of displaced people, 117; refugee, 174–176; the state sanctioning, 2

repatriation program, settlement subsidizing, 113–114
Resolution No. 689, 155
restitution, 175–176; for settled citizens, 134; settlement linked with, 154
restoration, reconciliation contrasted with, 120
"return to normal life" discourse, 122, 124
revolution, failure of, 1–2
reward and punishment regimes, 142; categorization informing, 25–26; citizen behavior structured by, 80
Rojava, the, 159
Rojava administration, 41
Russia, 37, 51–52, 71, 185; Syrian regime supported by, 41; United States and, 46–48
Russian military intervention, 2, 9, 10, 21, 39, 97, 109–110; battlefield shifted by, 44–45; "peace" following, 30–31; stalemate broken by, 33–34, 43–45; Syrian conflict ended by, 88–89
Russian Reconciliation Center for Syria, 28, 103, 108–109

Salafist-jihadist landscape, fragmentation of, 41
SANA. *See* Syrian Arab News Agency
Saudi Arabia, 176
SCC. *See* Syrian Constitutional Committee
SCND. *See* Syrian Congress of National Dialogue
SDF. *See* Syrian Democratic Forces
sectarianism, 17
security agencies, competition between, 82–83
Security and Military Committee, 99
security approval: power-of-attorney system subjected to, 155; real estate transactions requiring, 160
settled citizens, 122, 124; restitution for, 134; unsettled citizens contrasted with, 141

settlement, 116–119; adjudicating, 132–135; bifurcation through, 126; civil war, 167–168; as conflict management, 135–136; of deceived or psychologically unstable citizen, 114–115; moral-political order reconstructed through, 120; repatriation program subsidized by, 113–114; restitution linked with, 154; social repair framed by, 125–126; wanted category and, 35
settlement application, 127–130, 132–133
settlement centers (*markaz al tasaweeah*), 127, 132
settlement of status (*taswiyah al wad*), 113
settlement process, 4, 120–121, 170–171; as authoritarian alchemy, 119–126; categorization and, 135; citizen subjectivity and, 121, 131–132; as loyalty test, 35; social repair framed by, 121–122; as tool of inclusion and exclusion, 134; transitional authorities adopting, 192–193
Sharaa, Ahmed al-, 174–175, 176–178
siege warfare, 97–98
Single Syrian Registry (*al-Amanah al-Suriah al-Wahidah*), 146
smart cards, 152–153
smuggling networks, 9
SNA. *See* Syrian National Army
SNC. *See* Syrian Negotiation Committee
social death, 20, 25; Astana process and, 56–57; of disloyal subjects, 192
social dimension, 95
socialization, 95
social solution (*hal ijtam'i*), 87, 94, 115, 119
society of enmity, 24
spatial control of territory, political economy and, 21–22
spatial organization of conflict, 21
spectral terrorist, 34, 61, 63–67, 71–73, 78–79; antiterrorism policies under girded by, 141–142; commonsense

narrative and, 88; without loyalist counterpart, 104, 109; narrating, 68–69; political order organized around, 81; state enemies and, 80–81, 83–85
SSG. *See* Syrian Salvation Government
SSSC. *See* Supreme State Security Court
stained in blood, hands (*mmn lam ttltakh aydiyhm baldma*), 116, 117, 186
stalemate, 40–42; political and military, 10, 11; Russian military intervention breaking, 33–34, 43–45
state, the, of Syria, 1; absenteeism criminalized by, 153–154; categorization absorbed by, 4; citizen subjectivity constructed by, 6–7; civil committees backed by, 2; conflict management strategies of, 3; conflict narrative constructed by, 34; counterinsurgency campaign of, 13; disloyal subjects targeted by, 14; documents and archives of, 31–32; enmity and, 25, 64; expropriated assets funneled to elites by, 153; non-state authority erased by, 100; political hatred structuring, 25; population warred with by, 5, 15; production of knowledge by, 4; punishment enacted by, 152; reconciliation process of, 90, 119; repatriation sanctioned by, 2; study of, 31–33
state appropriation, of citizen assets, 157
state authority, 89
state employees, 150–152
state enemies, 89; enmity against, 7; spectral terrorist and, 80–81, 83–85; state practices for excluding and punishing, 18; terrorism and, 70–71; terrorism conflated with, 1–2; violence punishing, 13
state of emergency, 72
state officials, 93, 150; categorization by, 183, 188; Charter for National Reconciliation and Peace protecting, 89; commonsense narrative created by, 20; disloyalty framed by, 69, 80; friend/enemy binary constructed by, 80–81; Syrian conflict framed by, 68; violence and, 92
state of panic, 77–78
state oversight, civil committees outside, 28
state practices, state enemies excluded and punished by, 18
State Security Branch (*Fr' al Amn al Dualah*), 83
state violence, 5, 12–13, 14–15, 32, 81; counterterrorism and, 72; fear of, 135; reconciled factions and, 107
subjectivity, 23–26
subjectivization, categorization linked with, 189
supreme antagonism, 24
Supreme State Security Court (SSSC), xiv, 72–73, 77
sustained mode of governance, 19
Syria: civil war regime in, 5, 15, 19; as counterterrorist state, 72–79; economic destruction in, 174; future of, 191–193; GWOT embraced by, 68–69; mass violence in, 14–15; territorial fragmentation of, 8; transition in, 166–171, 180–181. *See also* battlefield, Syrian; population, of Syria; state, the, of Syria
Syrian Arab Army, 106
Syrian Arab News Agency (SANA), xiii, 112–113, 123
Syrian catastrophe, 7–9
Syrian civil war, 80
Syrian conflict, 9–11, 30, 33, 60–61, 162–163, 191; economic opportunities through, 187; international efforts to resolve, 45–46; Russian military intervention ending, 88–89; state officials framing, 68; UN not solving, 52
Syrian Congress of National Dialogue (SCND), xiii, 58–59

244 INDEX

Syrian Constitutional Committee (SCC), xiii, 52, 57–58
Syrian counterinsurgency campaign, 107
Syrian Democratic Forces (SDF), xiii, 113, 166, 169, 179–180; Astana process excluding, 57; Türkiye attacking, 59
Syrian National Army (SNA), xiv, 44, 164
Syrian National Coalition, 46
Syrian National Council, 46
Syrian National Dialogue Conference, 179
Syrian Negotiation Committee (SNC), xiv, 58
Syrian Public Funds Collection, 151
Syrian refugees, displaced Syrians contrasted with, 8
Syrian refugees, in Türkiye, 7–8
Syrian regime: collapse of, 36; conflict management by, 166–167, 182–183; GWOT instrumentalized by, 70–71; Iraqi regime contrasted with, 27; peace crafted by, 89; political order created by, 3; Russia supporting, 41; study of, 31–33. *See also* Assad, Bashar al-
Syrian Salvation Government (SSG), xiv, 146–147, 164, 166, 168–169, 180
Syrian Socialist National Party, 93
Syrian Trading Establishment, 152–153
Syrian uprising, 2–3

Takamo (company), 153
taswiyah al wad. See settlement of status
tenure laws, ownership requirements and, 156
territorial fragmentation, of Syria, 8
terrorism, 20, 63, 78, 183, 186; categorization of, 84; displaced by, 116–117, 128; fluidity of definition of, 71; Law No. 19 redefining, 73; property confiscation tied to, 154–155; state enemies and, 70–71; state enemies conflated with, 1–2. *See also* counterterrorism; Counter-Terrorism Court; spectral terrorist

transitional authorities, settlement process adopted by, 192–193
transitional justice, 171–174
trials, 75–77
tripartite power, 54–55
Trump administration, 178
Türkiye, 37–39, 44, 51–52, 176, 185; SDF attacked by, 59; Syrian refugees in, 7–8
tusaleeh. See reconciliation

UN. *See* United Nations
UNHCR. *See* United Nations High Commissioner for Refugees
unilateral forgiveness, 125
United Nations (UN), 11, 37–40, 45–52, 56, 71; Astana process sidelining, 51–52; constitutional reforms and, 57–58; liberalism and, 38; Syrian conflict not solved by, 52
United Nations Development Programme, 174
United Nations' Economic and Social Commission for West Asia (ESCWA), 86
United Nations High Commissioner for Refugees (UNHCR), xiv, 7, 8
United Nations Security Council (UNSC), xiv, 46, 50
United Nations Security Council resolutions (UNSCRs), xiv, 45–46; 2254, 48–49, 56; 2118, 47
United States (US), 37, 46–48, 70, 71, 178
universalist liberal ideas, post-conflict transitions and, 45
unreconciled subjects, 104–109
UNSC. *See* United Nations Security Council
UNSCRs. *See* United Nations Security Council resolutions
unsettled citizens, settled citizens contrasted with, 141
UN Supervision Mission in Syria, 45
US. *See* United States

victim/perpetrator narration, 87, 90, 121–122, 172, 192
Violations Documentation Center (CTC), 75
violence, 12–13, 40, 65–66, 186; Astana process sanctioning, 59; displacement and, 140; multidirectionality of, 81–83; necro-, 147; political economy incentivizing, 42; state enemies punished with, 13; state officials and, 92. *See also* mass violence; state violence

wanted category (*matloob*), 75, 112, 115–116, 129–130, 138, 148; disloyal subjects and, 160–161; settlement and, 35

war: as bureaucratic governance, 26–27; as counterterrorism, 83–84; individual experiences of, 11
war casualties, 7
war on terror, 2, 71, 186, 188. *See also* global war on terror (GWOT)
war system, 42
"We Are All for the Homeland" (*kulna lil watan*) (poetry marathon organizer), 94
women-led households, 145
Wzrat al Dulah Lshun al Musalahat al Wataniyah. See Ministry of National Reconciliation

Yekîneyên Parastina Gel. See People's Defense Units
YPG. *See* People's Defense Units

GPSR Authorized Representative: Easy Access System Europe, Mustamäe tee
50, 10621 Tallinn, Estonia, gpsr.requests@easproject.com

www.ingramcontent.com/pod-product-compliance
Lightning Source LLC
Chambersburg PA
CBHW022046290426
44109CB00014B/1005